THE
HOLY
SPIRIT

THE HOLY SPIRIT

W.H. Griffith Thomas

Foreword by
Howard F. Sugden

KREGEL PUBLICATIONS
Grand Rapids, Michigan 49501

Library of Congress Cataloging-in-Publication Data

Thomas, W. H. Griffith (William Henry Griffith),
1861-1924.
  The Holy Spirit.

  Reprint. Originally published: The Holy Spirit of
God. 4th ed. Grand Rapids, Mich.: W.B. Eerdmans
Pub. Co., 1913.
  Bibliography: p.
  Includes indexes.
  1. Holy Spirit. I. Title.
BT121.T35   1986   231'.3   86-7209
ISBN 0-8254-3835-7

CONTENTS

PART III

THE THEOLOGICAL FORMULATION

Chapter 17

Chapter 18

Chapter 19

Chapter 20

Chapter 21

Chapter 22

Chapter 23

PART IV

THE MODERN APPLICATION

Chapter 24

FOREWORD

If there is any overwhelming desire in the heart of one who is a student of the Word of God, it is the desire to have available some resource material: careful exposition that will enlighten the mind, strengthen and deepen faith and place rock beneath our feet. When one opens this priceless volume he feels that he has in his possession the wealth of the ages on the subject, THE HOLY SPIRIT OF GOD.

Lord Bacon tells us that some books are to be tasted, others swallowed, and some few to be chewed and digested. Certainly this volume falls in the latter category.

One turns to this remarkable treatise with great expectation, realizing that Dr. W. H. Griffith Thomas rested his case on every theological subject on the certainty of Divine revelation. In his book, *The Stronghold of Truth* he affirms, "If God has spoken to us in the Bible, and if this Divine revelation is our supreme authority, it is of course essential that we should know its contents, what it says, what it means to us—in a word, its message." An acquaintance with his writings gives eloquent proof that Thomas had come to know well and handle wisely "the word of truth."

W. H. Griffith Thomas made his entrance into the life that would be filled with service for the King in 1861. Before he stepped into the presence of the One he served so well, he published some fifty volumes of booklets and larger works. All his writings bear the stamp of heaven and true greatness upon them. His zenith of Bible exposition is certainly reached in this work! In a day when a spate of books is available on this theme, think of the unspeakable privilege of opening this volume and being met with this carefully-arranged and well-documented study that brings a depth of spiritual enrichment. Here we find "The biblical revelation." Linked with this

"The historical interpretation." Each of the thirty-two chapters is like an "apple of gold in a picture of silver."

The life of a casual reader will be blessed, but here the careful student will add a new dimension to his knowledge of the work of the Spirit of God. May the lives of all who read and study be deeply blessed.

HOWARD F. SUGDEN

PREFACE

FOR several years past the reading and collection of books on the Holy Spirit has been a matter of great interest to me, and when the invitation came to deliver the Stone Lectures at Princeton it seemed a favourable opportunity for putting together the available material. The object I had cherished for some time was to provide a Monograph for students, with references and Bibliography. In *The London Quarterly Review* for April, 1905, Dr. W. T. Davison, in an article on ' The Person and Work of the Holy Spirit,' described almost exactly what had been in my mind.

' The treatise for which the Church waits must be comprehensive enough to include branches of it which have been treated in a disconnected and fragmentary way, whilst sufficiently instinct with spiritual life to blend them into one living and organic whole. It should briefly trace the development of revelation through the Old Testament, showing what fresh light on the Person and Work of the Holy Spirit is shed by the New. The bearing of the doctrine on the interior relations of the Godhead should be expounded, so far as Scripture gives guidance on a profoundly mysterious subject. The offices of the Spirit in relation to Christ and the believer can more easily be explained and illustrated. On the question of the relation between the Spirit and the Church widely different opinions are held by different sections of Christendom, and it is on this ground that so many divergent paths have been taken by " heretics " of various schools. . . . A complete treatise on the work of the Holy Spirit should show the significance of these several religious movements and the measure of truth and falsity in each.'

' This kind of work has, however, been undertaken, and more or less imperfectly accomplished. What has not been attempted is a study of the chief " building eras of religion," under the guidance of the Spirit, as this is understood by Protestants and all who do not accept the Romanist doctrine of infallibility. . . . With these topics should be combined a careful inquiry into the relation between the illumination bestowed by the Spirit on the living Church of each generation on the one hand, and Holy Scripture as inspired by the same Spirit on the other. The measure of light and grace granted to the world outside the Christian Church, the operation of the Spirit in convicting the world of sin by the proclamation of the Gospel, and the work of the same Spirit in the initiation and conduct of all aggressive enterprise, are themes which greatly need to be thought out and expounded afresh by wise Christian teachers. Closely connected with them is the question of intermittent operation to which we have referred. The hindrances which prevent the Church of Christ from being " filled with the Spirit," and which therefore terribly retard the accomplishment of the great task of evangelization entrusted to her, together with the ways in which the Spirit Himself is seeking to remove these obstacles, need to be studied as a portion of the same great theme—manifold in its diversified parts, but one in its central conception and significance.

It will be said that the sketch thus outlined covers almost the whole field of dogmatics and Church history. . . . The answer is obvious. Only those aspects of Church thought and life should be considered which concern the direct operation of the Holy Spirit, and they should be treated from that point of view alone. . . . They have not been sufficiently considered from one special point of view and in the unity which that would give them.'

It was only after working for some time at the subject that I came across this article, and I desire to acknowledge with gratitude the help and guidance found in it. Of course, I make no claim to the realisation of this splendid ideal, but I have kept the aim before me and have endeavoured to frame my work on these lines. The plan is here reproduced in an available form for others, in the hope that they may bring the issue to fuller success.

It will soon be seen that there is no attempt at originality, but only the effort to call attention, within the compass of one volume, to some of the most important aspects of the truth. In the list of books found at the beginning of each chapter, in the numerous quotations scattered throughout the work, and in the Bibliography, the character and extent of my indebtedness will readily be noticed. Indeed, I should like to forestall some criticism by saying that the definite purpose of my book is to be seen from the frequent and full quotations especially in the earlier chapters. As the ground had already been so adequately and ably covered by writers of the eminence of Dr. Swete and others, I felt that it would have been wholly superfluous to re-state what had been thus effectively set forth. Instead of this, therefore, I have endeavoured, by means of quotations and references, to direct students to works in which the particular topics have been thoroughly discussed.

Another point seems to call for special mention. My lectures were delivered at Princeton and the substance of the book was completed before I read Dr. Forsyth's *Faith, Freedom, and the Future* and *The Principle of Authority*, and Dr. Mullins' *Freedom and Authority in Religion*. But I am particularly glad to be able to include quotations from and references to these valuable works, and especially to find some of my own conclusions confirmed by two such great authorities. Even though Dr. Forsyth's distinction between the Word of the New Testament and the Word of the Gospel is not here followed, there does not seem to be any fundamental difference between the position for which he and I contend in regard to the constant and close association of the Word and the Spirit.

I had hoped to be able to utilise the latest and best works in French and German on the subject of the Holy Spirit, and in order to make the book as complete as possible I wrote to several leading theologians for information and guidance. Unfortunately, time has prevented me from doing what I wished, unless the issue of this volume were to be seriously delayed, but I have included all the recommendations in the Bibliography for the guidance of other students, and I desire to express my obligations to Dr. Forsyth, Professor H. R. Mackintosh, Professor Denney, and Professor Knowling, for their valuable information and suggestions.

It remains to add two matters of a more personal nature. I am deeply indebted to the Faculty of the Princeton Theological Seminary for the invitation to deliver the Stone Lectures, and not least for the honour of being, I believe, the first Anglican to lecture on that Presbyterian Foundation. My visit to Princeton and my intercourse with the Faculty and the students were a privilege and an enjoyment which will long be a happy memory. Then, again, I have inscribed this volume to seven well-known names, first, in order to acknowledge with thankfulness my great indebtedness in various ways to their writings ; and, second, to call attention to and emphasise something of that essential unity of Christian scholarship which is perhaps doing more than anything else to pave the way for the still larger unity of the Churches for which our Master prayed, and without which the world will not be impressed with the things of the Spirit. In this connection, I would like to make my own the closing words of the *Times'* notice of Professor Swete's book, *The Holy Spirit in the Ancient Church* :

' It is part of the irony of history that whereas all Christians have believed that the Holy Spirit was given to the Church in order to bind its members together into one Body, the disputes which arose concerning the Person or Persons through Whom the Spirit was given to the world were a chief cause of the disruption of the Church. We would fain believe that the increasing recognition of the work of the Holy Spirit within the Christian Church and throughout the world which has been a marked characteristic of recent years will prove to be the prelude to the complete reunion of Christendom.'

CHAPTER 1

INTRODUCTION

OVER forty years ago that great scholar, Bishop Thirlwall, expressed the opinion that

'the great intellectual and religious struggle of our day turns mainly on this question, Whether there is a Holy Ghost.'

When it is remembered that the Bishop was one of the ablest thinkers of his time, we can appreciate the insight and foresight of this statement. Still nearer our own day, Bishop Westcott, referring to Bishop Thirlwall's remark, said :

'I will venture to define this statement more closely and say that the struggle turns upon our belief in a Holy Ghost sent in the Name of Jesus Christ according to His own emphatic promise.'

The prominence and emphasis given in the New Testament to the Holy Spirit are at once the cause and the vindication of these utterances, and we may legitimately argue that the importance of the subject can be rightly measured by the place given to it. Other doctrines of great importance, as, for example, those of the Church and the Sacraments, do not obtain anything like the notice given in the New Testament to the Holy Spirit. No one can fail to be impressed with the frequency, variety, fulness and prominence of the references to the Spirit all through the New Testament Scriptures. Instead of stopping with the Resurrection, the New Testament leads on to the subject of the Holy Spirit and His work.

In truth, the Holy Spirit is in several ways the unique and ultimate Fact and Force in Christianity. He is the culmination of everything in the revelation of Divine redemption. Other religious systems have their founders, their sacred books, their ethics. But not one has anything corresponding to the New Testament doctrine of the Holy Spirit. The Holy Spirit is the only means of guaranteeing religion as personal communion with God. The Divine revelation given historically in the Person of Christ is mediated and made real to the soul by the Holy Spirit. This, again, is a mark of uniqueness in Christianity, since only therein is religion realised as a matter of personal communion with the Deity.

The Holy Spirit is also the true *articulus aut stantis aut cadentis ecclesiae.* John Owen regards the Holy Spirit as the touchstone of faith to-day just as the Persons of the Father and of the Son respectively have been tests in days past.[1] Thomas Arnold said it is

' the very main thing of all. We are living under the dispensation of the Spirit; in that character God now reveals Himself to His people. He who does not know God the Holy Ghost cannot know God at all.' [2]

The Holy Spirit is the unique element of Christianity as a living power to-day. The vindication of the Gospel of Christ will never be accomplished merely by the presentation of a moral ideal, still less by any statement in terms of philosophic thought. It is only as a ' dynamic ' that Christianity will recommend itself to the life of to-day, and, according to the New Testament, this ' dynamic ' is only possible by the presence and grace of the Holy Spirit.[3]

The question at once arises whether the subject of the Holy Spirit has received due attention compared with that given to other doctrines of the Faith, *e.g.* Christology or Ecclesiology. After making every allowance for historical circumstances, it is surely not without significance that the Apostles' Creed contains ten articles on the Person and Work of Christ, with only one on the Holy Spirit. And when we consider the scarcity of references in the New Testament to the Holy Communion, contrasted with the

---

[1] *Pneumatologia*, Book I. ch. i. Quoted by Moule, *Veni Creator*, p. 1 f.

[2] *Sermons*, 1st Series, XXVIII. Quoted by W. L. Walker, *The Holy Spirit*, p. 7.

[3] W. L. Walker, *The Holy Spirit*, ch. i.

prominence given to it in the history of the Church, we have another significant illustration of the comparative neglect of the doctrine of the Holy Spirit. Indeed, the principle of cause and effect seems to obtain here, for probably if the Church had realised more of the meaning of the Holy Spirit, there might have been less need of controversy on the Holy Communion. In the *Expository Times* ten years ago, the Editor remarked : ' The doctrine of the Holy Spirit still suffers neglect among us.' [1] And even the valuable books published since then cannot be said to have adequately redressed the balance.[2]

Many considerations tend to make us emphasise the special importance of this subject at the present time. Materialism in science and also in commerce bulks largely in many lives. The teaching of Haeckel in Germany, and the recent suggestion of Professor Schäfer in regard to the solution of the problem of life by means of chemistry alone, show a distinct but happily receding trend of modern scientific thought. And in commercial life, the craving to ' get rich quick,' the power of Trusts, and the over-mastering force of speculation in Real Estate constitute another serious element in the practical materialism of to-day. It will only be by the incoming of the New Testament message of the Holy Spirit that Materialism will be overcome and prevented in future.

In the opposite direction we cannot fail to observe the revolt against Materialism in such movements as Christian Science, Spiritualism, Theosophy. We are bound to recognise the truth behind these tendencies, which seem to be in great measure due to a reaction from the blank agnosticism of the days of Huxley, Spencer, and Tyndall. And yet no mere denunciation will suffice to meet their dangers. The craving for the non-material, the emphasis on mind rather than matter, and the belief in the reality of the spiritual world expressed in one way or another by these movements can only be adequately met by an insistence on the doctrine of the Holy Spirit.

Nor dare we forget the purely negative criticism of Christ

---

[1] May, 1903.

[2] *E.g.* Swete, Downer, Davison, Humphries (see references later).

and Christianity from the time of Strauss to the present day. All such efforts of thought have tended towards a naturalistic Christ, robbed of everything distinctively Divine and supernatural, and brought within the limits of our own humanity. While processes of reasoning and historical scholarship will do much to meet this criticism, it remains true that only by the Holy Spirit shall we be fully enabled to see the futility and fatality of such a conception of our Lord.

The problems arising out of Modernism and Mysticism constitute another appeal to the doctrine of the Holy Spirit. Modernism with its efforts to cut loose from miraculous Christianity while retaining a belief in religion, and Mysticism with its endeavour to sublimate the Gospel into a religion free from all connection with the past, both tend towards the essential destruction of vital Christianity. And it is only in the presence and power of the Holy Spirit of God that such dangers can be met. A purely intellectual and natural religion can never satisfy the human heart, while philosophy, however true, cannot form, and never yet has formed, the basis of religion. The Holy Spirit applying to the soul the reality of God's revelation in Christ can alone suffice for the foundation of true religion.

The emphasis laid on the Church and Sacraments in certain quarters tends to the undue exaltation of the community in relation to the individual, to the exaggeration of the specific place and proper proportion of the Sacraments in relation to the other means of grace, and to a check on the spiritual liberty of the individual. The various ecclesiastical problems will find their true solution only as proper attention is given to the full New Testament teaching on the Holy Spirit.

There are those who charge Christianity to-day with failure as a vital force. The Bampton Lectures by Archdeacon Peile are perhaps the most striking recent discussion of this view.[1] There is only one way of demonstrating Christianity as a supernatural religion, and that is by a constant insistence on the presence and work of the Holy

---

[1] *The Reproach of the Gospel.*

Spirit. If we are to have a safeguard against fluctuating experiences of the Church, as seen through the centuries, and if we are to keep the Church immune from spiritual weakness, disease, and death, we must make much of the Divine Spirit.

The subject can perhaps best be studied along the lines of the following plan :

1. The Biblical revelation as the spiritual foundation of the doctrine.

2. The historical interpretation of the doctrine in the history of the Church.

3. The theological formulation of the doctrine in the Creeds and Confessions, and its spiritual presentation in the Christian life of the individual and the community.

4. The modern application of the doctrine to the various movements of to-day.

And so in different ways and from several quarters the call comes to us for a fresh enquiry into the meaning of, and a fresh emphasis on the value of that Article in the Creed, ' I believe in the Holy Ghost.' The supreme requirement is that the subject be considered from the standpoint of one who knows the realities of the Spirit by personal experience, not by intellect only.

' While lack of spiritual experience is a drawback in the study of any department of theology, it is absolutely fatal here. Critics may discuss Christology from the point of view of history or of literature ; but, when they come to deal with the work of the Holy Spirit, without spiritual knowledge they are so far at a loss that they give up the attempt with a sneer at its futility.' [1]

---

[1] W. T. Davison, *The Indwelling Spirit*, p. 30.

PART I

THE BIBLICAL REVELATION

CHAPTER 2

THE HOLY SPIRIT
IN THE OLD TESTAMENT

THE doctrine of the Holy Spirit is clearly a Bible doctrine, and cannot be derived from any other source.

' The notion that God is a Spirit can be traced in more religions than one, but the conception of a Spirit in God is in any developed form, found only in the Scriptures.' [1]

' The doctrine of the Holy Spirit is distinctively a doctrine of revelation. It belonged to the Holy Spirit to expound His own work. Beyond that authoritative exposition no one has been able to take a sure step, although reason has spared no lawful effort, and mysticism has put forth every desperate or delighted endeavour to break through the Bible's bounds.' [2]

It is particularly important to observe this because of the dangers of non-Christian rationalism, and of certain aspects of Mysticism which tend in different ways to separate the doctrine of the Spirit from the Scriptures.

The subject is naturally not so prominent in the Old Testament as in the New, but there are said to be eighty-eight direct references to the Spirit in the Old Testament.[3] It is clearly mentioned in about half of the thirty-nine books, though in sixteen of them there is no direct reference.

---

[1] Humphries, *The Holy Spirit in Faith and Experience*, p. 3.

[2] E. H. Johnson, *The Holy Spirit*, p. 2.

[3] Elder Cumming, *Through the Eternal Spirit*, p. 50.

LITERATURE.—A. L. Humphries, *The Holy Spirit in Faith and Experience*, chs. i., ii. ; I. F. Wood, *The Spirit of God in Biblical Literature*, p. 3 ; Welldon, *The Revelation of the Holy Spirit*, ch. i. ; Denio, *The Supreme Leader*, pp. 5-25 ; Smeaton, *The Doctrine of the Holy Spirit*, pp. 9-39 ; Downer, *The Mission and Ministration of the Holy Spirit*, ch. ii. ; Elder Cumming, *Through the Eternal Spirit*, pp. 19, 50 ; J. S. Candlish, *The Work of the Holy Spirit*, p. 11 ; Redford, *Vox Dei*, p. 21.

And whatever date we may assign to Genesis, the fact remains that the idea of the Spirit is mentioned in ch. i. 2 as though quite familiar, just as in Matt. i.

It is noteworthy that the New Testament identifies the Holy Spirit of the New Testament with the Spirit of God in the Old Testament. This shows that there is no fundamental difference between them. Indeed, the New Testament conception of the Spirit rests on the Old Testament as its basis, and much in the former is only intelligible when read in the light of the latter, since no explanation is afforded in the New. Thus, St. Luke iv. is identified with Isa. lxi., Acts ii. with Joel ii.; and the work of the same Holy Spirit in both Testaments is clearly indicated in such passages as Acts vii. 51, 1 Pet. i. 11, 2 Pet. i. 21. Later books of the Old Testament show direct contact with New Testament doctrine, so much so that it can be said that 'the Old Testament is in closest genetic relation to the New Testament doctrine of man's renewal by the Spirit.'[1] In both Testaments, God is regarded as at work by His Spirit.

But it is of course essential to examine more particularly the Old Testament doctrine of the Spirit of God. The subject is found largely in outline in the Pentateuch and Historical books. Fuller treatment is seen in Isaiah and Ezekiel. Indeed, Isaiah has an almost complete doctrine of the Spirit,[2] while Ezekiel has been said to express in his teaching a unity of all the varied Old Testament lines.[3] But the mere fact of frequency or infrequency of reference is no guide to the history of the doctrine, since the Spirit is mentioned in Numbers, though not in Leviticus; in Judges, though not in Joshua; in Nehemiah, though not in Ezra; and in about half of the Minor Prophets, though not in the rest.

The Hebrew word for 'Spirit' calls for special attention, together with its Greek and Latin equivalents, πνεῦμα and *spiritus*. The original usage of רוּחַ was applied to

---

[1] H. W. Robinson, *The Christian Doctrine of Man*, p. 65.

[2] Smeaton, *The Doctrine of the Holy Spirit*, p. 32.

[3] Kleinert. Quoted in *Presbyterian and Reformed Review*, Vol. VI. p. 666.

' breath ' and ' wind.' Some authorities consider that the
' blowing ' of wind, and then of man ' panting ' for breath,
was the primary conception.[1] But others take the opposite view, and think that the idea of ' breath ' is closer to
the fundamental conception than the invisible ' wind.'

' It seems doubtful whether the living breath is not more close
to the basal idea than the invisible, immaterial wind. Early religious ideas more often start with a conception of a living power than
with a lifeless force.' [2]

(It is noteworthy that the two ideas of ' wind ' and
' breath ' are found in connection with the Holy Spirit in
St. John iii. 8 and xx. 22.) From this came the thought
of רוּחַ as the principle of life, emotional and spiritual, the
highest psychical nature of man (Gen. vii. 22 ; Job. xvii.
1 ; Ezek. xxxvii. 5, 6, 8). Then these elements were
attributed to God, and the word is found 134 times, all
referring to supernatural influences acting on man, and
rarely on inanimate objects (Gen. i. 2). This attribution
to God is probably anthropomorphic, expressive of the
Divine activity, just as the רוּחַ of man is the principle
of his life (Psa. cxxxix. 7). It is significant that Nephesh,
' soul,' is never applied to God. Thus the idea of the
Spirit of God seems to be formed on the idea of the spirit
of man. As man's spirit is man himself, so the Spirit of
God is God Himself active and energetic on man's behalf.[3]

There are three main lines of Old Testament teaching on
this subject, and the results are not essentially affected by
either view of the Old Testament, critical or conservative.
There are differences as to the stages of the process, but
no vital difference as to the latest and fullest teaching of
the Old Testament in relation to the Spirit of God, or as
to the contact of the doctrine there stated with the fuller
revelation in the New Testament.[4]

1. *The cosmical, or world relations of the Spirit of God.*

---

[1] Robinson, *op. cit.* Index, *Pneuma, Ruach, Spirit* ; Wood, *The
Spirit of God in Biblical Literature*, p. 32, note ; Humphries, *op. cit.*
p. 4.

[2] Wood, *op. cit.* p. 32, note.

[3] A. B. Davidson, *Theology of the Old Testament*, p. 117.

[4] H. W. Robinson, *The Christian Doctrine of Man*, p. 65.

The Spirit is associated with creation (Gen. i. 2 ; [1] Job. xxvi. 13) : with human life as a whole (Gen. vi. 3 ; Job. xxvii. 3 ; xxxii. 8 ; xxxiii. 4) : with intellectual and artistic capacity (Exod. xxxv. 30) : with Divine providence (Psa. civ. 29, 30 ; Isa. xl. 7) : and with other natural phenomena (Ezek. xxxvii. 9). Thus the Spirit in the world is concerned with man's physical life, intellectual powers, and executive ability (Deut. xxxiv. 9). This action of the Spirit is generally expressed by the term ' Spirit of God ' as indicative of the natural and universal influences of God on man and the world. And yet in all this there is not the slightest approach to Pantheism or any absorption of God in creation. Although God may be spoken of in these respects as immanent in the world, His transcendence is never in question, whatever may be said of Him in relation to His creation.

2. *The theocratic or redemptive relations of the Spirit of God.* In the period of the Exodus, in Judges and elsewhere, the Spirit is the author of Divine power and energy, coming on man for the performance of special duties (Jud. iii. 10 ; vi. 34 ; I Sam. xi. 6 ; xviii. 10. Cf. Numb. xi. 17-25). Later on, in the Prophets, the Spirit is the author of Divine revelation and inspiration (Isa. lxi. 1 ; Ezek. ii. 2 ; Mic. iii. 8 ; Zech. vii. 12 ; ix. 30. Cf. Numb. xxiv. 2). In harmony with these, and as the culmination of the redemptive or theocratic gift, we find the picture of the Messiah as one endowed with the gifts and graces of the Spirit of God, providing Him with insight and ability for His work (Isa. xi.). All these aspects of the covenantal or theocratic gift may be called official, since they are regarded as bestowed upon the special organs of the Divine purpose of redemption. They are gifts of office rather than of personal grace. The term used is invariably the ' Spirit of Jehovah,' which, as contrasted with the ' Spirit of God,' is the covenantal title. The gift is also plainly supernatural in every case, and there is no possibility of confusion between it and the personal powers of the recipients. It was not a permanent and continuous power, but a Divine gift for special work at special times. It

---

[1] See Driver on Gen. i. 2 ; H. W. Robinson, *ut supra*, p. 64 f.

represented an unique inspiration and endowment above and beyond the general uniqueness of the nation. While this aspect of the Spirit is at once abnormal and normal in expression, it is inaccurate to say that the greatest proof of the Spirit in the early ages was its association with abnormal phenomena, but that later the normal prevailed without the accompaniment of physical accessories.[1] The accompaniments of dreams and visions are found throughout the whole period of Old Testament prophecy.[2] And no distinction can be drawn between the earlier and the later prophets, as though the latter separated themselves from everything ecstatic. Nor is it correct to say that frenzy and raving were the usual accompaniments of Old Testament prophecy, and therefore of the work of the Spirit. No doubt the men of the world considered the prophet as ' crazed,' but this is very different from the idea that raving and insanity were the accessories of Divine communication.[3] The truth is that Israel is regarded throughout as an inspired supernatural people,[4] and the Spirit is given to the leaders of the theocracy for the purpose of accomplishing their divinely appointed tasks. It is, therefore, more correct to regard Israel as abnormal, than to say that the characteristic feature of the Spirit is its abnormality. Israel was the depository of the Divine truth, the instrument of Divine purpose for the world, and the Spirit is the vehicle of the Divine revelation and the Agent of the Divine will. While the cosmical aspects of the Spirit naturally come first in order, the redemptive, covenantal, theocratic elements are far more prominent, and it is probably true to say that subsequent to the entrance of sin, the working of the Spirit of God is invariably limited to Israel as the people of God, whether as a community or as individuals.[5] The Divine purposes were

---

[1] Humphries, *The Holy Spirit in Faith and Experience*, pp. 49-51.

[2] Beecher, *The Prophets and the Promise*, p. 115.

[3] Beecher, *op. cit.* pp. 35, 72, 74, 75.

[4] Humphries, *op. cit.* pp. 22, 23, note.

[5] Warfield, ' The Spirit of God in the Old Testament,' *Presbyterian and Reformed Review*, Vol. VI. p. 669, and note 1.

to be realised only through Israel, and for this the work of the Spirit was essential.

3. *The individual, personal relations of the Spirit of God.* Later on in the history the relation of the Holy Spirit to man's spiritual life is evident. It is possible that Gen. vi. 3 and 1 Sam. x. 6 have this ethical idea, but there is no question as to its existence in the later books. In the Pentateuch and Historical books the cosmical and official aspects are almost solely prominent ; the Psalms introduce the ethical, while the Prophets have both the ethical and prophetical aspects.[1] The idea of holiness is not usually associated with the Spirit in the Old Testament as it is in the New Testament. The term ' Holy Spirit ' occurs only three times (Psa. li. 11 ; Isa. lxiii. 10, 11), but we have ' good Spirit ' twice (Neh. ix. 20 ; Psa. cxliii. 10). The idea of holiness was probably implicit in the idea of the Spirit from the first, even though the term ' holy ' is not so often used. When we look at the *kind* of work the Spirit does, and not simply at the terms used, we see the dispositions He inspires, and the nature of His operations. He strives with men, He puts exalted utterances into the mouth of Balaam (' God is not a man,' Numb. xxiii. 19), and generally fits man for holy service. The root of קדש is to ' cut,' ' separate,' and therefore implies Divine transcendence, unapproachableness, purity, so that the thought of holiness, as attributed to the Spirit in Psa. li. 11, indicates a union of immanence and transcendence.

It is, however, mainly in regard to the Messianic days that this individual, personal, and ethical relation of the Spirit of God is found (Isa. xi. 2-5 ; lxiii. 10, 11 ; Ezek. xxxvi. 27 ; xxxvii. 14 ; Joel ii. 28-32). Nor is this surprising in view of the fact that the national elements were more plainly emphasised in Old Testament times, while the spiritual and universal aspects were quite naturally left for Messianic days. But speaking generally, we may say that from Genesis to Malachi the Spirit of God is never far away. God's life is seen in active operation on man's behalf, and this naturally becomes fuller in the later books because of the principle of development and the more

---

[1] Warfield, *ut supra*, p. 669.

detailed anticipations of Messianic times. A. B. Davidson says that there are two ways in which God exercised His rule in Israel and His guidance in all spheres of life. (1) By the external manifestation of Himself in the Angel of the Lord; and (2) by His Spirit.[1] So that the 'Spirit of Jehovah is Jehovah Himself within men, as the Angel of Jehovah is Himself without men.' Hence 'the Old Testament doctrine of God is not more strongly monotheistic than it is theistic and not deistic.'[2] Kleinert says that 'the doctrine of the Spirit of God is the most powerful vehicle of the Old Testament monotheistic contemplation of the world.'[3]

These three lines of teaching are in general accord with the progress of Divine revelation in the Old Testament.[4] God is regarded as actively working (a) in the world, (b) in the theocratic community, (c) in the individual soul. And they are united, because (a) the cosmical work of the Spirit prepares the world as the home of man, (b) the theocratic work prepares men as the Divine society, (c) the personal work prepares individuals as members of the redemptive community.[5]

The question now arises as to whether there are indications of development in the Old Testament doctrine of the Spirit of God. In the earlier history the Spirit is depicted as a Divine energy. In the later books there seems to be something like an approximation to the doctrine of the Spirit as a personal Being. Thus in Isa. lxiii. 9, 10, He is said to be 'grieved,' and in Isaiah xlviii. 16, which A. B. Davidson remarks, 'is of some significance,' He is either subject or object. A similar conception is found in Zech. iv. 6. Perhaps the words of Davidson carry us as far as we can go:

' This way of speaking is much developed in the Old Testament, so that we may say the beginnings at least of the distinction between the Lord and His Spirit, are to be seen.'[6]

---

[1] A. B. Davidson, *op. cit.* p. 116.

[2] A. B. Davidson, *op. cit.* p. 120.

[3] Quoted in Oehler, *Theology of the Old Testament*, Vol. I. p. 173.

[4] Dale, *Christian Doctrine*, p. 318.

[5] Denio, *The Supreme Leader*.

[6] A. B. Davidson, *op. cit.* p. 128.

The Old Testament teaching may therefore be summarised thus : the Spirit is a Divine agent and energy rather than a distinct personality. God is regarded as at work, and, as in the New Testament, the Spirit is 'the executive of the Godhead.' He is not a gift separate from God, but God Himself in and with men ; a Power rather than a Person. The Spirit is always a Person in activity, not an influence at a distance from God Himself, and not a substance communicated to man.[1]

' The question whether the Old Testament teaches the personality of the Spirit of God is not one that should be raised apart from the other, what is its conception of the Spirit of God ? ' [2]

The Old Testament is moral and practical, not metaphysical and philosophical. The supreme thought is ' the relation of a living, active personal God to the world and men.' [3] Beecher's words are also noteworthy :

' The Spirit is effluent energy from Yahaweh the infinite Spirit. But if we stop with this, the answer is incomplete. This effluent energy is spoken of in terms of personality. . . . In fine, this Spirit that inspires the prophets is presented to us as a unique being, having personal characteristics, effluent from Yahaweh the supreme Spirit of the universe, at once identical with and different from Yahaweh.' [4]

From this it is clear that the doctrine of the Spirit is really the doctrine of a Divine immanence placed side by side with the predominant Old Testament thought of the Divine transcendence. As such, it implies a profound enrichment of the idea of God, and is a definite preparation for the doctrine of Divine providence and the specific New Testament idea of the indwelling of the Spirit of God. Indeed, without this preparation the New Testament revelation is hardly conceivable. But we have no right to expect more. The special work of Israel was to emphasise the Divine unity and transcendence, and the Old Testament is therefore only preparatory to the fuller manifestation of the New Testament. As Westcott says :

---

[1] A. B. Davidson, *op. cit.* p. 127.
[2] A. B. Davidson, *op. cit.* p. 115.
[3] A. B. Davidson, *op. cit.* p. 115.
[4] Beecher, *The Prophets and the Promise*, pp. 114, 115.

' The Spirit of God is not yet made known as a distinct Person with Whom man can hold communion, though the scope of the energy foreshadows the nature of the Person. . . . The Spirit was in the fulness of the Divine Nature, but not in that personal relation with the Church and with the believer which followed on the exaltation of the Saviour.' [1]

One aspect of Old Testament teaching remains for brief, separate consideration. Several passages speak of a ' Spirit from Jehovah ' in connection with evil and untruth (1 Sam. xvi. 14; 1 Kings xxii. 19-23). These statements are admittedly very difficult, but they cannot set aside the general and predominant thought of the Spirit as identical with God at work on behalf of His people. They probably are intended to express in an extreme Oriental form God's judicial action against wilful sin.[2]

---

[1] Westcott, *Historic Faith*, p. 104 f.

[2] For the critical view, see Humphries, *op. cit.* p. 14; Wood, *op. cit.* pp. 6, 12. For the conservative view, see Beecher, *op. cit.* p. 114.

CHAPTER 3

THE HOLY SPIRIT
IN THE APOCRYPHA

IT is impossible to avoid asking whether there was any
movement of thought and life on the subject of the Holy
Spirit in the centuries between Malachi and Matthew.
Prophecy had given place, first, to the priesthood, and then,
to the work of the Scribes, whose duty was the exposition
of the Law and its application to daily life. Then, again,
contact with Greek thought at Alexandria had its effect
on Judaism. What effect, if any, had all this on the doctrine of the Spirit. Is any modification found during this
period? There was modification, certainly, but no real
additions to the doctrine.

Dr. Swete says :

' In the non-canonical literature of Palestine, references to the
Divine Spirit are rare, and when they occur are little else than echoes
—sometimes broken and imperfect echoes—of the canonical teaching. . . . The growing angelology of the Pharisees may possibly
have obscured the Biblical conception of the Divine Spirit as the
operative force in nature and in man. . . . When prophecy ceased,
it seemed as if the presence of the Divine Spirit had been suspended
or withdrawn.' [1]

At Alexandria Jewish thought took a somewhat different
form.

---

[1] Swete, Article ' Holy Spirit,' Hastings' *Bible Dictionary*, p. 404.

LITERATURE.—Humphries, *The Holy Spirit in Faith and Experience*, ch. iii. ; Wood, *The Spirit of God in Biblical Literature*, p. 60 ;
Welldon, *The Revelation of the Holy Spirit*, p. 50 ; Denio, *The
Supreme Leader*, p. 26 ; Swete, *The Holy Spirit in the New Testament*, p. 398 ; Article ' Holy Spirit ' in Hastings' *Bible Dictionary*,
p. 404 ; Redford, *Vox Dei*, p. 171 ; H. W. Robinson, *The Christian
Doctrine of Man*, p. 71.

' The old consciousness of the perpetual activity of the Spirit of God survived, associating itself with the philosophical thought of Hellenism, and growing in its influence into new forms of belief.' [1]

This was seen more particularly in the connection of Wisdom with the Spirit, a connection found in the Canonical books, but carried much further in the thought of Alexandrian Judaism. But it was mainly intellectual not moral and ethical.

' Of the ethical aspect of the Spirit's work in man Philo has little to say. . . . Of the Spirit as restoring the moral nature of man we hear nothing. . . . The omission may be partly due to the circumstance that he employs himself chiefly about the Pentateuch ; but it is more probably to be traced to the predominance of the intellectual interest in Alexandrian thought.' [2]

With this agrees the view of another modern writer, that the eschatological development forms the chief contribution of later Judaistic theology, and that

' the chief lacuna in the religious experience generated by Judaism . . . is the absence of any adequate development of the Old Testament idea of the Spirit of God.' [3]

In the same way, Humphries says :

' So far as the doctrine of the Holy Spirit is concerned, there was practically no advance made. One thing which strikes us, as we read the literature of the period, is the paucity of its references to the Spirit. And the few which we find seem to be echoes rather than new and living voices.' [4]

On the other hand, Denio considers that the evidence is slight but real for a tendency during this period ' to neglect the conception of the Cosmic Spirit and to think more of the personified Spirit of God.' [5] But he admits that the language of Wisdom (ch. vii. 22-27), where the Spirit of God is personified under the name of Wisdom, ' is coloured by Greek philosophy, and the personification is doubtless suggested from Proverbs viii.' [6]

---

[1] Swete, *ut supra*, p. 404.

[2] Swete, *ut supra*, p. 405.

[3] H. W. Robinson, *Christian Doctrine of Man*, p. 74.

[4] Humphries, *The Holy Spirit in Faith and Experience*, p. 96.

[5] Denio, *The Supreme Leader*, p. 26.

[6] Denio, *op. cit.* p. 27.

Wood sums up the position as follows :

(a) ' The concept of the Spirit as the essential substance of human life is nowhere clearly stated. It would seem that God had become too far removed from the world of human error and frailty for this idea to be wholly acceptable.'

(b) ' The small part which the idea played in the thought of this period is indicated by the narrow range of literature in which the term occurs. In the books of the Apocrypha it is found only in Judith, Sirach, Susanna, Second Maccabees, and Fourth Maccabees.' [1]

If it be said that Jewish devotion and patriotism must have come from the Spirit of God, still an explanation of the silence of these books as to the Spirit is required. May it not have been found

' in the growing tendency to put God far away from the world and to avoid any phrase which had an anthropomorphic relation ? The angel of Jahveh had disappeared. . . . In place of it a hierarchy of angels had been developed. This accounts for the meagre use of the Spirit as applied to human experience.' [2]

Instead of the Old Testament doctrine of the Spirit, there was a speculation on the relation of the Spirit of God to the created universe by means of intermediate beings. But, as it has been well said,

' in these fantastic speculations, which were an attempt to safeguard the transcendence of God, and yet to provide for some part of supernatural contact with the world, we are far removed from the simple faith in God's nearness to man which we find expressed in some of the Psalms, and which came to re-birth in the teaching of Jesus.' [3]

The chief contribution of this period was the personification of the Spirit as Wisdom, following Greek rather than Hebrew thought. Of this several things need to be said. In the Old Testament the two conceptions of the Spirit and Wisdom occupy different spheres and stand for different realities. The Spirit is concrete ; Wisdom is abstract. The Spirit meant power ; Wisdom meant knowledge. It is true that in the cosmical aspect of the Spirit the outcome was wisdom and knowledge (Gen. xli. 38, 39 ; Deut. xxxiv. 9 ; Isa. xi. 2). But the conception of Wisdom in the Old

---

[1] Wood, *The Spirit of God in Biblical Literature*, p. 67.

[2] Wood, *ut supra*, p. 72.

[3] Humphries, *op. cit.* p. 98.

Testament never attains to the prominence given to the Spirit, and within the limits of the Old Testament the two ideas never approach identity. This was only effected in the period now under consideration in connection with the fusion of Hebrew and Greek thought in Alexandria. Yet the union was not effected without serious modification and the loss of distinctive elements of the Old Testament :

> ' Here at last the Hebrew idea of the Spirit of God was identified with that of Wisdom, yet no longer the aphoristic, common-sense wisdom of the Hebrew sages, but a universal cosmic principle, bearing marks of the influence of the great unities of · Greek philosophy.' [1]

And speaking of this book of Wisdom, the same writer remarks :

> ' At last the old Hebrew antithesis of supernatural Spirit, and natural world-Wisdom is overcome, but in a one-sided way ; not by the synthesis of the two ideas into a higher conception, retaining the force of both, but by the absorption of the one into a more abstract form of the other. Nothing of Spirit remains save the name ; and Wisdom is no longer a quality of the practical, concrete morality which the Hebrew sage knew, but a world-reason, a universal law whose point of contact with experience and reality is difficult to discover.' [2]

Farrar says :

> ' On the Divine side, Wisdom is the Spirit of God, regarded by man under the form of Providence ; and, on the human side, Wisdom is trustworthy knowledge . . . regarded by God as manifested in moral life. But one set of terms does service to express both the intellectual and the moral wisdom. The ' wise ' man means the righteous man ; the ' fool ' is one who is godless. Intellectual terms that describe knowledge are also moral terms describing life.' [3]

All this only goes to confirm the truth with which our study commenced, that the doctrine of the Spirit is a Biblical doctrine, and can only be derived from and protected by the Divine revelation. With the cessation of the Divine work of prophecy there was, and could be, no guarantee of protection against error in thought and practice. It is

---

[1] Rees, ' The Holy Spirit as Wisdom,' *Mansfield College Essays*, p. 294.

[2] Rees, *ut supra*, p. 298.

[3] Farrar, ' Introduction to Wisdom,' *Speaker's Commentary*, Vol. VII. p. 419.

the difference between revelation and discovery ; between Divine knowledge and human speculation ; between spiritual experience and intellectual abstraction ; between God's sunshine and man's candlelight.

' Speculation was able thus to run riot in the region of the supernatural, because there was no immediate experience which was felt to correspond to what the older faith had recognised as the distinct product of the Spirit. Of all the activities attributed by the Old Testament to the Spirit of God, none had been so impressive as the gift of prophecy. But during the period which we are now considering the voice of prophecy was dumb.' [1]

It should also be observed that another influence was at work in the tendency to identify the Hebrew Wisdom with the Greek Reason (*Logos*), so that Wisdom, Reason, and Spirit became convertible terms. But in the process the blend of Jewish philosophical thought of Alexandria did not remain true to the old conception of the Hebrew prophets. While unity was gained in one direction practical reality was sacrificed in another.

' The word " Spirit," which meant to the Hebrew thinker the realised operation of a personal God, so that there was always the possibility of the Spirit being itself conceived as personal, was rendered almost superfluous. The religious interest was sacrificed to the intellectual, and a vital element in religion thereby imperilled.' [2]

We may therefore conclude that for all practical and spiritual purposes the period of the Apocrypha made no real contribution to the doctrine of the Holy Spirit.

' The doctrine of the Holy Spirit's nature or operation makes no important progress in Apocryphal literature. It remains where it was ; or rather, the stream of thought regarding it flows underground for two or three centuries, until it re-emerges in the fulness of our Lord's own teaching.' [3]

It was reserved for the New Testament revelation to correct the dangers of mere intellectual abstraction and to reassert, only with greater clearness, depth, and fulness of meaning, the doctrine of the Spirit of God.

---

[1] Humphries, *op. cit.* p. 98.

[2] Humphries, *op. cit.* p. 107.

[3] Welldon, *The Revelation of the Holy Spirit*, p. 51.

CHAPTER 4

THE HOLY SPIRIT
IN PAUL'S EPISTLES

GREAT prominence is given to the subject of the Holy
Spirit in the New Testament. It is found in every book
except three short and personal ones : Philemon, 2 and 3
John.

' It may be said that to understand what is meant by the Spirit
is to understand two things—the New Testament and the Christian
Church. . . . In them and in their mutual relations we have the
only adequate witness of what the Spirit means for Christians ; to
the men who wrote the New Testament and to those for whom they
wrote the Spirit was not a doctrine but an experience. . . . In
some sense this covered everything that they included in
Christianity.' [1]

The human and literary sources of the New Testament
doctrine are the Old Testament and Palestinian Judaism ;
there is little, if anything, of Alexandrian Judaism.

The doctrine may be derived by one or other of two

---

[1] Denney, Article ' Holy Spirit,' *Dictionary of Christ and the
Gospels*, p. 731.

LITERATURE.—The Holy Spirit in the New Testament. Hum-
phries, *The Holy Spirit in Faith and Experience*, ch. iv. ; Wood,
The Spirit of God in Biblical Literature, Part II. ; Swete, *The Holy
Spirit in the New Testament* ; Winstanley, *Spirit in the New Testa-
ment* ; Bullinger, *The Giver and His Gifts* ; W. T. Davison, *The
Indwelling Spirit*, ch. ii. ; Denio, *The Supreme Leader*, pp. 28-54 ;
W. L. Walker, *The Holy Spirit*, ch. ii. ; J. S. Candlish, *The Work
of the Holy Spirit*, p. 21 ; Elder Cumming, *Through the Eternal
Spirit*, pp. 31, 60 ; A. B. Simpson, *Power from on High*, Vol. II.
The Holy Spirit in St. Paul's Writings. Humphries, *op. cit.*
ch. viii. ; Wood, *op. cit.* p. 198 ; Welldon, *The Revelation of the Holy
Spirit*, p. 177 ; Moule, *Veni Creator*, chs. ix.-xii. ; Downer, *The
Mission and Ministration of the Holy Spirit* ; Smeaton, *The Doctrine
of the Holy Spirit*, pp. 57-85 ; Redford, *Vox Dei*, p. 259.

methods of approach, or we can take both in turn. We can study the New Testament as it is, in five or six distinct groups ; the Synoptic Gospels ; the Fourth Gospel ; the Acts ; the Pauline Epistles ; the Catholic Epistles ; and the Apocalypse. But this has already been done adequately, and in some respects finally.[1] Or we can study it in approximate chronological order. The latter is perhaps preferable for our present purpose, since it will enable us to keep closely in touch with the spiritual experience of the primitive Church, and also with modern critical thought as to the New Testament.

The earliest New Testament documents are included in the writings of St. Paul, making his teaching a suitable starting-point for the New Testament doctrine of the Holy Spirit. A remarkable fulness of teaching is seen therein ; it is much fuller than in any other part of the New Testament.

' It is to the Epistles of St. Paul that we must turn for the fullest treatment which the doctrine of the Spirit receives within the limits of the New Testament.' [2]

' In St. Paul's Epistles the Holy Spirit is mentioned nearly 120 times, and may be said to have a prominence and importance which it has nowhere else in the New Testament.' [3]

The teaching touches every part of his message. The Spirit is regarded as essentially characteristic of the New Covenant.

' The work of the Holy Spirit enters so largely into the life of the Church, and held so great a place in the thought of the first age, that no Apostolic letter to the Churches could ignore it altogether ; and references to it will be found in all the Epistles attributed to St. Paul with the exception of the short private letter to Philemon.' [4]

' In studying the New Testament teaching concerning the work of the Holy Spirit in the individual man, His methods and processes in the training of each soul for God, we naturally turn to St. Paul. He has made this subject his own. Other writers have touched upon it, he has developed it and led the theological thought of the Christian Church in reference to it for centuries.' [5]

---

[1] Swete ; Smeaton ; Downer ; Simpson ; *ut supra.*

[2] Swete, Article ' Holy Spirit,' Hastings' *Bible Dictionary*, p. 409.

[3] Denney, *ut supra,* p. 738.

[4] Swete, *The Holy Spirit in the New Testament*, p. 226.

[5] Davison, *The Indwelling Spirit*, p. 59.

This is the more remarkable because we usually think of St. Paul mainly and almost entirely as the Apostle of righteousness by faith. But his doctrine of the Spirit is the necessary, vital, and essential complement of his doctrine of justification.[1]

In harmony with the methods of modern thought several attempts have been made to discover and trace the source of the Pauline doctrine of the Spirit, and the greatest possible differences of opinion exist. According to Sanday and Headlam, ' the doctrine of the Spirit of God, or the Holy Spirit, is taken over from the Old Testament.' [2] With this agree Wendt and Gloel. Gunkel derives the doctrine from St. Paul's own experience and originality, with very little connection with the Old Testament. Pfleiderer and Holtzmann connect it with Hellenistic thought, especially with the Book of Wisdom. Stevens,[3] after quoting the above, thinks that the root is in the Old Testament, but that personal experience and originality had greater importance in determining development. Swete speaks of St. Paul's treatment as characterised by

' an insight, a freshness, and a precision due partly to his unique experience, partly to the intensity of his interest in the Gospel and its workings upon human nature.' [4]

It is hardly possible to doubt that the Old Testament and also the specific revelation of Jesus Christ in St. Paul's own experience combine to give this doctrine both its contents and form.

The teaching is found in each group of the Epistles under special aspects.

' There is a manifest progress in the apostle's handling of this subject which corresponds to the progress in his own life and work.' [5]

The first group consists of 1 and 2 Thessalonians, and here ' he scarcely exceeds the usual teaching of the first generation ' [6] (1 Thess. i. 1, 5, 6 ; iv. 7, 8 ; v. 19 ; 2 Thess.

---

[1] Moule, *Veni Creator*, pp. 164-167.

[2] Sanday and Headlam, *Romans*, p. 199.

[3] Stevens, *The Theology of the New Testament*, p. 432, note.

[4] Swete, Article ' Holy Spirit,' Hastings' *Bible Dictionary*, p. 409.

[5] Swete, *ut supra*, p. 409.

[6] Swete, *ut supra*, p. 409.

ii. 13). Two points of special interest are (1) the reference to man's nature as 'spirit, soul, and body' (1 Thess. v. 23), and (2) the statement that the Holy Spirit is associated with the truth (2 Thess. ii. 13).

The second group includes Galatians; 1 and 2 Corinthians, Romans. Of these Swete remarks:

'The next group of letters (Rom., 1, 2 Cor., Gal.) carries us into the heart of his teaching on this subject and we find ourselves in the midst of what is largely a new revelation.'[1]

Starting with Galatians iii. and v., we see the force of the statement that

'the Epistle to the Galatians furnishes ample ground for the student who would follow St. Paul's exposition of the things of the Spirit.'[2]

The three special points of interest and importance in 1 Corinthians are (1) the relation of the Holy Spirit to spiritual insight (ch. ii.); (2) the action of the Holy Spirit in the formation of the Church (ch. xii. 13); (3) the great question of spiritual gifts in relation to the Holy Spirit (chs. xii., xiv.).[3] In 2 Corinthians the Holy Spirit is associated very largely with the Apostle's ministry. In Romans, while there are allusions in chs. v. and xv., the most important place is ch. viii., which may almost be called the Apostle's *locus classicus* of the subject.[4] No single passage is so full. While concerned almost entirely with the relation of the Holy Spirit to the believer's deliverance through the victory over sin, the treatment is remarkably varied and complete.

'There is perhaps nothing in the whole range of New Testament Pneumatology which carries us so far into the heart of the Spirit's work. He is seen here in His most intimate relations with the human consciousness, distinct from it, yet associated with its imperfectly formed longings after righteousness, acting as an intercessor on its behalf in the sight of God, as the glorified Christ does; not however in heaven, but in the hearts of believers. The mystery of prayer stands here revealed, as far as it can be in this life; we see that it is the Holy Spirit Who not only inspires the filial spirit which is the necessary condition of prayer, but is the author of the " hearty desires " which are its essence.'[5]

---

[1] Swete, *ut supra*, p. 409.　　　　[2] Davison, *op. cit.* p. 75.
[3] See note P, p. 282.　　　　[4] See note A, p. 274.
[5] Swete, *The Holy Spirit in the New Testament*, p. 221.

The third group consists of Colossians, Ephesians, and Philippians. Uniting these and the later Pastoral Epistles, Swete remarks :

'We find the Apostle's point of view somewhat modified. The intensity of his interest in the individual life has now been supplemented by a new interest in the unity and catholicity of the Church. He touches on the relations of the Spirit to the individual with a freshness of conception which shows that he is as keenly impressed as ever with their primary importance (Eph. i. 13, 14 ; iv. 30 ; vi. 17, 18 ; Phil. i. 19 ; Col. i. 7 ; 2 Tim. i. 14) ; yet it is as the Spirit of the universal Church that he now specially delights to contemplate the Holy Ghost.'[1]

In Colossians the only reference to the Spirit is found in ch. i. 8. In Philippians the teaching is also only occasional and incidental. But in Ephesians the doctrine is remarkably full, both in regard to the individual and also to the community.[2] It should never be forgotten that Ephesians is the next place in the New Testament after Matthew where the Church universal, as distinct from the Church local, is treated. In 1 Corinthians he is dealing with the *Ecclesia* of a single city, but in the Epistle to the Ephesians he is dealing with the universal *Ecclesia*.[3]

The fourth group is formed of 1 Timothy, Titus, 2 Timothy. The teaching as to the Holy Spirit in these Epistles is concerned almost entirely with the ministry (1 Tim. iv. 1 ; 2 Tim. i. 6, 7, 14). Although there is a natural and inevitable difference in these Epistles by reason of the very different topics of discussion, yet

'even in the Pastoral Epistles Pauline theology is not unpresented, and in particular they contain several characteristic allusions to St. Paul's doctrine of the Spirit.'[4]

As we study these four groups, it is impossible to avoid noticing that the main and important elements of the Apostle's teaching are found in Galatians ; 1 and 2 Corinthians ; Romans ; Ephesians. From these Epistles alone we are able to derive the specific outline of his doctrine of the Holy Spirit.

---

[1] Swete, Article 'Holy Spirit,' Hastings' *Bible Dictionary*, p. 410.

[2] See note A, p. 272.

[3] Hort, *Christian Ecclesia*, p. 141.

[4] Swete, *The Holy Spirit in the New Testament*, p. 243.

When we endeavour to combine and correlate the various aspects of teaching, we find that they can clearly be resolved into the two main aspects of the Work of the Spirit and the Nature of the Spirit. Each of these needs careful attention.

A. *The Work of the Spirit.* Swete says :

' By far the larger number of St. Paul's references to the Spirit in these Epistles are concerned with His operations on the spirit of man.' [1]

Indeed, His operations may perhaps be best understood by commencing with St. Paul's idea of the human spirit in relation to the Spirit of God. Bruce remarks that

' the great question for him was not, what the Holy Spirit is, but what He does in the soul of a believing man.' [2]

In every part of a believer's life the Holy Spirit is made prominent. From beginning to end He is all, and nothing seems to be outside His operations.

Smeaton says :

' When we survey the names or titles of the Spirit in St. Paul's Epistles they are numerous. . . . If we survey His titles as derived from the benefits and blessings which He confers, and of which He is the immediate author, He is called the Spirit that dwelleth in us (Rom. viii. 11), the Spirit of grace (Heb. x. 29), the Spirit of wisdom and revelation in the knowledge of the Lord Jesus (Eph. i. 17), the Spirit of adoption (Rom. viii. 15), the Spirit of life (Rom. viii. 2), the Spirit of meekness (Gal. vi. 1), the Spirit of power, and of love, and of a sound mind (2 Tim. i. 7).' [3]

Denney speaks of

' what is characteristically Pauline in the conception of the Spirit, namely, a possession of the Spirit which is beyond all particular " gifts " or " operations " of a spiritual kind, which is, in short, identical with Christian life.' [4]

The following points seem to be the most important, and to call for special notice.

1. He is the Source, Principle, and Support of the spiritual life. (*a*) In relation to the past He is the Spirit

[1] Swete, Article ' Holy Spirit,' Hastings' *Bible Dictionary*, p. 409.

[2] Bruce, *St. Paul's Conception of Christianity*, p. 242.

[3] Smeaton, *The Doctrine of the Holy Spirit*, p. 58.

[4] Denney, Article ' Holy Spirit,' *Dictionary of Christ and the Gospels*, p. 738.

of sonship (Rom. viii. 15), and liberty (2 Cor. iii. 17).
(*b*) In relation to the present He is the Spirit of holiness
Whose presence is the guarantee of ' fruit ' (Gal. v. 22).[1]
(*c*) In relation to the future life He is the Spirit of heirship
as the earnest of our inheritance (Eph. i. 14 ; cf. Rom.
viii. 23), and the guarantee of our resurrection (Rom.
viii. 11).

2. There is a fundamental distinction between the
' flesh ' and the ' spirit.'[2] According to St. Paul the
' flesh ' is either physical or ethical. In the latter sense
it is the sphere, seat, instrument, but not the principle of
sin. This remarkable contrast

' pervades the Apostle's writing, and is conspicuous in such
passages as Rom. viii. ; Gal v." [3]

3. The use of ' spirit ' to describe both Divine and
human elements.[4] In several passages where this is
discussed

' it is not easy to determine whether by πνεῦμα the Apostle means
the Spirit of God in man, or the spirit of man under the influence of
the Spirit of God.' [5]

Probably in several of the doubtful passages we are to
understand πνεῦμα ' as the human spirit influenced by and
so far identified with the Spirit of God.' [6] It would seem
as though no hard and fast rule can be laid down, especially
in such a passage as Rom. ch. viii.[7] A similar difficulty
arises in connection with the adjectives πνευματικός and
ψυχικός (1 Cor. ii. 14 ; xv. 44). The former is the man
under the control of the πνεῦμα ; the latter under the control of the ψυχή. But it would seem as though the former

---

[1] Davison, *op. cit.* ch. v.

[2] Swete, *The Holy Spirit in the New Testament*, p. 193.

[3] Denney, *ut supra*, p. 739. Cf. Bruce, *St. Paul's Conception of Christianity*, p. 262 ff.

[4] Davison, *op. cit.* ch. iii. ; Fletcher, *The Psychology of the New Testament*.

[5] Swete, Article ' Holy Spirit,' Hastings' *Bible Dictionary*, p. 410.

[6] Swete, *ut supra*, p. 410.

[7] Cf. Sanday and Headlam, *Romans*, p. 196.

must mean the highest nature of man as possessed and ruled by the Holy Spirit of God. One thing is quite clear ; the πνεῦμα is a faculty that belongs to the unregenerate, and cannot be limited to the regenerate only. 2 Cor. vii. 1 is conclusive on this point.

' It must be said, however—in opposition to some highly respected authorities, including Delitzsch, Neander and others—that there is no ground for the view that the πνεῦμα in St. Paul is a faculty of which the natural man is destitute, and which is only imparted in regeneration. It is contrasted with " flesh " in many cases where regeneration has not taken place ; it is used in connection with such words as disobedience and cowardice ; and its occurrence in 2 Cor. vii. 1, " Let us cleanse ourselves from all filthiness of flesh and spirit," shows that both parts of man's nature have been stained with sin, and that both may be cleansed and renewed by grace.' [1]

Discussion has often been rife as to the meaning of spirit, soul, and body in 1 Thess. v. 23.[2] Is man tri-partite or bipartite ? There are great names on both sides, and certainly in passages like Luke i. 46, 47 there is no essential difference between soul and spirit. Perhaps we may say that 'spirit' is that element or aspect of human nature which is capable of fellowship with God ; 'soul' is that non-material part which includes the thoughts, emotions, and volition, while 'body' is the physical element.

' The preferable view, now very generally adopted, would seem to be that spirit, soul, and flesh are in St. Paul, as elsewhere in the Bible, not three natures, but man's nature viewed in three aspects. The spirit is the self-conscious life-principle given by God, in virtue of which man thinks and feels and wills. The soul is the personal being so constituted, and is descriptive of man's natural, earthly life ; while man, as flesh, inherits a frail, perishable body, which represents him on the outer and lower and material side. The whole man—body, soul, and spirit—is redeemed by Christ, and is to be completely sanctified by the renewing power of the indwelling Spirit of God.' [3]

Summing up the whole question of the relation of the Divine to the human 'spirit,' we may remark that they are so intimate as to be indistinguishable, although their union

---

[1] Davison, *op. cit.* p. 70.

[2] Denney, ' Thessalonians,' *Expositor's Bible*, p. 255 f.

[3] Davison, *op. cit.* p. 70.

is always regarded as equivalent to communion, never to identity.[1]

4. A clear distinction is drawn between the grace and the gifts of the Spirit, between the ordinary and the extraordinary; between χάρις and χάρισμα. It has been thought that while the Apostle fully accepted the χαρίσματα, he saw their spiritual danger, and thereupon was led to emphasise more definitely the ordinary graces of the Spirit. There is no doubt whatever that he held quite as firmly as any of his contemporaries the supernatural manifestations of the Holy Spirit in the form of miraculous gifts.

'Paul shared to the full the belief of the primitive Church on this subject. He himself enjoyed a measure of the common gift of the Spirit that was greater, it would seem, than that which fell to any other, uniting in himself in a singular degree the various endowments that were conferred on believers by this new power. He was in the most entire agreement with his fellow-Christians as to the superhuman origin of the gift and as to its paramount value for the religious life.' [2]

'It is not intended to suggest that the Apostle broke entirely away from the earlier charismatic theory. He not only did not doubt or deny, he earnestly believed in the reality of the miraculous charisms. He even sympathised with the view that in their miraculousness lay the proof that the power of God was at work.' [3]

His teaching as to the relation of spiritual gifts to the normal graces of the Spirit clearly shows his view of their relative value and importance (1 Cor. xii. 31; xiii. 1; xiv. 1).[4] But although he emphasises the normal element of the Christian life, he is none the less emphatic as to the source of everything being the Holy Spirit.

'The fact that the ordinary graces of Christian character were ascribed by him to the Spirit of God, is of itself a testimony to the

---

[1] An able modern writer, Dr. J. Moffatt of Oxford, recently remarked that, 'The psychology of the "spiritual" man, in Paulinism, is an extremely difficult problem, and the general relation of "flesh" and "spirit," in the apostle's teaching, involves a pretty accurate knowledge of the rabbinic doctrine of the evil impulse, if it is to be appreciated aright' (*British Weekly*).

[2] Somerville, *St. Paul's Conception of Christ*, p. 114.

[3] Bruce, *op cit.* p. 248.

[4] Cf. Stevens, *The Theology of the New Testament*, pp. 433-436.

superhuman worth and Divine origin that were felt to belong to
true and noble character in apostolic times.' [1]

5. The doctrine of the Holy Spirit in the Church is
based on the doctrine of the Holy Spirit in individuals.
Because He dwells in individuals, He is therefore in the
community ; the Church has the Spirit because individuals
have the Spirit.

As we review the teaching of the Apostle on the Work
of the Holy Spirit, we see that

' the life in the Spirit is the counterpart of that justification by
which the believer was accepted and forgiven. With Paul these
are inseparable elements or aspects of the process of salvation. They
are organically related to each other. Justification opens the way
into the new life ; sanctification is the development of that life
through the union with Christ which is entered into by faith.' [2]

And so

' when the religious ideas of the apostolic age are considered, this
correlation of the Spirit with man's ethical and practical life seems
to be Paul's greatest contribution to the doctrine under consideration.' [3]

B. *The Nature of the Spirit.*[4] As already noted, the
great majority of St. Paul's references to the Spirit are
concerned with His Work rather than with His Nature,
and it is only as we combine and correlate the references
to the Work that we can really derive his doctrine of the
Nature. It is asserted that

' Paul's language does not furnish us with the materials for an
accurate definition of the Spirit.'

Though the writer adds that it is certain

' that the Spirit was to him an objective divine reality and
power. . . . His language is, for the most part, general and practical, and does not lend itself to our aid in the metaphysics of the
subject.' [5]

But we must still face the problem :

' Regarding the personality of the Spirit, the question should be,
not whether Paul thought of the Spirit as a person distinct from

---

[1] Somerville, *op. cit.* p. 116.

[2] Stevens, *ut supra*, p. 437.   [3] Stevens, *op. cit.* p. 439.

[4] For different opinions of St. Paul's view of the Nature of the
Spirit, see Stevens, *ut supra*, p. 441, note 1.

[5] Stevens, *ut supra*, p. 444.

God and Christ, but whether what he says of the Spirit naturally involves that conclusion *for us.*' [1]

The main teaching can be thus summarised :

1. A close relation of the Holy Spirit to God. He is called the Spirit of God (Rom. viii. 9), and the Spirit of Him that raised up Jesus from the dead (Rom. viii. 11). The same results are attributed to Him as to God (Rom. xv. 16 ; 1 Thess. v. 23). Thus in some way the Spirit is regarded as possessing a Divine objective reality.

2. An attribution of Divine personal activities. That the Spirit is personal is seen from the fact that He can be grieved (Eph. iv. 30 ; 1 Thess. v. 19) ; and can inhabit human lives (1 Cor. vi. 19). A further proof of the same idea is the distinction between the Father, the Son, and the Spirit, and yet the possession of identical names and work (1 Cor. ii. 10 ; ' searcheth ' ; 1 Cor. xii. 4-6 ; 2 Cor. xiii. 14 ; Eph. iv. 4-6). It is impossible to speak of these statements as implying merely a personification.

' By some this personification of the Spirit is regarded as purely poetical and rhetorical. It is, however, quite certain that there are important differences between Paul's personifications of sin and death and his personification of the Spirit. The operations of the Spirit are, in any case, really personal whether the Spirit is distinguished from God and Christ or not. To say that the Spirit is a power, as Beyschlag does, defines nothing. It is to take refuge in an abstraction. God is also called a power (Matt. xxvi. 64) without detriment to the conviction of His personality. I am confident that no such co-ordination with God and Christ as we observe in the case of the Holy Spirit in the three passages above cited (2 Cor. xiii. 14 ; 1 Cor. xii. 4-6 ; Eph. iv. 4-6) can either be found, or even reasonably imagined, in the case of any of Paul's other personifications. It seems to me that reflective thought can most naturally construe the functions of the Spirit, as Paul describes them, upon the view that the Spirit is a self distinct from God and from Christ.' [2]

3. The relation of the Spirit to Christ is more difficult, because it is something altogether novel and strange.

' The relation of God and the Spirit is not one difficult to understand. We have the entire history and literature of the Jewish nation to aid us, as well as innumerable analogies from other religions. Not so with the relation of Christ and the Spirit. This has

---

[1] Stevens, *ut supra*, p. 444.

[2] Stevens, *op. cit.* p. 445.

no parallel elsewhere. It was a problem new to the Christian Church.' [1]

The Titles must be noticed : of Christ (Rom. viii. 9) ; of His Son (Gal. iv. 6). The Spirit is the unseen Agent by Whom Christ is made real to the believer.

' He is a Person Who represents Jesus Christ to His disciples. In the absence of Jesus Christ His presence is more than equivalent to the personal presence of the latter (John xvi. 7-15), and in the Christian economy He, the Holy Spirit, is as the personal God (2 Cor. iii. 3-11).' [2]

' The Spirit is for St. Paul specifically Christian. It is not the power or the life of God *simpliciter*, but the power or the life of God as God has been manifested in Christ, and especially in His resurrection and exaltation. He calls it expressly the Spirit of Christ (Rom. viii. 9) ; it is an epistle of Christ that is written on men's hearts by the Spirit of the living God (2 Cor. iii. 3) ; he even goes so far as to say, the Lord is the Spirit (iii. 17), and he who is joined to the Lord is one spirit (1 Cor. vi. 17). The presence of the Spirit is, it may be said, the spiritual presence of the Lord ; it is not an indefinite power of God, but the last Adam who has become lifegiving spirit (xv. 45).' [3]

The activity of Christ as the Redeemer and Head of the Church is regarded as continued by the Holy Spirit Who is at once transcendent and immanent, Lord and Life. The Spirit of God is identified with the Spirit of Christ (Rom. viii. 9-11) ; the Spirit is given through Christ ; the Spirit reveals Christ and makes Him real to the believer ; the Spirit is the active principle of Christ's personality. The value of this as a criterion of alleged spiritual phenomena is evident. The supreme question is whether such phenomena come from Christ. The one and only purpose of the Spirit is to reveal and glorify Christ.

Then there is a close association of the Spirit of God and the Spirit of Christ with the Person of Christ. No line of demarcation is drawn between Christ and the Spirit. The great passage is 2 Cor. iii. 17, ' Now the Lord is the Spirit.' So close is the association that Bruce is able to say, ' The Spirit is the Alter Ego of the Lord.' [4]

---

[1] Wood, *The Spirit of God in Biblical Literature*, p. 228.

[2] Denio, *The Supreme Leader*, p. 45.

[3] Denney, Article ' Holy Spirit,' *Dictionary of Christ and the Gospels*, p. 738.

[4] Bruce, *op. cit.* p. 254.

And yet with all this intimacy of association they are never absolutely identified ; they are distinguished and yet united ; united and yet distinguished.

' Being " in Christ " and " being in the Spirit " are the same thing, and in the thought of the Apostle, " Christ," the " Spirit of Christ," and " the Spirit of God " are practically synonymous. . . . His personal influence and working being, to the entire exclusion of every lower element, the influence and working of the Holy Spirit, He, Himself personally, might be spoken of as the Lord, *the Spirit.*' [1]

' He recognised no hard and fast line between what he owed to Christ and what he owed to the Spirit of God.' [2]

' The transformation into the image of the Lord, accomplished by beholding and reflecting His glory, is essentially a spiritual operation. Only the Holy Spirit can effect it. Yet the whole process is so essentially that of Christ the Lord, Whom the Spirit is glorifying in the believer, that the subtle and paradoxical expression, " as from the Lord Who is the Spirit," or " the Spirit Who is the Lord," is permissible. It is readily understood by the devout heart while it may be open to the cavils of the critical mind.' [3]

And so it is possible to say that

' this practical identity of Christ and the Spirit of God is the ground or reason of that union between Christ and His people that is so characteristic a feature of the experience of the Christian life described in the Epistles of Paul, and that sets his thought of Christ in so original a light.' [4]

4. The implications of the doctrine of the Trinity are obvious. While we find nothing approaching a definite, metaphysical, ontological Trinity in the New Testament, it is impossible to avoid observing the contributions made by St. Paul to the Christian doctrine of the Trinity. The association of God the Father, Christ the Son, and the Holy Spirit with Divine operations carries its own definite implication, however far this may be from any systematic or philosophic expression.

' Though the Apostle attempts no metaphysical synthesis of the doctrine of the Trinity, he certainly affirms the fundamental Trinitarian ideas. Thus, for example, in the benediction he directly indicates both the Divinity and the threefold existence of Father, Son, and Holy Ghost (2 Cor. xiii. 14).' [5]

---

[1] Somerville, *op. cit.* p. 118.   [2] Somerville, *ut supra*, p. 113.

[3] Davison, *op. cit.* p. 74.   [4] Somerville, *op. cit.* p. 121.

[5] Adeney, *The Theology of the New Testament*, p. 184. Cf. Wood, *op. cit.* p. 231 f.

We may perhaps sum up the Pauline doctrine by distinguishing the following uses of the word ' Spirit.'

(a) The Spirit of God. This is in the direct line of the Old Testament thought, though with significant developments. In the Old Testament the Spirit is revealed as mainly temporary for endowment, but leading up to the idea of a permanent element for life. The latter becomes normal in St. Paul though the former is still visible in the New Testament idea of spiritual gifts. H. W. Robinson says :

' But Paul has brought together the Old Testament doctrine of the Spirit, and the Old Testament aspiration after mystic fellowship with God, and made them real, vital, personal, by his conception of Christ as the mediator of the Divine Spirit.' [1]

(b) The Spirit of Christ, i.e. as sent by Christ, and revealing Him. Christ is the Son of God ; the medium of God for us, Whom the Spirit could use, and to our consciousness both are one and the same (Gal. ii. 20 ; 1 Cor. vi. 17, 19 ; Rom. viii. 10, 11). Christ dwelling in us by the Spirit is the essential truth for the believer's life.

(c) The spirit as a human faculty (1 Cor. ii. 11 ; v. 5).

(d) The spirit as a human faculty renewed by grace (Rom. viii. 10, 15).

(e) The Spirit in the Church as proved by the phenomena of graces and gifts.

(f) The Spirit in individual Christians indwelling, working, and transforming.

(g) The Spirit with the genitive, e.g. ' Spirit of life,' ' Spirit of adoption.' But this is not to be understood in the modern sense of ' disposition,' or temperament, a usage which is almost certainly not found in the New Testament.[2]

We must never forget that St. Paul's doctrine of the Spirit is uniformly practical, not speculative. It is conceived and maintained in close and constant connection with his own personal Christian experience.

---

[1] ' Hebrew Psychology in Relation to Pauline Anthropology,' in *Mansfield College Essays*, p. 285. See the same idea elaborated in his *Christian Doctrine of Man*, pp. 125-129.

[2] Humphries, *The Holy Spirit in Faith and Experience*, p. 261, and note 2.

' Paul's psychology is not a matter of inference and certainly not of philosophy, but of his own personal experience.' [1]

' Nothing is more certain than that his whole conception of the Spirit was religious, and had its root in his experience of the fruits of the Spirit in his inner life.' [2]

As we leave this subject it is again essential to call attention to the prominence and importance of the doctrine of the Spirit of God in the writings of St. Paul. It is scarcely possible to exaggerate its significance for a true conception of essential Christianity.

' Among the many contributions of Paul to the developed thought of Christianity only one, that of the universality of the Gospel apart from the law, is more striking in itself or more far-reaching in its effects than his theory of the Spirit.' [3]

Gloel remarks that ' the Apostle's entire thinking stands under the influence of his estimate of the Spirit.' The possession of the human spirit by the Spirit of God ; its purification, control, guidance, assurance, and transformation constitute the very heart of the Pauline doctrine of the indwelling of Christ by the Spirit, and there will never be any practical difficulty in the relation of the human to the Divine Spirit if both are kept in constant contact with the reality of a living experience.

' The gracious ambiguity of some of St. Paul's expressions can deceive no one. The reason why in some passages it is difficult to say whether the immediate working of the Spirit of God is intended, or the result of His operation reflected in the human spirit, is that these two are strangely and deeply one. We are in the Spirit if He is in us. And without the Spirit of Christ Himself at work within us we can do nothing.' [4]

---

[1] Wood, *op. cit.* p. 218.   [2] Somerville, *op. cit.* p. 119.
[3] Wood, *op. cit.* p. 198.   [4] Davison, *op. cit.* p. 77.

CHAPTER 5

THE HOLY SPIRIT
IN THE ACTS OF THE APOSTLES

THE fulness of Pauline teaching clearly presupposes a genuine experience of the Spirit existing in the Christian community.

' That the Divine Spirit was present in the community of believers, revealing there His mighty power, was no discovery of the apostle Paul's. The fact was patent to all. By all accounts the primitive Church was the scene of remarkable phenomena which arrested general attention, and bore witness to the operation of a cause of a very unusual character to which beholders gave the name of the Holy Ghost.' [1]

Our next step, therefore, is to get behind St. Paul's teaching, and study the experience of the early Church. We can do this in the Acts, and attention to its teaching is essential to a proper understanding of the subject. Recent criticism bears ample testimony to the early date and historical character of the book, and also in particular to the historical value of the early chapters.

' While these chapters do not tell us all that we should like to know, they do furnish us a clear idea of the relations of the earliest Christians to their ancestral religion and of the principal points

---

[1] Bruce, *St. Paul's Conception of Christianity*, p. 243.

LITERATURE.—Humphries, *The Holy Spirit in Faith and Experience*, chs. vi. and vii. ; Wood, *The Spirit of God in Biblical Literature*, p. 151 ; Welldon, *The Revelation of the Holy Spirit*, p. 147 ; Smeaton, *The Doctrine of the Holy Spirit*; Davison, *The Indwelling Spirit*, ch. iv.; Downer, *The Mission and Ministration of the Holy Spirit*, chs. v. and vi. ; E. H. Johnson, *The Holy Spirit*, p. 158 ; Elder Cumming, *Through the Eternal Spirit* p. 168 ; Redford, *Vox Dei*, p. 259 ; Swete, Article ' Holy Spirit,' Hastings' *Bible Dictionary*, p. 407.

which they emphasised in their efforts to win men to belief in the messiahship of Jesus.' [1]

The first point to observe is the remarkable prominence given to the Holy Spirit in this book.

' No one can read the vivid and intense pages of the early chapters of the Acts without feeling that even the written record betrays a consciousness of unmeasured power, a heroic enthusiasm in the face of man and circumstance, an overmastering realisation of divine guidance swaying the leaders and the communities in ways unexpected and before unexperienced.' [2]

There are at least seventy references, and on this account the book has been called ' The Acts of the Holy Spirit.' Wood speaks of

' the superabundant use of the Holy Spirit in the literature of early Christianity. If that literature represents with any adequacy the life of the early Church, that life was full of the thought that the Spirit was an actual possession of the Christian. The Spirit manifested itself in every Church and was a part of the common experience of many Christians.' [3]
' So, also, the whole book glows in the light of this primary fact, and back to it all the activities of the Church as witness to Jews and Gentiles for salvation in the name of the risen Lord are traced. It might be termed " The Acts of the Holy Spirit " in and through Peter, Paul, and other leaders.' [4]

Another line of emphasis is placed on the Lord Jesus Christ as exalted.[5] This may be, and doubtless is, ' a very simple Christology,' [6] but it is sufficient to show the Divine position He held and the supreme authority He possessed in the eyes of the early Christians, as recorded in these chapters :

' The descriptions which they give of Christ's absolutely unique character and work appear to me to be quite irreconcilable with the humanitarian theory of His Person.' [7]

This twofold stress is the most remarkable feature in the book ; the prominence of the Divine over the human element in life and work. Denney says :

' The whole Pentecostal phenomenon . . . has the character of a testimony to Jesus . . . the gift and possession of the Spirit is the

---

[1] Stevens, *The Theology of the New Testament*, p. 258.

[2] Winstanley, *Spirit in the New Testament*, p. 130.

[3] Wood, *The Spirit of God in Biblical Literature*, p. 157.

[4] Winstanley, *op. cit.* p. 131.   [5] Stevens, *op. cit.* p. 265.

[6] Stevens, *op. cit.* p. 266.   [7] Stevens, *op. cit.* p. 267.

proof to the world of the exaltation of Jesus. It is His Divine power which is behind this incalculable elevation and reinforcement of the natural life. This is the New Testament point of view throughout.' [1]

We must now look more definitely at the teaching of the book. The first striking feature is the reference to the Holy Spirit in connection with the Great Forty Days of our Lord's post-resurrection earthly life. Christ's teaching and the disciples' expectations are seen to be concentrated on the Holy Spirit. The key-note is struck at once (ch. i. 2, 4, 8). It has been well pointed out that this first reference in Acts to the Holy Spirit ' is one of the most singular,' [2] because, although in the Gospel our Lord speaks and acts in the power of the Holy Spirit,

' there is no parallel to this expression. It seems to suggest that with the Resurrection the dispensation of the Holy Spirit began, and that the disciples were conscious, as they listened to the new and final charge of their Lord, that they were in contact, as they had never been before, with the powers of the world to come (He. vi. 5), the Divine inspiration of the Messianic age.' [3]

The second feature of the book is the prominence given to the Day of Pentecost. It is clearly to be regarded as unique both as the culmination of previous expectation, and also as the beginning of the new Society. For the purpose of the study of this important and pivotal event, the following points call for special study.

(*a*) The facts connected with the coming : the symbols and realities. The occasion was a Jewish Festival which necessarily brought together a vast concourse of people. The symbols of Fire, Wind, and Tongues were expressive of the testimony and service which were to be inaugurated on that day as the most important efforts thenceforward of the Christian community.

(*b*) The effects of the coming : the reception of the Spirit, with the testimony to Christ and its resultant impressions. The true interpretation would seem to be that all the disciples, and not the Apostles only, were filled with the Holy Spirit. The narrative does not warrant the view that

---

[1] Article ' Holy Spirit,' *Dictionary of Christ and the Gospels*, p. 737.

[2] Denney, *ut supra*, p. 736.

[3] Denney, *ut supra*, p. 736.

the Apostles alone were the recipients of the gift.[1]   The correct idea is that all the 120 who had been waiting in the Upper Room experienced the new power and blessing.

' The whole was a vision, as St. Luke is careful to explain, but a vision that corresponded to a great spiritual fact which at the same moment accomplished itself in the experience of all who were present.' [2]

(c) The first sermon : with the reference to Joel ii.   A careful comparison of the context in the Prophet shows that the primary meaning was essentially Jewish, whatever secondary and wider application the words may be supposed to have.   If Joel is taken just as it stands, Pentecost was not at all a full and complete realisation of the prophetic word.

' Neither the Prophet nor the Apostle who quoted him could have seen all that was implied in this prophecy, or how it would work itself out in the history of the Church.   In the thought of both, *all flesh* seems to have borne the narrow sense " all Israelites and all proselytes to the religion of Israel from among the Gentiles." ' [3]

(d) The effects of the preaching : the Holy Spirit offered and received.   After his quotation, St. Peter again refers to the coming of the Spirit as associated with the Ascension of Christ, and then definitely sets before his hearers the possibility of their experiencing the same Holy Spirit on the conditions of repentance and baptism.   The result was immediate, for on the acceptance of the Apostle's word the gift came, and with it the new life that was to be henceforth a predominant mark of those who were the followers of the Lord Jesus Christ.

' The closing verses of the second chapter of the Acts, with their picture of the simple, joyful, strenuous life of the newly baptized in the days that followed the Pentecost, reveal even more than the miracles of the Pentecost itself the nature of the Power which had come to dwell with the Church.' [4]

What then are we to understand as the meaning of this important Day of Pentecost ? [5]

---

[1] So Welldon, *The Revelation of the Holy Spirit*, p. 149.

[2] Swete, *The Holy Spirit in the New Testament*, p. 71.

[3] Swete, *ut supra*, p. 75.   [4] Swete, *ut supra*, p. 80.

[5] Swete, *The Holy Spirit in the New Testament*, p. 73 ; A. J. Gordon, *The Ministry of the Spirit*, p. 27 ; Elder Cumming, *Through*

1. First of all, it was the vindication of Christ to the Jews. It was the demonstration of His character and claim (ch. ii. 22-36).

2. Then, it brought a new power among the disciples. Pentecost was not their regeneration, for they were already disciples; it involved a new era and operation of the Holy Spirit, such as never existed before (John vii. 37). In the Old Testament and the Gospels we have the record of the Holy Spirit as already at work, but this is a fuller manifestation, and its newness lay in the relation of the Holy Spirit to Christ. To the disciples the gift of the Holy Spirit at Pentecost may be said to be analogous to the descent of the Holy Spirit on Christ at His baptism; it was the initiation into, and consecration to specific service for God. And with this came the bestowal of power, as in their Master's case, adequate to the new demands that were so soon to be made upon them.

' The descent of the Holy Spirit on the disciples at Pentecost was to them what the descent of the Holy Spirit upon our Lord at His Baptism was to Him. It was their initiation into an official ministry. As in His instance, so too in theirs, it occurred on the threshold of public responsibility. After His Baptism He was no more a private man, living in quietness and retirement, but the definite claimant to Messiahship. And they too, after the Pentecost, were no more timid, shrinking, reticent, half-hearted men, no more gathered apart from society in a small room, but bold as lions, the strenuous advocates of the greatest of all causes, the invincible evangelists of the world.' [1]

' The Peter of the Day of Pentecost is a new man, far other than the Peter of the Passover. . . . And in courage and general understanding of the new situation Peter was not alone; the whole company of believers was filled with the same spirit; the rest of the Twelve stood up with him, identifying themselves with his words. From that day forward a new strength, which was not their own, marked all the sayings and deeds of the Apostolic Church. It is in this great change of mental and spiritual attitude rather than in the external signs of wind and fire or in strange powers of utterance that we recognise the supreme miracle of the day of Pentecost.' [2]

the Eternal Spirit, chs. vii.-ix.; J. M. Campbell, After Pentecost, What? ch. i.; Kuyper, The Work of the Holy Spirit, p. 112; E. H. Johnson, The Holy Spirit, p. 160; Stevens, The Theology of the New Testament, p. 432; Welldon, The Revelation of the Holy Spirit, p. 147; Humphries, The Holy Spirit in Faith and Experience, pp. 155, 183; Joseph Parker, The Paraclete, p. 10.

[1] Welldon, op. cit. p. 153.   [2] Swete, ut supra, p. 76.

3. By the same gift the new body was constituted. While we may say, literally, that the birthday of the Christian Church was that occasion on which the two disciples of the Baptist heard their master speak and followed Jesus (John i. 37), yet the Day of Pentecost may be rightly called the commencement of the Christian Church among the Jews by the coming and indwelling of the Holy Spirit as the gift of the Ascended Christ.

4. Above all, Pentecost was the entrance of the Holy Spirit into human life, to make real the work of Christ. All through His earthly life, and especially in its later stages, our Lord had spoken of a Kingdom and a coming gift, and even after His resurrection His followers were told to wait until they were endued with power from on high (Luke xxiv. 49 ; Acts i. 4, 5). Then after the Ascension and the prayerful waiting during the ten days, the Gift came, with its bestowal of light and power. What their Master had said to them now became instinct with meaning, and they entered into a new experience of their crucified and risen Lord. Thus it was not until the Day of Pentecost that the reality of the work of redemption became fully vital in their experience.

The third feature of the book is the prominence given to the Spirit of God in the early Church. This is seen in almost every part from beginning to end.

' The early history of the Church recorded in the Acts is a kind of extended Pentecost. On that day a pellucid spring of new life is seen pouring forth from the mountain-side, and the first years of the Church show us the course of the stream, in its pristine freshness and purity, the first effervescence of what can only be described as a Vita Nuova, a New Life.' [1]

It is only possible to look at this in outline.

(a) The Bestowal of the Spirit. There are six accounts of the gift of the Spirit as representative examples of His coming. In ch. ii. we have the commencement of the Jewish Christian Church ; in ch. iv. 31, a special bestowal for special testimony ; in ch. viii. the extension of the Church to the Samaritans ; in ch. ix. the conversion of the Apostle of the Gentiles ; in ch. x. the extension of the

---

[1] Davison, *The Indwelling Spirit*, p. 81.

Church to the Gentiles ; and in ch. xix. the special occasion at Ephesus.

(b) The Work of the Spirit. This is found in almost every aspect of the life of the Christian community, and in particular whenever the Church is called upon to extend its sphere. Thus in ch. vi. 3, the appointment of the Seven is bound up with the fulness of the Spirit ; in ch. xiii. 2, the Spirit calls men to missionary service ; in ch. xv. 28, the Holy Spirit is associated with the decision of the Council at Jerusalem ; in ch. xvi. 6, the Holy Spirit's guidance is given as to the proper sphere of labour.

'It was plainly an accepted canon of judgment that any new departure or policy was right which either was initiated by the Spirit, or was subsequently endorsed by Him.'[1]

'The author of the book of Acts assigns to the Spirit the guidance of the Church in its progressive expansion.'[2]

'The Holy Spirit is a great reality in Luke's thought-world, it dominates his conceptions. He is the Divine guiding power in the Church's growth throughout.'[3]

(c) The Gifts of the Spirit. These are found at almost every juncture, and are of various kinds. There is the gift of tongues on three occasions (chs. ii., x., xix.) ;[4] the gift of healing (ch. iii.) ; the gift of prophecy (ch. xix. 6) ; and some manifest tokens of the Spirit which are not described in detail (ch. viii. 18).

All this shows how true it is that the book is dominated throughout by the Holy Spirit, and that the life of the primitive Church is possessed, inspired, and controlled by His Divine presence and power.

But there is one great problem to be faced. Modern writers often distinguish very clearly between the revelation of the Holy Spirit in the Acts and that found in the Epistles of St. Paul. This distinction is one of the most prominent features in several recent books, and calls for thorough consideration. It is urged that the first Christians realised the presence of the Spirit only in extraordinary and supernatural phenomena, and that this

---

[1] Humphries, *The Holy Spirit in Faith and Experience*, p. 190.

[2] Wood, *op. cit.* p. 182.

[3] Winstanley, *op. cit.* p. 135.

[4] See note B, p. 275.

tendency to favour the preternatural resulted in a very partial, one-sided view of the work of the Spirit of God.

'It was in phenomena of this sort, preternatural effects of some great power, that the first Christians saw the hand of God. The miraculousness of the phenomena was what they laid stress on. The more unusual and out of the ordinary course, the more divine. In accordance with this view, the Spirit's work was conceived of as transcendent, miraculous, and charismatic.'[1]

According to this view, the Spirit in Acts is a Spirit of power rather than a Spirit of holiness ; the author of gifts ($\chi\alpha\rho\acute{\iota}\sigma\mu\alpha\tau\alpha$) rather than of grace ($\chi\acute{\alpha}\rho\iota\varsigma$).[2] This interpretation is adopted by a number of writers. Thus Stevens says :

'The extraordinary and the marvellous were the marks of the Spirit's presence and power.'[3]

Wood even goes so far as to say that

'the Spirit was never regarded in the pre-Pauline Church as an essential part of the ordinary Christian life, but as a *donum superadditum*. . . . Nowhere in the book of Acts is there proof that the author regarded the Spirit as the basis of the ordinary religious life.'[4]

This is interpreted to mean that there was a fundamental misconception in this emphasis on the abnormal, which the Apostle had to remove,[5] and that he thereby saved the Church from a very real danger.[6] This work of the Apostle is said to be 'one of Paul's most ingenious and truly spiritual conceptions.'[7] To the same effect is the following statement :

'It is one of the defects which, as a legacy from the Old Testament, long attached to the doctrine of the Spirit in the primitive Church, that Christians seemed unable to realise His presence save through some arresting appeal to the senses.'[8]

The writer adds that 'the corrective was supplied by the Apostle Paul.'[9] It is therefore regarded as one of the

---

[1] Bruce, *op. cit.* p. 244.   [2] Bruce, *op. cit.* p. 245.

[3] Stevens, *op. cit.* p. 431. See also Humphries, *op. cit.* p. 239.

[4] Wood, *op. cit.* pp. 186, 187.   [5] Humphries, *op. cit.* p. 239.

[6] Humphries, *op. cit.* p. 243.

[7] Gunkel ; quoted by Humphries, *op. cit.* p. 243.

[8] Humphries, *op. cit.* p. 164.

[9] Humphries, *op. cit.* p. 164, note.

most obvious truths that the thought of the Holy Spirit in the Acts is inextricably bound up with the abnormal, the spectacular, and the dramatic, and with that alone. ' Until Paul taught them a truer view they saw Him nowhere else.' [1] The supernatural phenomena of Acts are said to imply a defect which the Apostle corrected, and that this involves an advance in Paul's doctrine.

' The community regards as pneumatic the extraordinary in the life of the Christian, Paul the ordinary ; they that which is peculiar to individuals, Paul that which is common to all ; they that which occurs abruptly, Paul that which is constant ; they that which is special in the Christian life, Paul the Christian life itself. Hence the value which the primitive Church attaches to miracles, Paul attaches to the Christian state. No more is that which is individual and sporadic held to be the Divine in man ; the Christian man is the spiritual man.' [2]

The issues are thus made perfectly plain and have to be faced. First of all, this must surely be said. It is not quite correct to state in so unqualified a way that the abnormal is the only element in the conception of the Holy Spirit in the Acts, because the presence of the normal is admitted :

' We are not to suppose that anyone meant deliberately to exclude the Holy Ghost from the properly spiritual sphere, and to confine His agency to the charismatic region. That the author of Acts had no such thought may be gathered from the fact that he ascribed Lydia's openness of mind to the Gospel to Divine influence.' [3]

Again, and chiefly, while these writers are correct in their facts, they seem to be incorrect and misleading in their deductions. There is indeed a great difference between Acts and St. Paul, but the explanation is to be sought for elsewhere and otherwise. The true view is pretty certainly to be found in a fresh and fuller consideration of the Acts in relation both to what precedes and follows. As a commencement, let us contrast the earlier and later parts of the book. Nothing is more striking than the Jewish features in these early chapters, which link on the Day of Pentecost to that which precedes. While a new dis-

---

[1] Humphries, *op. cit.* pp. 191, 194.

[2] Gunkel ; quoted by Humphries, *op. cit.* p. 243.

[3] Bruce, *op. cit.* p. 246.

pensation has begun, the emphasis is rather upon Pentecost as the close of a former than the opening of a new era. In a word, Pentecost is really transitional, and almost everything found at least in the first twelve chapters bears out the principle of the Apostle, ' To the Jew first.' The fact is that Acts is almost entirely Jewish until the time of Stephen's martyrdom, followed by Saul's conversion, and even then the Jewish element does not materially recede, but is found more or less fully until the end of the book. So that the key to the proper understanding of Acts is to regard it primarily as the record not of the founding of the Christian Church in its wide sense, but rather as the account of the last offer to, and the wilful sin of the Jewish nation.[1]

This is all the more striking when we remember that Luke, the writer of Acts, was a companion of Paul, and must surely have known the Apostle's characteristic doctrines of grace. Thus it has been remarked on this point :

' The truly Pauline level of teaching is unattained, the doctrine of the Spirit as the moulder and fashioner of the Christian's inner life continually, as it confronts us in the Apostle's letters, is unassimilated. Thus Luke, after all, reflects a less developed form of teaching in his writings than his greater fellow-traveller ; he edits his sources in the light of the Spirit's work, but that work is still to him almost solely confined to the equipment of the Messiah, of those who prepare His way, and of those who lead on the continuation of His saving mission. The guidance is occasional, mostly external or by " tongues " and " prophecy," the daily religion of the believer is not yet by Luke expressly regarded as the sphere of the influence of the Spirit of God or of Christ.' [2]

The admitted fact of this inadequacy of teaching compared with ' the truly Pauline level ' ought to have received more attention from students, because therein we may find the solution of our problem. This view of the book is fully borne out by a careful study of its contents.

(a) The first chapter is concerned with the Kingdom of God in relation to *Israel*, thereby indicating the last chapter of Israel's history rather than the first chapter of Church history ; the close of an old dispensation rather than the beginning of a new.

[1] Anderson, *The Silence of God*, pp. 49-58, 72-78, 172-177.

[2] Winstanley, *op. cit.* p. 136.

(b) The same Jewish features are strikingly evident in the story of the Day of Pentecost. Not only was the date one of the Jewish Festivals, and Jews were the original recipients of the Holy Spirit, but the Apostle's address is to ' men of Judea, and all that dwell in Jerusalem,' with a special use of an Old Testament prophecy (Joel ii. 28-32). The more the context of Joel ii. is studied, the more fully it will be seen to refer to Israel rather than the Church.

(c) Then, again, a comparison of the references to purely Jewish matters and to miraculous gifts during the time of the Acts with those found afterwards produces some very striking results. Thus in the Acts there are twenty-five references to the Jews, while afterwards there is only one ; in Acts fourteen to Israel, but afterwards only two ; in Acts nineteen allusions to Abraham, but afterwards none at all. So also in regard to gifts. They are seen to be in operation up to the end of Acts, but not afterwards, for while, for example, the gift of healing is found throughout Acts, we have no trace of anything of the kind afterwards ; on the contrary, Epaphroditus is spoken of as dangerously ill, Timothy is given medical advice, and Trophimus is left at Miletus sick. The same contrast is seen if we take the Epistles of St. Paul written before Acts xxviii. (1 and 2 Thess. ; 1 and 2 Cor. ; Gal. ; Rom.), and compare them with those written during the Roman captivity. In the former there are twenty-five references to the Jew, and only one in the latter ; twenty-two references to tongues, and none in the latter ; nine allusions to gifts as opposed to two ; thirteen references to prophecy as a gift, with none in the latter.

These facts, and more that could be adduced, seem to show that the miraculous gifts recorded in Acts were specifically and solely for Israel ; that they were demonstrations of power to vindicate the Messiahship of Jesus of Nazareth, but not intended for permanent exercise in the normal conditions of the Christian Church when Christ had been rejected by Israel. When these remarkable differences between Acts and St. Paul are thus viewed historically and dispensationally, they are seen to be explicable on these grounds, and do not in any way involve either a defect in the Acts or a correction of the defect by St. Paul. When once it is realised that the Pentecostal period was transitional, and was more closely connected with the Jewish past than with the universal Christian future, everything becomes quite clear. The key is found in Acts iii. 19-21, which plainly teaches that if only the Jews had there and then repented, Jesus Christ would have come back according to His own promise, but as they wilfully refused to accept Him, and maintained this refusal on every occasion when the offer was made, the supernatural manifestations of the Holy Spirit came to an end, and the normal graces of the Spirit became naturally more prominent in the Gentile Christian Church and as associated with the Apostle Paul.

If this view of the character of the Acts is correct, it settles by rendering unnecessary the discussion of several questions often raised to-day, including :

(*a*) The relation of Pentecost with its gifts to the normal Christian life.[1]

(*b*) The question of the gift of tongues.[2]

(*c*) The laying on of hands in association with the bestowal of the gifts of the Spirit (Acts viii., xix.). Any connection, as is sometimes instituted, between this laying on of hands and what is known as confirmation necessarily falls to the ground.[3]

(*d*) Even the question of what is known as ' the baptism of the Spirit '[4] finds its truest interpretation in connection with the specific Jewish character of the Acts, especially as in the Epistles the term descriptive of the work of the Spirit is not ' baptism,' but ' fulness ' and its cognates. The baptism, whether regarded as miraculous or normal, is evidently to be considered (like its analogue of water baptism) as an initial gift which is not to be repeated, while the soul may be ' filled ' with the Spirit again and again.

---

[1] Kelly, ' Gift and Gifts,' *Lectures on the Doctrine of the Lord's Supper*, p. 162.

[2] See note B, p. 275.   [3] See note C, p. 275.

[4] See note D, p. 276.

CHAPTER 6

THE HOLY SPIRIT
IN THE SYNOPTIC GOSPELS

IT is necessary, however, to go still further back. The experience recorded in Acts has itself to be accounted for. Did it not come from Christ Himself? To answer this we examine the Gospels.

It is now usual to distinguish in the Synoptic Gospels between the teaching of Christ and the narratives of the writers. This is only possible in a general way, and even so, it is not always a simple matter.[1] Old Testament ideas are clearly presupposed as familiar, and there is no trace of novelty or hint of change. The very way in which the subject is mentioned in the earliest verses shows the importance of continuity in understanding the doctrine (Matt. i. 18; Mark i. 8; Luke i. 5).

The opening pages of the Gospels indicate a special Divine movement at the time of our Lord's birth. Swete says St. Luke's

"narrative reveals the fact that the birth of the Baptist was accompanied by a manifestation of the Spirit unparalleled in the life of the Jewish people since the days of the Maccabees.'[2]

---

[1] Wood, *The Spirit of God in Biblical Literature*, p. 124.

[2] Swete, *The Holy Spirit in the New Testament*, p. 12.

LITERATURE.—Humphries, *The Holy Spirit in Faith and Experience*; Wood, *The Spirit of God in Biblical Literature*, p. 124; Welldon, *The Revelation of the Holy Spirit*, p. 57; Redford, *Vox Dei*, p. 189; Denney, Article ' Holy Spirit,' *Dictionary of Christ and the Gospels*; Swete, Article ' Holy Spirit,' Hastings' *Bible Dictionary*; *The Holy Spirit in the New Testament*, pp. 11-61, 113; E. H. Johnson, *The Holy Spirit*, p. 76; Joseph Parker, *The Paraclete*, p. 7.

' As we open the pages of the Gospels, we find ourselves at once in an atmosphere swept by spiritual currents.' [1]

' All the events of this period are transacted, so to speak, in an atmosphere agitated by the Spirit.' [2]

The references to the Holy Spirit are very full and definite in connection with the persons mentioned as associated with the period of our Lord's birth.

' The Gospel history opens with an outburst of prophecy. As the moment of the Incarnation drew near, men and women in Israel found themselves lifted up by the Spirit into new regions of thought and endowed with new powers of expression. The movement began in the family of a priest. A child was born of whom it was foretold that he should " be filled with the Holy Spirit from his mother's womb " ; and the inspiration was shared by his parents. Others were touched by the same current of Divine energy. . . . Such a revival of prophetic gifts had not occurred since the days of Ezra and Nehemiah ; even the Maccabeean age had looked for it in vain.' [3]

All this is in accord with the view of the Holy Spirit seen in the Old Testament.[4] And the entire conception of the Spirit in these Christian records is a striking testimony to the truth of the Gospel story at the precise moment of our Lord's appearance when compared with the post-Pentecostal teaching, and particularly in view of the fact that the record is given by men who wrote after the unique event of Pentecost.

' It is among the evidences of the substantial truth of the Gospel records that the last of the prophets of Israel is represented as inspired by the Spirit of the Old Covenant, and not as he would have been depicted by the imagination of men who had tasted of the Pentecostal gift.' [5]

The special feature of the record at this point is the association of the Holy Spirit with the Incarnation. The answer of the Angel to Mary is stated in the language of the Old Testament,[6] and Matthew's account is also couched

---

[1] Humphries, *The Holy Spirit in Faith and Experience*, p. 124.

[2] Denney, Article ' Holy Spirit,' *Dictionary of Christ and the Gospels*, p. 736.

[3] Swete, Article ' Holy Spirit,' Hastings' *Bible Dictionary*, p. 405.

[4] Swete, *The Holy Spirit in the New Testament*, p. 21.

[5] Swete, *ut supra*, p. 22.

[6] Swete, *ut supra*, p. 26.

in Old Testament language, though equally associated with the Holy Spirit. On the one hand, it is like the Old Testament manifestations of power, and yet, on the other, it has an element of uniqueness.[1] The Birth itself is regarded as natural, but the Conception is associated with manifestations of the Holy Spirit. Both the Sonship and the Sinlessness of Christ are referred definitely to the Holy Spirit.

' The Angel's words base the sanctity and Divine sonship of Mary's child not on His pre-existence but on His conception by the Divine Spirit.'[2]

' The miraculous conception reminds us that the absolutely perfect life must not only be begun, continued, and consummated in the Spirit, but anticipated likewise. So richly was the Spirit given to Christ that His holy influences were pulsing in those rudimentary stages of life which precede all signs of consciousness and moral responsibility.'[3]

All this is intended to teach the superhuman, supernatural, Divine origin of the Personality of the Son of Mary.

' This is the conviction which—not to speak of historical evidence —sustains the stories of the birth of Christ. He must always have been what Christians eventually knew Him in their own experience to be : He must always have been Son of God. If it is the Spirit which makes Him Son, then behind the baptism with the Spirit must lie a birth in which the Spirit is equally important : not only the equipment of this personality, but its origination, must be traced directly to God. And it *is* the origination of the personality of Jesus with which both Matthew and Luke are concerned. Neither of them betrays any idea that the Son of God pre-existed, and that they are only narrating the mode in which He came from another order of being into this ; and, difficult as it may be to understand how a companion and friend of St. Paul could ignore such an idea, we must abide by the facts as they are before us. No act of man, but only the power of God, lies behind and explains the existence of Jesus Christ in the world.'[4]

The next stage of the subject is the opening of our Lord's ministry. This was preceded by the preaching of John the Baptist.

---

[1] Swete, *ut supra*, p. 27.

[2] Swete, *The Holy Spirit in the New Testament*, p. 28.

[3] Selby, *The Holy Spirit and Christian Privilege*, p. 28.

[4] Denney, *op. cit.* pp. 735, 736.

' There is one section of the Gospel narrative which represents
entirely Jewish thought, except as it may have been coloured by
the Christian medium through which it has passed. This is the
preaching of John the Baptist. The Jewish element is seen in all
the concepts of John's teaching.' [1]

' The ministry of the Baptist was a link between the old order and
the new, and when Jesus began to teach He took up the thread
which John had been compelled to drop. In the Baptist the prophetic Spirit uttered its last testimony to Him that was to come,
completing the witness of the Old Testament at the moment when
the Christ was ready to enter upon His work.' [2]

There were three occasions in this period where the
presence and work of the Holy Spirit were emphasised.

(a) At the Baptism.[3] This may be called the Messiah's
consecration. While it was ' official ' it was not public.
It was the Divine recognition and acceptance of the Messiah's fulfilled righteousness, and at the same time there
came new powers with a new consciousness of God's
purpose and mission.

' Two things make that event a crisis in the life of Jesus, for it
marked the realisation by Him of His Messianic vocation, and His
reception of the Divine equipment for it. The conviction was
mediated by a Divine communication to the soul of Jesus ; the
equipment consisted in His baptism by the Holy Spirit.' [4]

(b) At the Temptation. This may be termed the
Messiah's testing, for having been anointed with power He
was ' driven by the Spirit ' into the wilderness to be proved
as to His fitness for the Divine work to which He had been
called.

(c) The Preaching at Nazareth. This may be described
as the Messiah's equipment, and although the incident may
belong to a later stage in the ministry, its place in St.
Luke's Gospel seems to strike a keynote in regard to the
Messiah's work.

' The words spoken at Nazareth disclose the consciousness of a
unique relation to the Spirit which is presupposed by all that Jesus
taught about Him.' [5]

---

[1] Wood, *op. cit.* p. 138.

[2] Swete, *The Holy Spirit in the New Testament*, p. 22. See also
note H, p. 279.

[3] E. H. Johnson, *The Holy Spirit*, p. 97.

[4] Humphries, *op. cit.* p. 132.

[5] Swete, *The Holy Spirit in the New Testament*, p. 115.

The course of the ministry has several references to the Holy Spirit that need attention.

(*a*) The ministry in general was marked by the two elements of teaching and miracles. The former does not seem to be associated anywhere with the Holy Spirit, although, as we have seen, it is found in the passage from Isaiah, applied by Christ to Himself at Nazareth. But the miracles are in one place associated with the power of the Spirit (Matt. xii. 28, ' Spirit of God ' = Luke xi. 20, ' finger of God '). And prophecy which anticipated the Spirit for the Messiah (Isa. xlii. 1) is regarded as having been fulfilled in the Gospel (Matt. xii. 18).

(*b*) The blasphemy against the Holy Ghost was another point of great importance (Mark iii. 29). The context clearly shows the true meaning of this much-discussed expression.

' It consists in attributing to a malign power acts of beneficence which clearly had their source in the Spirit of God.' [1]

' In principle it is the everyday sin of finding bad motives for good actions ; carried to its unpardonable height, it is the sin of confronting the Divine holy power which wrought so irresistibly and so intensely in Jesus, and saying anything—the maddest, most wanton, most malignant thing—rather than acknowledge it for what it is. . . . This was the depth which malignity in them had reached. . . . The Holy Spirit is specifically God's. . . . To withstand what is so unambiguously the redeeming power of God, and to do so deliberately and malignantly, in the spirit which will kill Jesus rather than acknowledge Him as what He is, is the unpardonable sin.' [2]

(*c*) Certain aspects of teaching about the Holy Spirit must be noted ; *e.g.* Luke xi. 1-13, where the Holy Spirit (Matt. vii. 11, ' good things ') is promised to them that ask the Heavenly Father.

(*d*) The instructions to the Apostles include a reference to the Holy Spirit as the Spirit of Inspiration (Matt. x. 20 ; Mark xiii. 11 ; Luke xii. 12). According to Wood,[3] this is the most central point of the Synoptic teaching for Christ's view of the work of the Spirit.

---

[1] Humphries, *op. cit.* p. 147.

[2] Denney, *op. cit.* p. 733. See also note G, p. 278.

[3] Wood, *op. cit.* p. 130.

(e) The association of the Holy Spirit with the inner personal life of Jesus Christ is very rarely noticed. Indeed, one writer goes as far as to say that

'there is no passage in the Gospels connecting the Holy Spirit with the inner and religious life of Jesus, nevertheless the existence of such a connexion may be assumed.' [1]

But Luke x. 21, R.V., clearly points to the presence and power in His ministry of that Spirit which had been associated with Him in the earlier parts of the Gospels.[2]

The period after the Resurrection must now be noticed.

(a) Among the parting instructions and counsels of the risen Lord is the promise of the Holy Spirit (Luke xxiv. 49), where

'the Risen Saviour describes it as "the promise of My Father," and as "power from on high." The last word, therefore, brings us back to the first. The fundamental idea to be associated with the Spirit is that of Divine power : how the Divine power is to be further characterised, what it is ethically, and to what issues or in what temper it works, we can see only in the life of Jesus. He is the key to the interpretation of a term which of itself is indefinite indeed.' [3]

(b) The baptismal formula also calls for special attention. As to the authenticity of the saying, many agree with Wood, who will not allow it to be regarded as one of the genuine words of Christ.[4] But the balance is overwhelmingly on the side of those who accept it.

'The evidence has been examined at length by the present Bishop of Ely, and few who have read his investigation will disagree with his finding that the whole evidence "establishes without a shadow of doubt or uncertainty the genuineness of Matthew xxviii. 19."' [5]

In this last command Christ brings together the Father, the Son, and the Spirit into one, thus uniting all the lines of His earlier teaching, and associating the Three Persons in their unity with the work which His disciples were to

---

[1] Humphries, *op. cit.* p. 148.

[2] E. H. Johnson, *op. cit.* p. 123 ; Robson, *The Holy Spirit the Paraclete*, p. 73.

[3] Denney, *op. cit.* p. 735.

[4] Wood, *op. cit.* p. 135.

[5] Swete, *The Holy Spirit in the New Testament*, p. 123.

do from that time forward.[1] This seems to be the only possible interpretation of these words as they stand.

'They certainly carry the Synoptic doctrine of the Spirit far beyond the point hitherto reached. For the Spirit is now seen to be not merely God in action, but God in relation to God, and we approach a mystery which belongs to the Divine Life itself. Yet this great step is taken in the interests not of scientific but of practical theology.' [2]

When we endeavour to summarise the teaching of the Synoptic Gospels we are led along three lines :

(a) The Holy Spirit in relation to Christ Himself. At each stage of His earthly manifestation the Holy Spirit is associated with Him ; at His Birth, Baptism, Temptation ; in His Life, Work, and Teaching.[3]

(b) The Holy Spirit in relation to the life of others. The time had not come for much to be said on this.

(c) The teaching of Christ.

'The teaching of Christ upon this subject, so far as it is reported by the Synoptists, goes but a little way beyond that of the Old Testament.' [4]

It is only, as we have seen, in connection with the baptismal formula that the teaching marks a distinct advance. Apart from this we may summarise the teaching in the Synoptists as follows :

'The Spirit is a manifest revelation of God, present in the work of the Messiah and guiding His action. It will also furnish needed Divine power to the members of the Messianic kingdom when Christ is absent and their own powers no longer suffice. It is not a new life or the basis of a new life, but a special gift, superadded to the ordinary life.' [5]

The general idea in the Synoptic Gospels is of the Holy Spirit as the Divine power at work on Christ, and promised to the disciples for the fulfilment of the Divine purpose of redemption. But the main stress is naturally laid upon the relation of the Spirit to Christ Himself as the Messiah.

---

[1] Swete, *The Holy Spirit in the New Testament*, p. 124.

[2] Swete, *ut supra*, p. 125.

[3] W. L. Walker, *The Holy Spirit*, ch. iv.

[4] Swete, Article ' Holy Spirit,' Hastings' *Bible Dictionary*, p 408.

[5] Wood, *op. cit.* p. 136.

But even on this point opinions differ. On the one hand we read :

' We find then in the teaching and conversations of our Lord, as reported by the Synoptists, no direct assertion that is well established claiming the Holy Spirit as the inspirer of His message and work. There must be some reason for this silence. . . . May it be that the immediacy of His communion with the Father was such that He did not need to speak of His endowment with the Messianic Spirit, and that in His training of the Twelve He led them to treasure a direct access to the Father in prayer during the days of His flesh ? Hints we possess, indeed, of allusions to the Holy Spirit when His bodily presence was to be removed, as teaching and inspiring the disciples in days of coming stress, as their unseen Pleader before men ; in some such converse briefly reported, we find the link which binds events in the Acts and discourses in the Fourth Gospel to the teaching of our Lord Himself. The Holy Spirit would inspire His followers according to their need for the continuing of His work among men.' [1]

To the same effect another writer remarks :

' The small part which the Spirit plays in the teaching of Christ needs explanation. It certainly cannot be taken as indicating that Christ placed little value on the idea which that term represented. The intimate relation between God and man which this term had indicated in the Hebrew literature was exactly that which Jesus was most concerned to bring about. It may very possibly be His clear realisation of this relation that led to the rare use of the term " Spirit of God " to express it. Christ taught a perfect harmony with God. He Himself stood in such a relation. He desired it for His followers. He would have His disciples brought into direct and immediate connection with God Himself. . . . It is significant that in no case does Christ speak of the Spirit as acting upon His followers while He is present with them. He would keep the thought of the disciples fixed upon Himself as the revelation of the Father.' [2]

But a different view is taken :

' In their reports of Christ's work the Synoptists rarely mention the Spirit by name, even Luke isolating simply one incident in Christ's experience—a mood of rapturous emotion—by associating it with the Spirit. But this very silence has its significance. The meaning is that from the Baptism the presence of the Holy Spirit in Jesus, instead of being viewed as occasional or fitful, as was sometimes the inspiration of the prophets, was regarded as permanent, and as the power in which all His Messianic duties were

---

[1] Winstanley, *Spirit in the New Testament*, pp. 128, 129.

[2] Wood, *op. cit.* pp. 136, 137.

discharged. And in taking this view the Evangelists were but expressing the mind of Jesus Himself.' [1]

We may perhaps sum up as follows :

' The general impression which this survey of Jesus should leave is that of the naturalness behind the supernatural. The Holy Spirit acted upon Jesus, not to the suppression, but to the intensification, of the human. Christ's humanity was not made one whit less real by the Divine presence within Him.' [2]

Nor need we be surprised at this comparative paucity of reference to the Holy Spirit in connection with Christ's earthly life and ministry. Indeed, this very fact is a testimony to the accuracy of the reports found in the Synoptic Gospels. The fuller teaching concerning the Spirit was yet to come.[3]

---

[1] Humphries, *op. cit.* p. 137.

[2] Humphries, *op. cit.* p. 151.

[3] Davison, *The Indwelling Spirit*, pp. 35, 36.

CHAPTER 7

THE HOLY SPIRIT
IN THE FOURTH GOSPEL

IN considering the subject as presented in St. John's Gospel, it is quite impossible to distinguish, even as far as we can in the Synoptists, between the teaching and the narrative.

' The Johannean author has so assimilated the teaching of Jesus, in both style and content, with his own theological thought, that no mere mechanical separation between the sections of Christ's discourses and the Gospel narratives will serve to distinguish between the thought of Jesus and that of the author.' [1]

But this is not intended to imply that the record of the Fourth Gospel is unhistorical, for the writer of the passage goes on to say :

' If we compare the use of the Spirit here with that in other New Testament literature, we find a difference of emphasis rather than a difference of content.' [2]

To the same effect is the position of Dr. Swete who assumes that the discourses attributed to our Lord are at least in substance His, and then adds :

' To assign to the Evangelist more than the *rôle* of an interpreter is to overestimate his genius or his inspiration, and to limit unduly the scope of Christ's mission as a Revealer of religious truth.' [3]

---

[1] Wood, *The Spirit of God in Biblical Literature*, p. 233.

[2] Wood, *op. cit.* p. 235.

[3] Swete, *The Holy Spirit in the New Testament*, p. 130.

LITERATURE.—Humphries, *The Holy Spirit in Faith and Experience*, ch. ix. ; Wood, *The Spirit of God in Biblical Literature*, p. 233 ; Welldon, *The Revelation of the Holy Spirit*, p. 88 ; Swete, *The Holy Spirit in the New Testament*, p. 129.

After making every allowance, we may regard the substance of the teaching as having emanated from Christ, even though we remember that the author is writing at a time when Pauline influences had been at work for many years in the Church. The limitations which we shall see in the course of our study, and also the pre-Pentecostal attitude adopted, both argue for historicity.

' The Johannine books cover all the literary forms known to the New Testament—Gospel, Epistle, Apocalypse—and the Spirit is prominent in all. To understand them it is necessary to remember that all the experience of the Pauline Churches lies behind them, and that the circumstances in which they originated have exercised a decided influence on their presentation of the facts and ideas with which they deal.' [1]

There is no reason to doubt the naturalness of the conversation on the subject of the Holy Spirit in Christ's farewell discourses.

' There is no adequate reason why the central thought of the charismatic Spirit may not belong to Christ's last talk with His disciples. In fact, such a thought as this would be a most natural, one might almost say an inevitable, element in a farewell discourse of Jesus to them. . . . Not only, then, is there no ground for rejecting from Christ's teaching the general doctrine of the Spirit in John xiv. to xvi., but there is every ground for retaining it.' [2]

The Holy Spirit is clearly related therein to the perpetuation of Christ's presence with His disciples.

' The most explicit teaching on the subject is found in Christ's discourses concerning the Paraclete in John xiv. to xvi. If these stood alone they might be represented as a comparatively late reflection of earlier doctrine peculiar to St. John. But St. Paul's Epistles are among the earliest New Testament documents, and Rom. viii. is equally emphatic on the personal characteristics—thought, feeling, and action—ascribed to the Holy Spirit throughout.' [3]

Nor can we reasonably question the possibility of earlier teaching with its subsequent illumination after the disciples had become partakers of the spiritual experience of Pentecost (ch. vii. 37-39).

---

[1] Denney, Article ' Holy Spirit,' *Dictionary of Christ and the Gospels*, pp. 739, 740.

[2] Wood, *op. cit.* pp. 242, 243.

[3] Davison, *The Indwelling Spirit*, pp. 41, 42.

It is particularly noteworthy that not only in the Synoptists, but in this Gospel also, there is an assumption of
familiarity with the Holy Spirit. Denney, speaking of
ch. i. 32 ff., says :

'What strikes us here is the assumption that every reader will
know what is meant by " the Spirit," or by " Holy Spirit." ' [1]
'Whence come these Johannean conceptions ? Many of them
occur in the discourses of Jesus. May it not be that the peculiar
Johannean view of the Spirit comes from the teaching of Jesus ?
If so, then the Pauline doctrine has some basis in the words of Jesus,
and the high-water mark of Christian thought on this subject was
reached by our Lord Himself.' [2]

There is, however, a distinct development of teaching
as compared with that in the Synoptists. In the Synoptists
(apart from the baptismal formula in Matt. xxviii. 19) the
Spirit is little more than the power of God active on man's
behalf, as in the Old Testament, though of course associated specifically with the Messiah. But in the Fourth
Gospel the Spirit is apparently (most writers would say
clearly) personal, and closely associated at all points with
the redemption of Christ. This may be due to the fact,
as held by some, that

'the teaching of Jesus concerning the Holy Spirit is, in a sense,
the counterpart of the Synoptic teaching regarding the parousia.' [3]
'The elaboration of the doctrine of the Spirit's personal nature
and of His offices in redemption is characteristic of that form of
Jesus' teaching which the fourth Gospel presents. It is the
Johannine counterpart of that aspect of the Synoptic teaching concerning the parousia which is expressed in the words of Jesus : " Lo,
I am with you alway, even unto the end of the world " (Matt.
xxviii. 20).' [4]

But Christ does not use *Parousia* of the present time.
His presence may truly be regarded as realised by the Holy
Spirit, but we must not confuse by calling it *Parousia*.

There is a definite progress of teaching within the Gospel
itself.

1. The Messiah's twofold office is stated as the Lamb of
God and the Baptizer with the Holy Spirit (ch. i. 32, 33).[5]

---

[1] Denney, *op. cit.* p. 740.   [2] Wood, *op. cit.* pp. 238, 239.

[3] Stevens, *Theology of the New Testament*, p. 213.

[4] Stevens, *op. cit.* p. 223.   See also *Johannine Theology*, p. 194.

[5] Clemance, *The Scripture Doctrine of the Holy Spirit*, p. 53.

2. The teaching of ch. iii. follows.[1] Whatever may be thought of the reference to Baptism in connection with the ' water ' of this chapter, it is clear that the mention of the Spirit is supreme.

' As the conversation goes on, too, while the water as merely symbolical, drops out (it only appears in v. 5), and the Spirit remains by itself (v. 8), attention is directed to the Son of Man. . . . Here we have the ideas introduced which define the Spirit—the experiences through which the experience comes to us with life-giving power.' [2]

Swete, while interpreting the ' water ' of baptism, says :

' Its omission in the true text of verse 8 shows that it is of secondary importance, the primary and essential source of the new birth being the Divine.' [3]

It may also be suggested that in the light of the subsequent references to ' water ' in chs. iv. and vii. the supreme emphasis is to be placed on the Holy Spirit.

3. The teaching of ch. vii.[4] This is clearly written from the standpoint of a post-Pentecostal experience. Pentecost was the inevitable sequel of the Passion and Resurrection.[5]

' The whole history of the Church and of the world from the Pentecost to the present time bears witness to their absolute truth.' [6]

4. The full teaching of chs. xiv.-xvi., especially the use of the new term ' Paraclete.'

5. The Resurrection gift of the Spirit (ch. xx.). The question has often been asked in what relation the gift of Easter Day stands to the gift of Whitsunday. Bishop Westcott, following Godet, replies that ' the one answers to the power of the Resurrection and the other to the power of the Ascension,' *i.e.* the one brought the grace of quickening, the other that of endowment. We cannot fail to recall the Divine ' breathing ' of Genesis ii. 7, expressive of life.

---

[1] Moule, *Veni Creator*, pp. 70-81 ; Ridout, *Person and Work of the Holy Spirit,* p. 45 ; Joseph Parker, *The Paraclete*, ch. ix.

[2] Denney, *op. cit.* p. 741.

[3] Swete, *op. cit.* p. 133.

[4] Moule, *Veni Creator*, p. 146 ; A. J. Gordon, *The Ministry of the Spirit*, p. 27 ; Tophel, *The Holy Spirit in Man*, p. 37.

[5] Denney, *op. cit.* p. 741.

[6] Swete, *op. cit.* p. 146.

But besides this, if we may judge from the words that follow, the Easter gift was specially connected with the future work of the Body of Christ.[1]

Two passages beyond all others call for special notice.

1. Ch. vii. 37-39 : ' But this spake He of the Spirit, which they that believe on Him should receive : for the Holy Ghost was not yet given ; because that Jesus was not yet glorified.' It has been pointed out that this is the first mention of the Spirit as a bestowal on all believers, but the reference to the future in its relation to the past and present is the important point. The first thing to notice is the symbol of water.

' The association of the Spirit with the gift of life, is very subtly intimated in St. John's Gospel under the Old Testament symbolism of *water*. St. John's explanation of one of Christ's sayings as referring to the Spirit Who " was not yet," ch. vii. 39—justifies us in seeing this reference in other sayings of the same character.' [2]

It is sometimes thought that the allusion to the Old Testament is to Isaiah xliv. 3. Then comes the plain, but difficult statement that ' the Holy Spirit was not yet given ; because that Jesus was not yet glorified.' The main idea ' is similar to that of the farewell address ; bodily presence renders spiritual presence unnecessary.' [3] It is obvious that ' not yet ' cannot mean ' unknown before,' but must be interpreted as ' not yet ' compared with Pentecost, because Christ was not yet ascended. In some way the Spirit's descent depended on Christ's ascension, and when Pentecost came, the Spirit was given only to disciples, and in intimate connection with the ascended Lord.

' The Spirit of God is the successor of the Son of God in His official ministry on earth. Until Christ's earthly work for His church had been finished, the Spirit's work in this world could not properly begin.' [4]

---

[1] Swete, *op. cit.* p. 167. See also Wolston, *Another Comforter*, pp. 131-134.

[2] Lowrie, *The Doctrine of St. John*, p. 170.

[3] Winstanley, *Spirit in the New Testament*, p. 101.

[4] A. J. Gordon, *op. cit.* p. 37.

The difference can also be seen in reference to the effects of the Spirit on those who were disciples of Christ :

' The previous activities, however splendid and abundant in their fulness, were incommensurable with the glory of His work, when, as the union of God and Man, He began to change our poor damaged nature into the nature of the glorified Jesus, from glory to glory ; to dwell in us, to abide in our poor life, to hallow and cleanse it down to its roots, to think through us, so that our thoughts and His thoughts are veritably blended, so that our desires are His purposes, our characteristic and personal functions become the glorious intentions of His Divine personality.' [1]

2. Chs. xiv.-xvi. Swete thinks that the references to the Holy Spirit in the earlier chapters are to the gift of the Spirit to individual men, while in the latter part of the Gospel, especially in the farewell discourses, the Church, as represented by the company in the Upper Room comes into view.[2] Three points need attention.

(*a*) The Nature of the Holy Spirit. He is designated as ' The Spirit,' ' The Holy Spirit,' ' The Spirit of Truth,' ' The Paraclete.' He is described as ' Another ' (ἄλλος not ἕτερος), that is, Someone distinct from Christ. He is to glorify Christ, and together with the neuter word ' Spirit,' there are the masculine pronouns αὐτός and ἐκεῖνος. All this clearly shows His personality, His distinctness from Christ, and His personal activities.

(*b*) The Work of the Holy Spirit. In relation to Christ He witnesses (ch. xiv. 26), and glorifies (ch. xvi. 14). In relation to believers He may be said to foster the Christian life in them in a variety of ways. In relation to the world He is said to convict of sin, righteousness, and judgment.[3] This is specific, not general (ch. xvi. 9-11), and is in con-

---

[1] Reynolds, ' The Witness to the Spirit,' *The Ancient Faith in Modern Light*, p. 402.

[2] Swete, *op. cit.* p. 148.

[3] Davison, *The Indwelling Spirit*, p. 47 ; Denney, Article ' Holy Spirit,' *Dictionary of Christ and the Gospels*, p. 743 ; Swete, *The Holy Spirit in the New Testament*, p. 157 ff.; Morgan, *The Ministry of the Holy Ghost*, p. 14 ; Robson, *The Holy Spirit the Paraclete*, p. 99 ; A. J. Gordon, *The Ministry of the Spirit*, p. 43 ; Moule, *Veni Creator*, p. 84 ; Elder Cumming, *Through the Eternal Spirit*, ch. vi. ; Tophel, *The Holy Spirit in Man*, p. 37 ; Ridout, *The Person and Work of the Holy Spirit*, p. 37 ; Joseph Parker, *The Paraclete*, chs. vii. and viii.

stant and close relation to Jesus Christ through believers.[1] This does not mean a denial of the general work of the Logos on the world, but it certainly seems to limit the specific work of the Spirit to and then through believers.

(c) The special title of Paraclete.[2] Denney says it is only the name which is new, since the idea is found already in the Synoptic Gospels. And yet

' No function more characteristic of personal life could have been attributed. . . . The personality of the Deputy is in fact essential to the Lord's reasoning ; no impersonal influence could supply the lack of personal guidance and probation which the Apostles would feel when the Lord was taken from them.' [3]

Most writers call attention to the remarkable association of the masculine term ' Paraclete ' with the neuter word ' Spirit,' and the masculine pronouns ' He,' ' His.'

' That which is of especial importance in this connection is that as soon as πνεῦμα ceases to be the *immediate* antecedent of pronouns designating the Spirit, masculine forms are employed. . . . It thus appears that John, when not prevented from so doing by the grammatical gender of πνεῦμα, uniformly designates the Spirit by masculine pronouns implying personality.' [4]

' It is this conception of the Paraclete as the teacher of the truth, which constitutes the most important element in St. John's doctrine of the Spirit, and which brings it into line with his philosophy of salvation.' [5]

Both the masculine pronouns, αὐτός and ἐκεῖνος, and also the function (' He shall teach ') represent the Holy Spirit as personal with a definiteness hitherto unnoticed.[6] It

---

[1] See p. 186.

[2] Hastings, Article ' Paraclete,' Hastings' *Bible Dictionary* ; Swete, Article ' Holy Spirit,' Hastings' *Bible Dictionary* ; Moss, Article ' Advocate,' *Dictionary of Christ and the Gospels* ; Moss, Article ' Comforter,' *Dictionary of Christ and the Gospels* ; Moss, Article ' Paraclete,' *Dictionary of Christ and the Gospels* ; *Expository Times*, Vol. XII. p. 445 (G. G. Findlay) ; Walker, *The Holy Spirit*, ch. ix. ; Davison, *The Indwelling Spirit*, p. 42 ; Swete, *The Holy Spirit in the Ancient Church*, p. 149 ; Lowrie, *The Doctrine of St. John*, p. 180.

[3] Swete, Article ' Holy Spirit,' Hastings' *Bible Dictionary*, p. 408.

[4] Stevens, *The Johannine Theology*, pp. 195, 196.

[5] Lowrie, *op. cit.* p. 169. See also Denio, *The Supreme Leader*, p. 45.

[6] Denney, Article ' Holy Spirit,' *Dictionary of Christ and the Gospels*, p. 742.

is particularly noteworthy that the same term ' Paraclete ' is used by St. John of Christ Himself (1 John ii. 1). So that there are two Paracletes, each possessing a relation to the life of believers, and both together completing the idea of eternal and permanent redemption.[1]

The general idea of the Johannine teaching concerning the Spirit may now be stated :

1. Christ's departure was to mean the removal of His bodily presence because of the gift of the Holy Spirit. No one can question that the Fourth Gospel represents the Spirit as ' a self distinct from Christ,'[2] and the arguments adduced in opposition to this do not seem to stand the test of thorough exegesis. Indeed, even Wood, who denies the distinctness, admits that

' had the doctrine of the Spirit begun with Christianity it must have meant either a representation of Christ or a distinctly separate person.' [3]

This is surely a fine testimony to the true meaning of the New Testament passages.

2. The Holy Spirit is a special gift of the New Covenant, bestowing Christ in His redemptive work of perpetuating His spiritual presence among His people.

(a) As a revelation of truth.

' In the relative independence which St. John ascribes to the Paraclete, we see reflected the high significance of the Spirit as the medium of revelation which the Jewish theology already dimly recognised, and which the Christian theology expressed in the trinitarian formula.' [4]

(b) As a bestowal of life.

(c) As an equipment for service.

Thus the Holy Spirit in the Fourth Gospel is represented as a Presence perpetual and permanent ; as the Spirit of Truth (ch. xiv. 17) ; of Remembrance (ch. xiv. 26 ; xvi. 14) ; of Revelation (ch. xvi. 12, 13) ; of Fellowship (ch. xvi. 22-27) ; of Testimony (ch. xv. 26, 27) ; of Conviction (ch. xvi. 8-11).

---

[1] Clemance, *The Scripture Doctrine of the Holy Spirit*, ch. ii. See also note I, p. 279.

[2] Stevens, *The Theology of the New Testament*, p. 217.

[3] Wood, *op. cit.* p. 255.   [4] Lowrie, *op. cit.* pp. 171, 172.

' A great part of the peculiarity of the Fourth Gospel is covered if we say that the word of the Risen Saviour, speaking by His Spirit in the heart of the Apostle, is presented as though it had been actually spoken on earth. And, little as this may agree with our ideas of a purely historical narrative, it is a precarious operation to set aside such a testimony based on Christian experience and contemplated by Christ, as though it could be merely irrelevant to the Christian religion.' [1]

---

[1] Denney, *op. cit.* p. 744.

CHAPTER 8

THE HOLY SPIRIT
IN OTHER NEW TESTAMENT BOOKS

THE main teaching on the Holy Spirit is found in the
writings of St. Paul and St. John. In the Epistle to the
Hebrews there are seven references to the Holy Spirit, but,
as Swete says, ' In Hebrews there is no theology of the
Spirit.' [1] And he quotes Westcott as finding a reason for
this in the design of the Epistle whereby

' the action of the Holy Spirit falls into the background . . . from
the characteristic view which is given of the priestly work of
Christ.' [2]

Denney goes so far as to say that

' the New Testament books which were written under Pauline
influence scarcely call for independent consideration.' [3]

The seven passages may be distinguished as three
referring to the Holy Spirit in relation to inspiration (ch. iii.
7 ; ix. 8 ; x. 15) : three referring to the Spirit in New
Testament times (ch. ii. 4 ; vi. 4-6 ; x. 29). This leaves
ch. ix. 13, 14, in which there is a reference to the ' eternal

---

[1] *The Holy Spirit in the New Testament*, p. 249.

[2] Westcott, *Hebrews*, p. 331. Quoted by Swete, *op. cit.* p. 249,
note.

[3] Denney, Article ' Holy Spirit,' *Dictionary of Christ and the
Gospels*, p. 739.

LITERATURE.—Swete, *The Holy Spirit in the New Testament*, p.
254 ; Welldon, *The Revelation of the Holy Spirit*, p. 213 ; Smeaton,
The Doctrine of the Holy Spirit, p. 86 ; Downer, *The Mission and
Ministration of the Holy Spirit*, ch. vi. ; Moule, *Veni Creator*, p. 158 ;
Downer, Article ' The Doctrine of the Holy Spirit in the Epistle of
St. James,' *Churchman*, June, 1906.

Spirit' in relation to the Atonement. Some writers interpret this of the Holy Spirit, by Whose presence Christ's offering became efficacious as the Atonement. But perhaps it is better to associate the term with our Lord's own spiritual nature, signifying that which gave to His sacrifice 'infinite worth and eternal validity.'[1] Swete refuses both as too definite, and prefers to take the words 'in a more general and non-technical sense,' implying that our Lord offered His sacrifice in a spirit not of the world, but one that 'takes its standpoint in the invisible and the eternal.'[2]

The references to the Holy Spirit in the Catholic Epistles do not call for much more than a bare mention.

(a) In James iv. 5, R.V., we have an interesting and novel thought about the Holy Spirit.

'The Spirit which God has planted within Christians yearns for the whole-hearted devotion of the hearts in which it dwells, with a jealous love which will not tolerate an intruder.'[3]

(b) In the Epistles of St. Peter the Spirit of God is associated with the Old Testament in 1 Pet. i. 11 and 2 Pet. i. 21; while the Spirit is associated with the Gospel in 1 Pet. i. 2, 12 and 1 Pet. iv. 12 ff.

(c) In the Johannine Epistles we have the unction of the Spirit in 1 John ii.; the test of the Spirit in ch. iv.; and the witness of the Spirit in ch. v. But it has been rightly said that the theology of the Holy Spirit in this Epistle does not call for separate treatment.

(d) The only allusion to the Spirit in Jude's Epistle is that in which they are mentioned who are 'sensual, not having the Spirit.'

The Spirit in the Apocalypse is depicted as related both to Christ and to the Church. The seven Spirits round the Throne seem to suggest the Spirit in His fulness as possessed by the Lord Jesus Christ;[4] while the Spirit in relation to the Churches implies the thought of a Divine personal address from the Throne to the people of God.'[5]

---

[1] Bruce, *Epistle to the Hebrews*, pp. 337, 347.

[2] Swete, *op. cit.* p. 252. [3] Swete, *op. cit.* p. 258.

[4] Swete, *op. cit.* p. 275. [5] Swete, *op. cit.* p. 276.

CHAPTER 9

SUMMARY OF THE
BIBLICAL REVELATION

THE perspective of truth in the Bible is clear and significant. There are three dispensations of the Divine revelation to man, involving a progressive economy of grace.[1]
First, God is revealed as transcendent, and exercises His
ministry either by prophecy, or by symbol, or by wisdom.
Then, the Father becomes manifested in the Incarnate
Son and God is revealed to man in Christ. Then, when
the work of the Incarnate Son is accomplished, the revelation of God to man becomes real and actual in the presence
and power of the Holy Spirit ; the ' other Comforter,' or
Advocate, Whose presence was only possible when the
first Advocate, Jesus Christ, had ascended into heaven.
We are therefore now living in what is called the dispensation of the Holy Spirit. Everything else was preparatory
to this, and the purpose of the two prior dispensations was
to prepare for the gift of the Holy Spirit whereby man
could be brought into fellowship with God, the power of
sin overcome, and human life in relation to God truly
restored.

' The dispensation of the Spirit, properly so-called, did not dawn
until the period of preparation was over and the day of out-pouring
had come. . . . It is not that His work is more real in the new
dispensation than in the old. It is not merely that it is more
universal. It is that it is directed to a different end . . . for the
perfecting of the fruitage and the gathering of the harvest. The
Church, to use a figure of Isaiah's, was then like a pent-in stream ;
it is now like that pent-in stream with the barriers broken down and
the Spirit of the Lord driving it. It was He who preserved it in

being when it was pent in. It is He Who is now driving on its gathered floods till it shall cover the earth as the waters cover the sea. In one word, that was a day in which the Spirit restrained His power. Now the great day of the Spirit is come.' [1]

As we review the teaching of the Bible on this profound theme, it is essential to remind ourselves again that the true way of approach is by means of personal experience.

' Certain it is that the language of the Holy Ghost can never be fully understood by an appeal to the lexicon. The heart of the Church is the best dictionary of the Spirit.' [2]

Four lines of teaching stand out with great prominence.

1. The intimate and essential relation of the Spirit to Christ. While in the later books of the Old Testament the Spirit becomes associated with Messianic prophecy, it is the unique feature of the New Testament revelation that the Spirit of God is the Spirit of Jesus Christ (Acts ii. 33). Most modern writers call special attention to this essential relationship of the Spirit to our Lord. Thus, Sanday says :

' With Paul as well as with John it is Christ Himself Who comes to His own in His Spirit.' [3]

And Moberly, similarly :

' Christ in you and the Spirit of Christ in you : these are not different realities, but the one is the method of the other. It is in the Person of Christ that the eternal God is revealed in manhood to man. It is in the Person of His Spirit that the Incarnate Christ is Personally present within the spirit of each several man. The Holy Spirit is mainly revealed to us as the Spirit of the Incarnate.' [4]

2. The Spirit is ' the Executive of the Godhead ' in and for the Christian Church. He is the Spirit of God, of Christ, of Truth, of Holiness, of Grace, of Glory, of Adoption, of Life, of Jesus, of His Son, of the Lord. By the Holy Spirit the work of Christ is applied and realised, and any subordination recorded is only in the sense of that self-abnegation which is true of each Person of the Trinity in relation to the others. Thus the Father glorifies the Son, and the Son the Father ; the Spirit glorifies the Son,

---

[1] Warfield, *Presbyterian and Reformed Review*, Vol. VI. p. 687.

[2] A. J. Gordon, *The Ministry of the Spirit*, p. 44.

[3] *Criticism of the Fourth Gospel*, p. 215.

[4] *Atonement and Personality*, p. 194.

and the Son sends the Spirit. No blessing comes to us from God apart from the Spirit of God.

3. The Deity of the Spirit. The association of the Spirit with the Father and the Son in the baptismal formula (Matt. xxviii. 19), and the Benediction (2 Cor. xiii. 14) clearly implies and teaches the Godhead of the Spirit. And yet no embarrassment is felt by New Testament writers from any contradiction with the unity of the Godhead. The Deity of the Spirit is always found in the closest association with Jewish Monotheism.

4. The Personality of the Spirit. This, again, seems clear, even if it be only by implication, in the New Testament. The Spirit is personal because God is personal, and Divine because God is Divine, and although it cannot be said that the Personality of the Spirit is made as clear as the Personality of the Father and the Son, yet it is impossible to think truly of the Spirit as impersonal, since definite personal attributes and powers are given to the Spirit.

'The New Testament and Christian experience are at one in teaching that the Christian conception of God includes all that is meant by Father, Son, and Spirit ; and as the omission of what is meant by any of these terms leaves the Christian conception unsatisfied, it may fairly be said that the doctrine of the Trinity is the fundamental doctrine of our faith. The Father, the Son, and the Spirit in their unity constitute the God Whom we know as the God of our salvation.' [1]

It will be seen from the foregoing that the distinctions in the Godhead involved in the New Testament doctrine of the Spirit are always connected closely with the Divine operations rather than with the Divine nature. There is nothing philosophical or speculative in the Biblical revelation. All is vital and personal.

'The evidence from the New Testament (Acts and Paul perhaps especially) teaches us that we must keep in view both aspects of divine-human relationship, the influence and the Person, the Giver and the Gift, the spirit and the Spirit ; we are conscious, as was the first age of Christians, of the work, then of the Worker, of the in-ourselves previous to the Not-in-ourselves.' [2]

[1] Denney, Article 'Holy Spirit,' *Dictionary of Christ and the Gospels*, p. 744.

[2] Winstanley, *Spirit in the New Testament*, p. 161.

Not the least significant point in the New Testament is the incidental and almost constant mention of the Holy Spirit. This feature is to be specially observed. It represents an atmosphere, a life. The Holy Spirit is regarded as normal in the life of the believer, who is enabled thereby to ' live ' and ' walk ' and even ' step ' in the Spirit (Gal. v. 16, 25, Greek).

6. The fundamental conceptions and experiences are the same throughout the whole of the New Testament. The only varieties are found in the types of thought and mental expression. It is impossible to trace any development of the doctrine of the Spirit through Ebionism to Orthodoxy. From the earliest to the latest the essential ideas are the same, however they may vary in aspect and degree of presentation.

' The Holy Spirit is, in the strict sense of the word, divine. No biblical writer yields any support to the Arian conception of a created Intelligence above the angels but inferior to the Son, to whom the name " Spirit of God " is improperly applied.' [1]

Everything connected with the Spirit of God in the Bible can be summarised in the one thought that from first to last the life of the believer depends upon God for its complete realisation, and this dependence is connected at each point with the Spirit of God. All that Jesus Christ was, and did, and is, becomes vital only by means of the action of the Spirit of God on those who are willing to receive Him.

' The essential thing, in summary statement, is that in relation to Christ men have to do with God, and may experience in themselves the energies of God. We have as much of God as we get through Christ ; we think of God as the God and Father of our Lord Jesus Christ. The Spirit of God, Whose presence in the believer's heart makes the new life of sonship, is the Spirit of Christ, or is Christ Himself, for the Spirit is God present with us, and we find Him present in and through Christ. Here, then, we have the dynamic of the Christian life, the power of God unto salvation ; the life of faith is essentially the life of dependence on Him Who dwells in the heart by its faith. There is here, obviously, an element of intelligent knowledge concerning Christ, and faith must have its preachers ; but the chief and central thing is the new dynamic, the whole resources of the Spirit of God through which not only

[1] Swete, Article ' Holy Spirit,' Hastings' *Bible Dictionary*, p. 410.

Christ is raised from death, but every one also who is crucified with Him in spirit.' [1]

And thus we see the force of the conclusion that

' the unification of all the religious life under the Spirit is the last stage in the biblical development of the idea. It is the last stage that ever can come in its development, unless there be retrogression ; for nothing more complete, in the relation of God to the human soul, can be conceived than the idea that the entire religious life originates from and is guided by God acting immediately on the human spirit. In biblical literature itself, then, the conception of the Spirit reaches its perfect end.' [2]

So that whatever lines of thought may be followed by the Church, and whatever avenues of experience may be entered, it will be impossible to arrive at any point, or to come upon any discovery, that is not in some way or other explicit or implicit in Holy Scripture.

' Conditioned as we are, we cannot really go beyond the New Testament doctrine of the self-witness of God through the Spirit in and through men.' [3]

---

[1] H. W. Robinson, *The Christian Doctrine of Man*, p. 324.

[2] Wood, *The Spirit of God in Biblical Literature*, p. 269.

[3] Winstanley, *op. cit.* p. 166.

PART II

THE HISTORICAL INTERPRETATION

CHAPTER 10

THE ANTE-NICENE PERIOD

It forms a natural transition from the Biblical revelation to the enquiry how the Christian consciousness has interpreted the Biblical data.

'No Christian doctrine, as it is now expressed, can be rightly understood without some knowledge of the history of Christian thought. The Christianity of the present day has not been evolved directly out of the New Testament, but is the product of the gradual assimilation of the original deposit by a long succession of Christian generations.' [1]

Opinions on the relation of the Spirit to the Church are so different, that it becomes essential to study with care the course and development of Christian thought and life. It is significant that so many movements in Christian history, which may be said to have developed into 'heresies,' have arisen in connection with the Holy Spirit. This fact alone makes it imperative to enquire as to the relation of Christian doctrine and history to the outstanding teaching of the Bible.

It is impossible, and in some respects unnecessary, to go into detail. For the purpose of arriving at true ideas on the subject, it seems better to concentrate on the chief eras of Church History. The progress of Christian thought

---

[1] Swete, *The Holy Spirit in the Ancient Church*, p. 4.

Literature.—Smeaton, *The Doctrine of the Holy Spirit*, p. 256 ; Denio, *The Supreme Leader*, p. 55 ; Moule, *Outlines of Christian Doctrine*, p. 119 ; Welldon, *The Revelation of the Holy Spirit*, ch. v. ; Swete, Article ' Holy Ghost,' *Dictionary of Christian Biography*, Vol. III. ; Orr, *The Progress of Dogma*, p. 124 ; *Mansfield College Essays*, p. 287 ; Warfield, Introduction to Kuyper's *The Work of the Holy Spirit*.

through the centuries seems to be characterised by the six landmarks indicated in these chapters.

Sub-Apostolic Christianity was characterised by a real Christian experience without much reflection on what was involved in that experience. The remarkable difference between the leading ideas of the New Testament and the thought of the sub-Apostolic age is observed by all writers. As Swete says, ' The spiritual giants of the Apostolic age are succeeded by men of lower stature and poorer capacity.' [1]

' From such literature of the next age within the Church as has been preserved to us, we find results that are sufficiently remarkable ; results which go to shew that the deepest and most ethical teaching, that which we cherish most now, that contained in Pauline and Johannine writings, is just that which is the least prominent.' [2]

In Clement of Rome and Ignatius the teaching seems to be solely personal and experimental, and only indirectly doctrinal, and the Shepherd of Hermas has the fullest of references to the Spirit of God.[3] But the fact that the threefold name of Father, Son, and Spirit was used in worship shows that implicitly and in practice the Deity and Personality of the Spirit were acknowledged. The experience of the Spirit was sufficient for the present.

' There was as yet no formal theology of the Spirit and no effort to create it ; nor was there any conscious heresy. But the presence of the Spirit in the Body of Christ was recognised on all hands as an acknowledged fact of the Christian life.' [4]

When we turn to the Apologists, we become conscious of the fact that the Logos doctrine occupies the first place, and that which the New Testament attributes to the Holy Spirit is usually connected with the Logos.

' The Greek apologists of the second century were so fully occupied with the endeavour to shew that the philosophical conception of a θεὸς λόγος was realised in the Person of the historical Christ, that they paid comparatively little attention to the doctrine of the Holy Ghost, and even ascribed to the Son operations and offices

---

[1] Swete, *op. cit.* p. 3.

[2] Winstanley, *Spirit in the New Testament*, p. 156.

[3] Swete, Article ' Holy Ghost,' *Dictionary of Christian Biography*, Vol. III. p. 114.

[4] Swete, *op. cit.* p. 31.

which the later thought of the Church referred to the Spirit of God.' [1]

'The Holy Spirit falls into the background in the theology, because it had not yet allied itself with any of the ruling ideas of the philosophy of the times ; and that factor of Christian experience which assumed the form of the Logos doctrine takes the supreme place.' [2]

'Those of the Apologists who were philosophers found it easier to develop the doctrine of the Logos than that of the Holy Spirit.' [3]

But it is quite clear that this immaturity of thought on the question of the Holy Spirit does not show any indication of error in experience, for,

'immature as the doctrinal language of the Church still was, no apologetic writer of the second century spoke of the Spirit of God as one of the creatures.' [4]

As in other cases, so here, it was heresy that compelled the Church to pay closer attention to the doctrine of the Holy Spirit. Gnosticism played some part in this process. Bishop Moule considers that the Gnostic systems bear a curious testimony to belief in the Personality of the Holy Spirit, since their ' Holy Spirit ' is as personal as their ' Christ,' though ' their theory is indeed wholly distorted from the Scripture view.' [5] Swete, however, remarks that, while the Gnostics who accepted the Gospels could not ignore the subject,

'it was not easy for Gnosticism to find a place in any of its systems for such a conception of the Holy Spirit as the Gospels present ; the attempt was made in various ways, but never satisfactorily. And though most of the Gnostic systems attached importance to the work of the Spirit, both in Baptism and in life, their view of the spiritual life led them to seek the sphere of His operations in the intellect rather than in the moral nature of man. For this reason the whole tone of Gnostic teaching on the Spirit differs widely from that of Catholic Christians in the second and third centuries.' [6]

---

[1] Swete, Article ' Holy Ghost,' *Dictionary of Christian Biography*, Vol. III. p. 115.

[2] T. Rees, ' The Holy Spirit as Wisdom,' *Mansfield College Essays*, p. 302.

[3] Swete, *The Holy Spirit in the Ancient Church*, p. 48.

[4] Swete, *ut supra*, p. 49.

[5] *Outlines of Christian Doctrine*, p. 147.

[6] *The Holy Spirit in the Ancient Church*, p. 66.

It was in Montanism that the subject came more prominently into notice, and there seems no doubt that the original impetus of this movement was a reaction in favour of the recognition of the presence and power of the Holy Spirit in a Church that was already tending to become too rigid in its intellectual conceptions and ecclesiastical organisation.

' For Tertullian, however, the interest of Montanism lay chiefly in the assurance which the New Prophecy seemed to give that the Holy Spirit was still teaching the Church. He is careful to insist that though the movement was a new one, the Spirit was none other than the Paraclete Who had been promised and already sent ; and that His teaching through the Montanist prophets was not essentially new.' [1]

' For Tertullian, and probably for many of its adherents both in East and West, Montanism stood for a recognition of the active presence of the Paraclete in the Body of Christ, and for a more spiritual and a more ascetic type of Church life than the official churches seemed to offer.' [2]

Unfortunately the movement developed along extravagant lines ; its original beneficent purpose became wholly lost, and it ' exerted no lasting influence over the thought of the Church.' [3] But notwithstanding the extremes into which Montanism went, it is also true that

' the obscure prophet of Phrygia had raised the eternal question of the ages. On the one hand, administration and order, the well-being of the Church in its collective capacity, the sacred book, the oral voice of the Master, the touch of the vanished hand, the perpetuation as of a bodily presence, some physical chain, as it were, which should bind the generations together, so that they should continue visibly and tangibly to hand on the truth and the life from man to man ; and, on the other hand, the freedom of the Spirit and the open heaven of revelation, . . . the vision by which each soul may see Christ for himself through direct and immediate communion with the Spirit of God—that Spirit Whose testimony within the soul is the supreme authority and ground of certitude, Who takes of the things of Christ and reveals them to· men with fresh power and new conviction, Who can at any moment authorize initiations of change and progress which yet do not and cannot break the succession of a continuous life of the Spirit in the Churches,—such were the terms of real issue between Catholicism and Montanism,

---

[1] Swete, *The Holy Spirit in the Ancient Church*, p. 79.

[2] Swete, *ut supra*, p. 83.

[3] Swete, Article ' Holy Ghost,' *Dictionary of Christian Biography*, Vol. III. p. 116.

which still wait, after eighteen centuries, for some larger or final adjustment.' [1]

Monarchianism also had a very definite bearing on the ante-Nicene doctrine of the Holy Spirit. It was impossible for Christian thought to ignore the relation of the Spirit to the Son in the face of the Christological teaching of the various schools of Monarchianism represented by Paul of Samosata, Praxeas, Noetus, and especially Sabellius, and it is to Tertullian, influenced by Montanism, that we owe the fullest ante-Nicene statement of the Holy Spirit's relation to the Father and the Son. [2]

The main ante-Nicene writers on this subject are Irenaeus, Tertullian, and Origen. Of Irenaeus, Swete writes as follows:

' The pneumatology of Irenaeus is a great advance on all earlier Christian teaching outside the canon. He does not use the term "Trinity," but the Father, Son, and Spirit form in his theology a triad which is anterior and external to the creation. . . . On the mission of the Holy Spirit or the Paraclete he is particularly full and clear. . . . Irenaeus has on this point caught the inspiration of St. Paul more nearly than any of his predecessors or contemporaries.' [3]

We have already seen Tertullian's testimony in connection with Montanism and Monarchianism. It is scarcely possible to exaggerate the importance of this writer, who ' lays the foundation of the Catholic doctrine of Divine processions,' [4] and who is described as far in advance of Western Christian thought. [5] It should be noted in passing that both in the Apologists and in Tertullian the doctrine does not seem to be as yet fully Nicene. The Spirit is Divine, but not eternal. [6] While it is true that the tendencies of Alexandria were speculative rather than dogmatic and practical, [7] yet it is ' in the writings of Origen we find

---

[1] A. V. G. Allen, *Christian Institutions*, p. 103.

[2] Swete, *The Holy Spirit in the Ancient Church*, p. 107.

[3] Swete, *The Holy Spirit in the Ancient Church*, pp. 92, 93.

[4] Swete, Article ' Holy Ghost,' *Dictionary of Christian Biography*, Vol. III. p. 118.

[5] Swete, *The Holy Spirit in the Ancient Church*, p. 107.

[6] Orr, *Progress of Dogma*, p. 125 f.

[7] Swete, *The Holy Spirit in the Ancient Church*, p. 124.

the first attempt, after Tertullian, at a scientific treatment of the doctrine of the Holy Ghost ' ; [1] and although Origen's daring mind led him into speculations,

' the Church and School of Alexandria in the third century contributed not a little to the clearing and quickening of Christian thought upon the doctrine of the Holy Spirit. If the results are less definite than those which come to us from North Africa, they go deeper, and their scope is less limited. It was by Origen rather than by Tertullian that the way was opened to the fuller discussion of the theology of the Spirit upon which the fourth century entered.' [2]

But the strongest confirmation of the true doctrine of the Holy Spirit in this non-reflective period is found in connection with the devotional life of the Church. Experience has often proved the best witness to what is in reality doctrinally implicit in the Christian community, and all the evidences we possess of the life of the Church of these days bear unquestioned testimony to the reality of the Holy Spirit of God.

(a) The earliest form of the Apostles' Creed is now acknowledged to date from the middle of the second century, and this is a record of facts rather than a theological interpretation.

(b) Doxologies and other hymns of praise bear the same testimony.

(c) In the ordinance of Baptism the Trinitarian form is found as early as the Didache, and whatever view we may hold as to the association of regeneration with the water, the testimony to the presence and power of the Spirit is unmistakable.

(d) In connection with the Lord's Supper, recent liturgical research goes to show that the earliest form of ' Invocation ' referred not to the elements, but to the communicant, thereby witnessing to an essential adherence to New Testament teaching, which never connects the Holy Spirit with the elements.[3] But this ' Invocation ' is sufficient to

---

[1] Swete, Article ' Holy Ghost,' *Dictionary of Christian Biography*, Vol. III. p. 119.

[2] Swete, *The Holy Spirit in the Ancient Church*, p. 143.

[3] Maclean, *Ancient Church Orders*, p. 51 ; R. W. Woolley, *The Liturgy of the Primitive Church* ; Upton, *Outlines of Prayer Book History*, pp. 16-19 and refs.

indicate what the Church of that day thought of the Holy Spirit. On the whole subject there can be no doubt that the devotional life and experience of the Church was the best and most convincing proof of what Christians believed concerning the Holy Spirit.

' The devotional language of the early Church was in fact on the whole in advance of its doctrinal system. Men like Origen still had intellectual difficulties in reference to the relation of the Spirit to the other Persons of the Holy Trinity ; but they could nevertheless associate His name in their prayers and praises with those of the Father and the Son. The worship of the Trinity was a fact in the religious life of Christians before it was a dogma of the Church. Dogmatic precision was forced upon the Church by heresy, but the confession and conglorification of the Three Persons arose out of the Christian consciousness, interpreting by its own experience the words of Christ and the Apostles and the primitive rule of faith.' [1]

---

[1] Swete, *The Holy Spirit in the Ancient Church*, p. 159.

CHAPTER 11

NICAEA TO CHALCEDON

IT was impossible for the non-reflective period concerning the Holy Spirit to continue in the light of the Christological controversies of the times, for when the Deity of the Son had been established, it was inevitable that thought would be turned in the direction of the Deity of the Holy Spirit. Even the heresy of Arius did not exclude the consideration of the Third Person, although the Nicene Council dealt only with the Deity of the Son, and ended its statement of belief with the simple words, ' And in the Holy Spirit.' But if the Son was not a Creator but ὁμοούσιος with the Father and therefore Divine, the Personality and Deity of the Holy Spirit would naturally be inferred, even though not specifically stated.

' Either the Church did not realise that the Person of the Holy Spirit was virtually included in the Arian attack upon the Person of the Son, or she was not prepared to pronounce a decisive judgment upon the Godhead of the Spirit ; or, as is more probable, she was not concerned to anticipate heresy, or to define the terms of Catholic communion more precisely than the occasion demanded. In any case the Council of 325 was content to assert the consubstantiality of the Son. Yet the sudden arrest of the Nicene Creed after the words " And in the Holy Spirit," gave warning that at some future time it might be found necessary to guard the Deity of the Spirit as the Deity of the Son had been guarded.' [1]

---

[1] Swete, *The Holy Spirit in the Ancient Church*, p. 165.

LITERATURE.—Orr, *The Progress of Dogma*, p. 126 ; For Athanasius ; Swete, *The Holy Spirit in the Ancient Church*, pp. 172-273 ; Article ' Holy Ghost,' *Dictionary of Christian Biography*, Vol. III. p. 124 ; for the Cappadocians, Gregory, Nazianzen, Orat. 31 (*Nicene and Post-Nicene Library*, Vol. VII. p. 319).

The question was not raised at once, although a controversy on subjects arising out of the Arian question was rife for thirty years after Nicaea. It is particularly interesting to notice that most of the later Arian Councils, up to 360, stated their belief concerning the work of the Holy Spirit in terms which were in thorough accord with the spiritual simplicity of Holy Scripture. So much is this the case, that Swete is able to write :

‘ The Church owes a debt, it may be freely admitted, to the Arian leaders who thus persistently called attention to the teaching and sanctifying influences of the Holy Spirit, at a time when there was grave risk of Christian thought being turned too entirely to theological controversy.’ [1]

But even this by itself did not prove satisfactory, for it would seem as though an exclusive emphasis on the work of the Spirit tended to a view of His inferiority in Person to the Son, and thus the Arian and semi-Arian statement of the mission and work of the Spirit, while admirable in itself, was in the outcome ‘ unsatisfactory and even misleading ; professing to be scriptural, it represents only one side of the teaching of Scripture.’ [2] As a consequence, a new controversy soon arose, and individuals ‘ everywhere begun openly to assert their unbelief in the Deity of the Spirit.’ [3] The controversy thus commenced lasted nearly thirty years, and was not settled until the Council of Constantinople, 381.

Meanwhile it is important to call attention to the names of leading writers during the period between Nicaea and Constantinople. The first is that of Eusebius, Bishop of Caesarea, who, as is well known, played a prominent part in the Nicene Council. His subordinationist view has tended to make modern writers think of him as unorthodox, but the verdict of Swete is probably correct :

‘ This is subordinationism in its most outspoken boldness, but it is the subordinationism of Origen rather than of Arius ; only, in passing through the mind of Eusebius, Origen’s conjectures have become dogmas. . . . It may be doubted whether, had Eusebius

---

[1] Swete, *op. cit.* p. 169.

[2] Swete, *op. cit.* p. 169.

[3] Swete, Article ‘ Holy Ghost,’ *Dictionary of Christian Biography,* Vol. III. p. 121.

lived to be present at the Council of 381, he would not have submitted as he submitted at Nicaea ; not going the whole way, perhaps, with the victorious party, but yet preferring conformity to separation from the Church. Certainly he would have hesitated to adopt the shibboleths of the Eunomians or the Pneumatomachi. . . . If this is far from the orthodoxy of an Athanasius or a Basil, it is certainly further from the irreverence of an Arius or a Eunomius.' [1]

Cyril of Jerusalem next calls for attention, and the importance of his testimony lies in the fact that he was a pastor and teacher rather than a theologian. His position has been well summed up :

' On the theology of the Holy Spirit, therefore, he is far from explicit ; but of the work of the Spirit no writer of the fourth century has spoken more fully or convincingly. Yet if the Catecheses had not survived, Cyril might have been known to us merely as a Semiarian leader who after a troubled episcopate sought rest late in life among the victorious Nicenes. The lectures shew that his true interests were religious and not controversial, and that in all essential respects he was from the first a Nicene in heart. His case suggests the hope that not a few of the Semiarian clergy of his age were men of devout minds, whose piety and pastoral labours fell little short of those of the best champions of the Nicene faith.' [2]

One of the greatest names is that of Athanasius, whose work during this period shows that he was just as capable of dealing with the Godhead of the Spirit as he had been with the Godhead of the Son, and both by his personal influence as well as by his writings he did a work of supreme and vital moment.

' It was of no little importance for the cause of the Nicene faith that when the Deity of the Spirit was for the first time explicitly denied, and the denial came from men who professed to believe in the Deity of the Son, the veteran champion of the Homoousion was ready to expose the futility of the attempt to accept the Homoousion unless it were extended to the Third Person of the Holy Trinity. The new heresy received in fact its death blow from the same capable hands that had despatched the earlier form of Arianism ; for though it struggled on for twenty years and more, the end was scarcely doubtful after the appearance of the *Letters to Serapion*.' [3]

Last of all, and in some respects greatest of all, are the three theologians popularly known as the Cappadocians ; Basil of Caesarea, Gregory of Nazianzus, and Gregory of

---

[1] Swete, *The Holy Spirit in the Ancient Church*, pp. 197, 198, 199.

[2] Swete, *op. cit.* p. 210.

[3] Swete, *The Holy Spirit in the Ancient Church*, p. 220.

Nyssa. It was due to them that the orthodox doctrine of the Holy Trinity ultimately prevailed throughout the Eastern Church.[1] Basil's important work is thus characterised :

'Others may have carried the doctrine of the Holy Spirit somewhat further, but no ancient writer either in East or West shews more sympathy with his subject, or treats it more worthily.' [2]

Gregory's sermon on the Holy Spirit is described as 'this greatest of all sermons on the doctrine.' [3] Of Gregory of Nyssa, Swete says :

'It may be doubted whether any subsequent writer, in East or West, has approached nearer to a satisfactory statement of the relation which, according to the laws of human thought, the Divine Persons may be conceived to hold towards one another.' [4]

The main line of orthodox teaching was that the Holy Spirit was Divine, or else the Son was not Divine. Basil and the two Gregorys developed this idea, and thereby prepared the way for the decision of the Council of Constantinople, 381.

The post-Nicene controversy on this subject arose directly out of the Arian troubles, and those who were unable to accept the Deity of the Holy Spirit were described by Athanasius as 'enemies of the Spirit,' who were afterwards designated 'Spirit-fighters,' Pneumatomachi. They were led by Macedonius, Bishop of Constantinople, and the controversy grew until at length it was found absolutely necessary for the Emperor Theodosius to deal with the subject, by calling a Council at Constantinople consisting of 150 orthodox Bishops, representing the East only. The result was the promulgation of the Creed now known as the Nicene, but which was in reality a Creed already used in Jerusalem several years before. The additions to the Nicene formula were a declaration after belief in the Holy Spirit as

'The Lord, the life-giver, that proceeds from the Father, that with Father and Son is together worshipped and together glorified.' [5]

---

[1] Swete, *op. cit.* p. 230. [2] Swete, *op. cit.* p 240

[3] Swete, *op. cit.* p. 240. [4] Swete, *op. cit.* p. 252.

[5] Swete, *op. cit.* p. 186.

It has been pointed out that the Creed used remarkable moderation in avoiding the term ὁμοούσιος to express the Spirit's oneness with the Father and the Son. He is not even called God, though the terms in which His work is described cannot possibly be predicated of any created being.

'The words served their purpose as well as if the Homoousion had been extended to the Third Person, for while no Semiarian who was in substantial agreement with the Nicene faith could stumble at them, they were sufficiently explicit to debar from communion any who refused to the Holy Spirit the honour due to God.' [1]

On this point a note by Dr. Swete is at once suggestive and significant :

'The Constantinopolitan Creed adds to its confession of the Person of the Spirit a clause recognising His work in the Old Testament Prophets (τὸ λαλῆσαν διὰ τῶν προφητῶν). It may be wished that the creed had proceeded, as most of the Arian creeds did, to speak of His office as Paraclete, and the Pentecostal effusion with its permanent results.' [2]

It is worthy of note that an orthodox modern scholar is able to argue in favour of the Catholic or orthodox party following the line taken earlier by the Arians and semi-Arians in emphasising the work of the Spirit.

The question of the Deity of the Holy Spirit was now finally settled, just as the Deity of the Son had been settled over fifty years before. Arianism, whether in relation to the Son or the Spirit, had no spiritual vitality. It was an illogical and impossible position, even from the intellectual point of view, while spiritually it had no basis at all. Whatever difficulties there may be in the orthodox view of the relations of the Son and the Spirit to the Father, it has one supreme advantage over every other theory ; it is rooted in a personal experience which has always proved its perfect safeguard against all foes. ' A living faith thrives under the stress and storm which thin the numbers of its adherents.' [3] But Arianism, ancient and modern, fails, simply because it is not ' a living faith.'

---

[1] Swete, *op. cit.* p. 187 ; Orr, *Progress of Dogma*, p. 127.

[2] *Op. cit.* p. 187, note 3.

[3] Swete, *op. cit.* p. 190.

Although the subject of the Deity of the Holy Spirit was decided by the Eastern Council of Constantinople in 381, it was still discussed and developed between Constantinople and Chalcedon both in East and West. It is impossible to do more than mention the Eastern names of Theodore of Mopsuestia (392-428) and Theodoret (432-458).

But some of the Western names call for more attention. Ambrose of Milan is the first of these, and to him

' belongs the merit of being the first Western writer who devoted a separate work of any magnitude to the doctrine of the Holy Spirit. It has no claim to originality ; the student who has read Athanasius, Basil, and Didymus on the same subject, will find little that is new in Ambrose.' [1]

Far greater is the name of Augustine of Hippo, whose treatment of the subject in his work, *On the Trinity*, is one of the profoundest in theological literature. Both as a theologian and as a deeply religious man his discussion of the Person and Work of the Holy Spirit is of supreme importance. His interest in the doctrine of grace would naturally lead to a consideration of this doctrine, for his own personal experiences tended to show him how at every point from the beginning to the end the Holy Spirit is needed by the believing soul. The way in which Pelagianism minimised the need of grace only led to the still stronger emphasis by Augustine on the need and power of the Holy Spirit of God. There are those who think that he went to extremes in his insistence on the sovereignty of God, but in the days in which he lived it is not surprising that he should have been led to concentrate attention on the Divine action in the revelation and bestowal of grace, and in spite of everything that may be said concerning Augustine, few will be found to disagree with Dr. Swete's conclusion :

' The whole Church owes a deep debt to Augustine for his insistence on the inability of the human will to choose that which is good without the co-operating power of the Spirit of God and of Christ.' [2]

In 451 the Council of Chalcedon, representing the Sees of Rome, Constantinople, Antioch, and Jerusalem, confirmed the decisions of Nicaea and Constantinople in regard

---

[1] Swete, *op. cit.* p. 317.   [2] Swete, *op. cit.* p. 338.

to Christian belief. This Council took care to say that the Nicene Creed was sufficient as a statement of the doctrine of the Trinity, and that the clauses added in 381 were only intended to make the Nicene doctrine more explicit as against those who, like the Macedonians, had endeavoured to deny the Deity of the Spirit. In harmony with this view, the Council endorsed both Creeds, and incorporated them in what is now known as the 'Definitio' of Chalcedon.

In reviewing the history of the period ending with Chalcedon, it is of course impossible to avoid the feeling of regret that such sacred subjects as the Person of the Son and the Person of the Holy Spirit and their relation to the Father should have been the cause of bitter controversy. But in spite of much that saddens us as we read the story of personal and synodical antipathies, we must not lose sight of the fact that all through there was a deep underlying spiritual experience of the realities of Divine redemption in the Person of Jesus Christ mediated by the Holy Spirit. Church History reveals to us intellectual controversy, but it is sometimes forgotten that spiritual experience was a reality throughout these times of storm and stress, and it is pretty certain that the experience did more than the definitions of theologians to keep the doctrine undiluted and undefiled.

'It is satisfactory to know that in those troubled years Eastern Christendom was not divided upon any great question connected with the office and work of the Paraclete. Arians who refused to call Him God, with a happy absence of logic recognised His function of sanctifying all the elect people of God. Catholics who differed among themselves on the subject of the Procession of the Spirit, were in full agreement as to His presence in the Church and His gracious workings in the Sacraments and on individual souls. A common experience accounts for this harmony, witnessing to the vital unity which in all sincere believers " underlies even serious differences of thought or creed." '[1]

---

[1] Swete, *op. cit.* p. 273.

CHAPTER 12

CHALCEDON TO THE REFORMATION

THE Deity of the Spirit was now fully and permanently established, but there still remained the important and mysterious question of His precise relation to the Father and the Son. The term 'Generation' was used to describe the relation of the Son to the Father, and the term 'Procession' was employed to denote the relation of the Spirit, but the question was whether this eternal 'Procession' or 'Forthcoming' was from the Son as well as from the Father.

The problem was Western, not Eastern, just as the question of the Deity was Eastern, not Western. This attitude indicates a difference which is explained by the conditions of the two Churches. The Eastern was faced with those who tended to regard the Spirit as inferior to the Son, because brought into human life through the Son's mediation. In order, therefore, to protect the full Deity of the Spirit, it was considered essential to represent Him as proceeding solely from the Father as the fountain (πηγή) of the Godhead. The Western Church, on the other hand, starting with the essential unity of the Son and the Father, desired to protect and preserve the truth that the Spirit is as much the Spirit of the Son as He is of the Father. Otherwise there could be no equality. This

LITERATURE.—Swete, *The Holy Spirit in the Ancient Church*, pp. 273-355 ; Swete, Article 'Holy Ghost,' *Dictionary of Christian Biography*, p. 126 ; Welldon, *The Revelation of the Holy Spirit*, ch. v. ; 'On the Doctrine of the Procession,' Swete, *op. cit.* pp. 151, 169 ; Denio, *The Supreme Leader*, p. 66 ; Moule, *Veni Creator*, ch. ii.

is the doctrine of Procession, and was expressed by saying that the Spirit ' proceeded ' from the Father and the Son. Not that the Greek writers were absolutely silent on the Procession from the Son, for it is found in both Didymus and Epiphanius.[1]   But it is in the West that the doctrine is made distinct, mainly by Hilary of Poitiers, but chiefly by Augustine.   It was the profound influence of the latter that almost wholly led to the endorsement of the doctrine by the Western Church.

The acceptance of the Augustinian doctrine of the Procession as a permanent part of Western doctrine is usually associated with the Council of Toledo in Spain, 589.   It was the incorporation of the doctrine into the Creed that led to its permanent acceptance in the West.

' Two causes co-operated to render the Spanish clergy painfully alive to the importance of a fuller symbolical statement of the Catholic doctrine.   Priscillianism disturbed the peace of the Church in Spain, from the end of the 4th century to the end of the 6th ; and amongst its other errors Priscillianism revived the Sabellian view of the Trinity (Aug. *c. Priscill.* 4), and, as it seems, confounded the Persons of the Son and the Spirit (Oros. *Comm. ad Aug.* 2). Further, at the beginning of the 5th century, the invasion of the Visigoths brought in a deluge of the worst form of Arianism, including the Eunomian doctrine of the creation of the Spirit by the Son.   These attacks upon the truth compelled the Spanish Church to formulate her faith in a series of confessions which abound in the most precise dogmatism upon the doctrine of the Holy Trinity.' [2]

At Toledo the authority of the first four Councils was acknowledged, and the Creeds of Nicaea and Constantinople rehearsed, and it is curious and mysterious that in this rehearsal the Synod imagined that the Latin Creed, which it repeated faithfully, represented the Greek original.   It is a matter of discussion how the words ' And the Son ' came into the Creed.   Some have thought this was due to a marginal gloss.   Dr. Burn adduces evidence from important Spanish MSS. to prove that the Council never added the words at all, that they are due to the blunder of a copyist of the Toledo text of the Constantinopolitan

---

[1] Swete, *The Holy Spirit in the Ancient Church*, pp. 224, 226.

[2] Swete, Article ' Holy Ghost,' *Dictionary of Christian Biography*, Vol. III. p. 129.

Creed.[1] In any case, the interpolation did not cause suspicion, but was repeated in Synod after Synod as the orthodox doctrine. It has often seemed surprising that the Council of Toledo should lay such stress on the point, and yet profess to keep the text of the Creed pure, but it would seem as though increasing error was already rendering further dogmatic definition necessary for proper interpretation.

' If the Holy Ghost is worshipped with the Father and the Son, such honour can only be rightly paid on the ground that He is coessential and coequal, as the Son has been acknowledged to be at the cost of the long Arian controversy. Therefore the Toledan Fathers were only drawing out what seemed to them latent in the Creed.' [2]

In reply to the argument that the Spanish Church acted in this way by reason of its controversy with Arianism and its intense desire to avoid attributing to the Father what the Son possessed, Dr. Burn says :

' It is more probable that without much reflection they were simply loyal to what had been a marked characteristic of Western teaching since the time of St. Augustine. It is important to make this fact quite plain. Eastern and Western thinkers started from two different points of view. Therein lies the justification for the age-long quarrel on this subject, which can never be composed until justice is done to the sincerity of both parties.' [3]

It is important and essential to distinguish between the doctrine of the Procession and its insertion in the Creed. There can be no doubt that however and whenever it was inserted, the addition was unwarranted, because it never received proper ecumenical authority. It was apparently due to the great influence of Gregory the Great that the Latin Church at last came to accept Augustine's doctrine of the Procession.[4] And yet it was a long time before the addition became part of the Roman version of the Constantinopolitan Creed.[5]

Referring once again to the East, the subject did not arise in connection with the fourth, fifth, and sixth Councils.

---

[1] *The Nicene Creed*, p. 40. [2] Burn, *op. cit.* p. 41.

[3] *The Nicene Creed*, p. 41.

[4] Swete, *The Holy Spirit in the Ancient Church*, p. 347.

[5] Swete, *op. cit.* p. 349.

In regard to the last-named, it is suggested that the question was perhaps purposely avoided by the Westerns out of regard for the peace of the Church.[1] But in the West the view was making progress, and it is thought probable that England received the doctrine from Augustine himself, who was sent by Gregory the Great. Nothing further occurred in connection with the doctrine of the Holy Spirit in the East until the time of John of Damascus, at the beginning of the eighth century. He has been rightly described as ' the last great theologian of the Eastern Church,' although he does not seem to have been a constructive theologian, but he is universally regarded as ' the recognised exponent of Greek patristic theology during the first seven centuries.' [2] Dr. Swete says that the effort of John of Damascus to systematise Greek theology ' has deserved well of Christendom,' and that

' it may be that when the time comes for the drawing together again of East and West, the writings of the Damascene will supply a starting point for the movement.' [3]

After Gregory the Great the Middle Ages may be said to set in, and ' scholastic theology gradually takes the place of the patristic type.' [4] During this period little or nothing occurred of importance in connection with the doctrine of the Holy Spirit. Semi-Pelagianism grew and developed in the West, though there were leading men who defended the Augustinian doctrines of grace. St. Bernard is the best representative of the Middle Ages, as anticipative of later and brighter days.

' At the beginning of the twelfth century a new creative epoch entered, and a new outpouring of the Holy Ghost, when religion though still mingled with foreign elements, decidedly revived among the nations. Bernard was the representative of that mystic or pectoral theology which runs through the mediaeval period wherever it shows spiritual elements. The stream of religious

---

[1] Swete, Article ' Holy Ghost,' *Dictionary of Christian Biography,* p. 131.

[2] Swete, *The Holy Spirit in the Ancient Church,* p. 280.

[3] Swete, *The Holy Spirit in the Ancient Church,* p. 285.

[4] Swete, *op. cit.* p. 350.

thought may be said to have divided in two from this time, the one more scholastic, the other more mystic.' [1]

After Bernard comes the period of Mediaeval Mysticism, when earnest souls were at once disturbed by the consciousness of their own sin and the consciousness of the powerlessness of the organised Church to provide spiritual deliverance. This led to a religion of personal, immediate contact of the soul with God, and the natural result was an emphasis on Christ and the Holy Spirit. Indeed, the very heart of Mysticism lies in fellowship with the personal Saviour, through the Holy Spirit, and this element, though limited to individuals who never broke away from the great Western Church, was undoubtedly a preliminary to, and a great preparation for, the Reformation. With all its limitations and inadequacy, Mysticism represents a genuine movement of the Holy Spirit of God.

At this stage it seems necessary to review the progress of thought, and especially to view it in the light of the New Testament. Three things were settled beyond all question, at least in the Western Church ; the Deity of the Son at Nicaea, the Deity of the Spirit at Constantinople, and the Procession of the Spirit from the Father and the Son in the Western Creed. But in passing from the simple yet significant experience of the New Testament, it is impossible to avoid the consciousness that the Creeds give us an intellectual and abstract statement of the truth that may easily be regarded as remote from spiritual realities. But the change of emphasis did not really involve any change of essential doctrine. Heresy, as already remarked, necessitated the intellectual, explicit statement of that which was spiritually implicit in the New Testament teaching and experience. It is often urged that the dogmas of the Creed are unwarranted when viewed in the light of the primitive simplicity of New Testament teaching, and it is said that they represent a corruption through the dogmatic strength of Greek philosophy.

' The truth is just the reverse. The novel element in the compound was not philosophy, but the Gospel. . . . The steps which

---

[1] Smeaton, *The Doctrine of the Holy Spirit*, p. 305.

led to the formulation of the doctrine of the Trinity are the steps by which the Christian spirit made for itself a home in the existing intellectual environment. However speculative in form, every one of them was due to a practical interest. . . . Putting ourselves back at the point of view of the men who made the decisions, and imagining ourselves faced with like questions, we should have been obliged to answer them in the same way.' [1]

It is of course vital to keep in mind the difference between a purely intellectual and even abstract conception, and the warm, vital experience of the believing soul. But there need and should be no contradiction between them, nor will there be if the Creed is regarded as a landmark rather than a goal, and as the explicit statement for the intellect of that which is implicit in the attitude of the believing, Christian soul to his God.

---

[1] W. A. Brown, *Christian Theology in Outline*, pp. 143, 145.

CHAPTER 13

THE REFORMATION

In the Middle Ages, Christian thought as to the Holy Spirit was mainly concerned with His Person and relation to the Deity ; scarcely anything seemed to be considered with reference to His work in individuals and the Church. It has been pointed out that in the East Christianity was mainly an intellectual system with no practical stress on the Holy Spirit, while the West had become concentrated under the authority of the Papacy, making Christianity little more than a mental and moral discipline. This tendency in the East was only the full flower of what had been dominant for centuries. Almost from the first the Greek Christian mind had superficial ideas of sin, and an exaggerated idea of philosophy, and this two fold tendency affected the entire theology.[1] The result was that the Eastern view of sin was essentially Pelagian long before the time of Pelagius.

' The Greek theology is not really Trinitarian, but Dualitarian. It thinks only in terms of God and His Logos ; and if the tradition and experience of the Holy Spirit still claim recognition, the system can only admit it as a shadowy repetition of the Logos, with no independent and effective function or principle of its own. The abstract dogma derived from Greek theology must, for its own self-preservation, for ever repress every movement of freedom, independence, and individuality, such as proceeds from a personal spirit ; this limitation of the Catholic theology, inherent in the form imposed upon it by Greek philosophy, lies at the root of its inadequacy to give either theoretical or practical expression to the Christian life ; and Christian theology has still to seek a synthesis

---

[1] Smeaton, *The Doctrine of the Holy Spirit*, pp. 264, 292.

of Spirit and Wisdom that will articulate a rational order, both physical and moral, issuing out of the activity of a free Spirit.'[1]

In the West, while the influence of Augustine was still at work in relation to the fact of sin and the consequent need of grace, yet the Church as a whole had become quite Semi-Pelagian, and this, together with the increasing sacerdotalism and its consequences, tended to keep the minds of men away from the question of the Holy Spirit of God. But, as we have seen, there were tendencies in Mysticism which went to emphasise the need of the Holy Spirit, and so far to prepare the way for the Reformation. The Reformation upheaval marks an epoch in connection with the Holy Spirit. While the Reformed Churches bore testimony in their formularies to a close adhesion to the doctrine of Chalcedon concerning the Deity, there was an entire change of view in regard to the Work of the Holy Spirit. His Deity was never in question, but the Reformation was revolutionary in regard to His Work.

The first aspect of this is associated with Divine revelation.

'During the long night of the Middle Ages the teaching of the New Testament was obscured by the huge shadow of the Church, a building which, intended to point men heavenwards, gradually blocked out from view the sun in its splendour and the azure of the sky. Reformers before the Reformation and the great leaders in the sixteenth century did much to clear the air and bring men face to face with God in Christ. It was not their fault, nor was it in itself an error, that they pointed chiefly to a Book ; for in this was the primitive record to which they appealed from the traditions which had obscured its meaning and stifled its teaching and influence. In reality they were building better than they knew. In vindicating the authority of the Scriptures against the encroachments of the Church they were helping to prepare the way for the complete supremacy of the Spirit.'[2]

Holy Scripture was no longer regarded as an ecclesiastical law book, needing to be interpreted by the Church and protected by the Hierarchy. It was the Word of God which once again spoke direct to the soul, and was to be received

---

[1] Rees, 'The Holy Spirit as Wisdom,' *Mansfield College Essays*, p. 304.

[2] Davison, 'The Person and Work of the Holy Spirit,' *London Quarterly Review*, April, 1905, p. 211.

by faith, and illuminated by the Spirit of God. The difference this made in men's conception of the Holy Spirit is profound and far-reaching.

Associated with this was the Reformation truth of peace with God on the basis of the Atoning Sacrifice received direct into the heart by faith. This doctrine, which Luther with true spiritual insight called the *articulus aut stantis aut cadentis ecclesiae,* at once set aside the need of priestly mediation, introducing the soul to God and providing the means of the Holy Spirit's presence and blessing. Here, again, the teaching was nothing short of revolutionary.

Not least of all, the controversies concerning Predestination and Freewill bore fruit in the same direction. There is nothing more striking or more characteristic of the Reformation from beginning to end than this emphasis on the Sovereignty of God, a doctrine taught as clearly by Melancthon as by Calvin.

' It is a striking fact that the Protestant theology of the sixteenth century both began and ended in strict theories of Predestination. . . . The severe doctrine of Calvin on the subject of Predestination is notorious ; but it should be remembered that the teaching of Melancthon in the first edition of his work was not less severe.' [1]

The explanation of this is seen in the fact that it is only by means of such a doctrine that man is brought to realise his own utter sinfulness and weakness, and his absolute and constant need of the grace of God. It was no mere philosophical problem of the Divine sovereignty and man's freedom, but a controversy which went to the heart of moral and religious realities.

' In proportion to the depth of men's moral and spiritual struggle, in proportion to the intensity with which they apprehend the height of the Divine righteousness and the Divine ideal, must there arise in them a sense of the utter feebleness of their own powers, of the weakness and servitude of their wills, and of their absolute dependence on Divine grace and the Divine will.' [2]

The bearing of all this on the need of the Holy Spirit is clear, and we are not surprised to find that the Reformation doctrine carried the twofold message, ' Without Me ye can do nothing ' ; ' I can do all things in Him Who

---

[1] Wace, *Principles of the Reformation,* p. 129.

[2] Wace, *op. cit.* p. 145.

strengtheneth me.' The Holy Spirit was seen to be beyond all else ' the Spirit of grace ' to those who were willing to receive Christ through simple faith.

Arising out of these three aspects of Holy Scripture, Justification, and Divine Sovereignty came the vital and fundamental difference in the relation of the individual to the community. Up to the time of the Reformation the characteristic and essential feature of mediaeval theology was ' through the Church to Christ,' but the Reformation reversed this method by a reinsistence on the New Testament principle of ' through Christ to the Church.' This, in some respects, is acknowledged on both sides to be the fundamental difference between Romanism and Protestantism. Protestantism has been truly described by a Roman Catholic authority :

> ' It took its stand upon a twofold antagonistic principle of its own—first, the principle of the immediate guidance of the soul by the Holy Spirit or private judgment which radically subverted all Church authority, and notably that of the Supreme Pontiff ; and secondly, the principle of justification by Faith alone, which practically subverted the whole Sacramental and Sacrificial system and with it the sacerdotium or priestly ministry that it postulates. Both these twin Reformational principles are at root logically one. . . . In the Catholic mind the order of Salvation stands as one, two, three—Christ, the Church, the Soul : that is to say, Christ living and acting in His Church teaches, saves, and sanctifies the soul. The work of Luther was to alter the order into that of Christ, the Soul, and the Church— or one, three, two. It is thus that in the Protestant mind the Church, falling into the third place, becomes something merely instrumental, instead of being as it is in the Catholic mind, something vital and permanently structural.' [1]

What has been said as to the precise relation of the individual and the Church does not ignore the obvious fact that our Christian heritage comes to us through the Christian Church, that faith is always mediated to the individual by the community or its members. But this is the work of a medium, not a mediator, and is spiritual not hierarchical. The fundamental difference between Roman Catholicism and Protestantism remains untouched.

---

[1] Moyes, ' The Mass and the Reformation,' *Eucharistic Congress*, 1908, pp. 37, 38.

It is unnecessary for our present purpose to refer specifically to individual Reformers, but there can be no doubt that both Luther and Calvin stand out supreme among Reformation theologians in their testimony to, and insistence on, the work of the Holy Spirit. Luther by his emphasis on Justification had much to say about the Holy Spirit as the Author of Divine Revelation mediated through faith, while Calvin brought into prominence those aspects of the work of the Spirit which are associated with the Divine Trinity and the operation of the Spirit in the heart and life of believers.

' There are three points in his teaching respecting the Holy Spirit which deserve notice : the Trinity, the work of the Spirit in renewal and sanctification, including His testimony to the sonship of believers, and the *testimonium Spiritus Sancti internum*, or the internal testimony of the Holy Spirit to the truth of the Scriptures and so to their Divine authority.' [1]

It has been said that we owe the doctrine of the work of the Holy Spirit more to Calvin than to anyone else.[2] This view has been made the subject of qualification, that it is true ' only in a very restricted sense,' namely, that

' Calvin was the first to give formulated expression to a description of the benefits bestowed by the Spirit on the individual believer.' [3]

But it is admitted that Calvin's ' Outline of New Testament teaching has been largely followed by Protestant Churches since his day.' [4]

It is also unnecessary to do more than refer to the fact that the various Reformed documents, the Augsburg Confession of 1530, the Anglican Articles of 1553, the Formula Concordiae, the Helvetic Confession, and, later on, the Westminster Confession, all bore testimony to the Deity of the Spirit following Chalcedon in its Western form, including the *Filioque*, and to the various aspects of the Work of the Spirit which had been brought into

---

[1] Denio, *The Supreme Leader*, p. 74.

[2] B. B. Warfield, Introduction to Kuyper's *The Work of the Holy Spirit*, p. xxxiii.

[3] Davison, Article ' The Person and Work of the Holy Spirit,' *London Quarterly Review*, April, 1905, p. 215.

[4] Davison, *op. cit.* p. 215.

prominence by the Reformation. Indeed, we may say that there was not a single vital doctrine connected with the personal life of the believer and the spiritual life of the Church which was not affected by the new and true emphasis on the presence and work of the Holy Spirit, and it is assuredly true that 'The developed doctrine of the work of the Holy Spirit is an exclusively Reformation doctrine.' [1]

---

[1] B. B. Warfield, *op. cit.* p. xxxiii.

CHAPTER 14

THE SEVENTEENTH AND EIGHTEENTH CENTURIES

IT is at once curious and saddening to observe the way in which almost every religious movement develops excesses and thereby provokes reaction. The outburst of religious experience connected with the Reformation was followed by a period of sad decline which took various phases in different parts of the Reformed Communions. All these aspects had a bearing on the true view of the Person and Work of the Holy Spirit.

In the Lutheran Church the controversy arose known as Synergism which, in its undue emphasis on man's free will and natural powers, tended more and more to set aside the need of Divine grace and the Holy Spirit. The Formula Concordiae endeavoured to bring this controversy to an end by stating in carefully balanced words the true relation of the Holy Spirit to the will of man.

In the Reformed Churches a much more serious trouble arose in connection with what is now known as Arminianism, from Arminius, a Dutch theologian of the latter part of the sixteenth century. Without entering into the controversy in general, involving, as it does, many theological and philosophical problems, it may be said for our present purpose that the whole tendency of Arminianism was to emphasise human effort and will, and to make salvation dependent upon man rather than upon God. It was essentially one with the Semi-Pelagianism of the Mediaeval Church. The Synod of Dort, 1618-19, met to deal with this question, and its Canons emphasised in the strongest possible way the need, working, and power of the Holy Spirit of God. But not even this great and important gathering prevented the growth of Arminian teaching, and in the English Church in particular this view was introduced and fostered under the influence of Archbishop Laud.

Another movement which may be said to have developed out of the Reformation, and yet for which the Reformation cannot be held responsible, was the tendency towards undue and unbalanced enthusiasm and Mysticism. The inevitable rebound from the authority of the Church produced excesses among those who failed to realise the intimate, constant, and necessary connection between Holy Scripture and the Holy Spirit. The result was the adoption of subjective principles, whether intellectual or emotional, which led the holders into unbalanced and dangerous extremes of thought and practice. When extremists taught that ' not the word of Scripture, but the Holy Spirit was to be the principle of the Reformation,' and that ' not only everything ecclesiastical, but also everything civil was to be spiritualised and reorganised,' we can readily see the serious dangers of such a subjective position. These excesses in their turn led to a further trouble, which must now be considered.

Whilst, on the one hand, the spiritually immature went to excesses in emotional life by appealing to the Spirit apart from Scripture ; on the other, those who were impressed by the reality of the Reformation movement, but who nevertheless were untouched spiritually by it, tended more and more towards a rationalism which ignored both the Scripture and the Spirit. Human nature let loose from the cast-iron fetters of the Middle Ages was too much for statesmen and thinkers. To this is due the various schemes of the seventeenth century for governing the fabric of humanity. In the Middle Ages the artificial power of Rome sufficed. Then came the break in the sixteenth century, and in the seventeenth the making of new artificial means to accomplish the same end. The Reformation assertion of individual freedom, of the direct relation of the individual to God, and the impossibility of any Society exercising absolute authority over individual consciences, could not help having its effect, and whether we think of the attempts of the Stuart Monarchy, or of Presbyterian rigidity, or of arbitrary government in France, or of such schemes as are represented by Hobbes, the problem is seen to be acute and pressing. In ordinary affairs these things work out by revolutions and wars, but in the realm of philosophy the matter is different. The result was that a school of philosophy arose, which attempted to construct an elaborate system, just as the Middle Ages had done, only that the latter drew their system from Christianity, while the former made its own. This took different aspects in different countries. In England it expressed itself in Deism, and was marked by all the practical earnestness of the English character. It soon passed over to France, and was seen in Infidelity, with Voltaire, a pupil of Bolingbroke, as its chief exponent. Thence in due course it reached Germany, and became Rationalism proper, marking an endeavour not only to explode but also to explain away Christianity. In all this Rationalism we see the inevitable tendency to ignore and even to oppose any appeal to Scripture and any submission to the Holy Spirit. Rationalism becomes either scholastic or naturalistic, and in Butler's great work we see the intellectual power which met the new philosophy, and at the same time the manifest limitations of the author's position, when judged in the light of the full Christianity of the New Testament. In the early part of the seventeenth century the general tendency of the Church was in the direction of a Christian scholasticism which, however valuable intellectually, was far removed from the full, strong personal Christian experience which gained the victory at the Reformation.

It must not be thought, however, that all the influences were in the wrong direction, for Puritanism in England during the time of the Commonwealth did not a little to call attention to the New Testament doctrine of Grace. But, here again, we are met with the fact of reaction, for this force passed away and gave place to the Restoration period, with ecclesiasticism in the Church of England and subjectivity in Quakerism.[1]   The English Church Restoration was essentially Arminian, in spite of the doctrines of the Articles, while the Quakers in their rebound from Ecclesiasticism tended to set aside the authority of Holy Scripture in their emphasis on the Holy Spirit as the ' Inner Light ' of the soul.   Two men, however, dealt with the subject of the Holy Spirit at this time, Thomas Goodwin and John Owen.   The former is said to

' mark an epoch in the progress of the comprehension of the relation of the Holy Spirit to the Christian life.   On its own peculiar theme, it is without a peer in Christian literature.' [2]

A larger and far better-known work is that of John Owen, which even yet has not been superseded.   In these works the authors set themselves to develop Reformation principles in relation to the Holy Spirit and Christian life, and it is impossible to exaggerate the value of the work rendered to theology and Christianity by the great writers of the Puritan period.[3]   But their efforts to stem the tide were unavailing, and the outcome of Anglican ecclesiasticism and Quaker subjectivity was spiritually dangerous, and had much to do with that blight which fell upon English Christianity in the later part of the seventeenth century and the early part of the eighteenth century.

But God does not leave Himself long without a witness, and both in Germany and in England movements of Revival took place.   In Germany the Pietist movement connected with Spener did much to reassert the true position concerning the Holy Spirit; [4] while still more important was the Methodist and Evangelical Revival in Great Britain and America under Wesley and Whitefield, then Romaine and Newton, and later on, Jonathan Edwards and others.   To Wesley in particular is due the insistence on what is generally called ' the witness of the Spirit,' the testimony borne by the Spirit to the heart of the believer, that he is ' accepted in the Beloved,' and a child of God.

---

[1] See Hodgkin, ' George Fox,' *The Trial of our Faith*, p. 239.

[2] Denio, *The Supreme Leader*, p. 95.

[3] Smeaton, *The Doctrine of the Holy Spirit*, pp. 326-330 ;   Denio, *op. cit.* ch. vi.

[4] Smeaton, *op. cit.* p. 333.

While the doctrine had not been overlooked before, it was certainly due to Wesley that it came to be regarded as one of the marks of the children of God. The effect of this Revival was seen almost everywhere, and the missionary expansion in England and America, which characterised the early years of the nineteenth century, was undoubtedly the result of this insistence upon the Holy Spirit in relation to the Gospel of Christ.

CHAPTER 15

THE NINETEENTH CENTURY

ONCE again the tide of spiritual life and power ebbed, and the Revival of the eighteenth century was succeeded by a period of spiritual dryness. Evangelicalism became largely spent in England; Germany, mainly untouched by Revival, continued in its Rationalism; and in America there was a decided reaction from the theology of Jonathan Edwards. All this movement, or lack of movement, naturally affected the relation of the Church to the Holy Spirit.

Then came a movement in Germany, represented by Schleiermacher. In opposition to the prevalent Rationalism, he rendered great service by emphasising the reality of personal religion as consisting of Feeling.

' Schleiermacher was as nearly original as a man can well be, yet his originality consisted rather in a novel combination of elements previously existing than in any great new discovery of his own. We can find in Spinoza, in Kant, in Novalis, in Zinzendorf, the separate threads which he wove together into his parti-coloured theology.' [1]

But, unfortunately, with this came the denial of the objective realities of the Incarnation, the Cross, and Pentecost. His doctrine of the Trinity is Sabellian; the Persons in the Godhead are only modes of manifestation. With regard to the Holy Spirit, He is not a Person distinct from the Son and from the Father, and His work

---

[1] Strong, ' The Theology of Schleiermacher,' *Miscellanies*, Vol. II. p. 13.

is defined as ' the collective Spirit of the new corporate life that was initiated by Christ.'

' The Holy Spirit is the union of the divine being with human nature in the form of the collective spirit which animates the collective life of believers.' [1]

It is therefore true to say that

' Schleiermacher knows nothing of a living Christ, nor of a living Holy Spirit ; he knows nothing of a continuous personal working of the exalted Redeemer, and nothing of a continuous personal working of the Holy Spirit, taking of the things of Christ and showing them to us.' [2]

The explanation of this is, of course, the fact that the subjective experience needs an objective reality for its basis.

' Unless the feeling of dependence has a proper object, it may be very irreligious. The heart needs a guide ; we must not apotheosize it, but must put it under rational control ; otherwise we may become a prey to most ignoble impulses. Schleiermacher's religion is not really Christianity, for it recognises no objective norm or revelation. It is a purely subjective phenomenon, a purely natural product.' [3]

While, therefore, it is possible and right to be profoundly thankful to Schleiermacher for his work and influence against the Rationalism of his day, a work which has affected German theology to the present time, yet from the standpoint of full Christianity in relation to the Deity of Christ and the Holy Spirit he is greatly wanting.

' In most respects he is a poor guide to follow. Charles Hodge has well said that Schleiermacher is like a ladder in a pit—a good thing for those who wish to get out, but a bad thing for those who wish to get in.' [4]

It may be convenient here to refer to two other names of great importance and prominence in Germany during the past century. The first is that of Hegel, who endeavoured to construe Christianity in the terms of pure thought and abstract philosophy. But beyond the mention of his

---

[1] Quoted, Paterson, *The Rule of Faith*, p. 356, note 4.

[2] Strong, *op. cit.* pp. 37, 38.

[3] Strong, *op. cit.* p. 17.

[4] Strong, *op. cit.* p. 56. For the most recent discussion of Schleiermacher, see W. B. Selbie's *Schleiermacher : A Critical and Historical Study*.

name as one who has widely and profoundly influenced all philosophical thought since his time, it is unnecessary to refer to his attempts to state Christian doctrine. As it has been rightly said, everything appears to be as Christian as before, and yet we cannot help feeling that nothing distinctively Christian is left.

' When once the Gospel has been severed from a historic person, and identified with a complex of metaphysical ideas, what it ought to be called is scarcely worth discussion ; that it is no longer Christianity is clear.' [1]

The other name of immense importance is that of Ritschl, whose position has been aptly summarised as ' theology without metaphysics.' His dominant thought was the Kingdom of God, and through this all the blessings of Christianity are mediated to the individual.[2] It is particularly interesting to notice how this view of the Kingdom has been seized by the Anglo-Catholic school in support of their theory of the Church, but in reality Ritschl's conception of the Kingdom is something far different from the sacerdotal idea of the Church as the mediator of blessing. Ritschl's avoidance of everything purely ontological necessarily affects his doctrine of the Trinity, and with it his view of the Holy Spirit. As to this, the following words seem to be true :

' In a doctrine of the Spirit the Ritschlian theology conspicuously fails. But the Evangelical theology unambiguously affirms His Personality, work, and abiding presence and power in the heart of the believer.' [3]

While, therefore, we may gladly accept the view that Ritschl has done much to emphasise some of the practical spiritual results of Christianity, yet his position must be regarded as ' deficient as a transcript of full Christian Faith.' [4]

' It is not easy to name any specifically Ritschlian doctrine of capital importance which has not in some former situation sought to establish itself in theology in a slightly different form, and which

---

[1] Mackintosh, *The Person of Jesus Christ*, p. 259.

[2] Paterson, *The Rule of Faith*, p. 380.

[3] Orr, *The Ritschlian Theology*, p. 269.

[4] Mackintosh, *op. cit.* p. 380.

did not evoke misgiving or solemn protest as impairing the efficacy or diminishing the security of the Christian salvation.' [1]

In England three movements call for attention in connection with this subject. The first of these is Tractarianism, which owed its initial impulse to a protest against ' Liberalism ' in Christianity and politics, and sought protection in the authority and continuity of the Christian Church as expressed and proved by Apostolic Succession. But its emphasis on this position tended, as sacerdotalism invariably does, to ignore the definite presence and spiritual power of the Holy Spirit. Whether we consider its Roman Catholic aspect, as represented by Newman and his fellow-converts, or its Anglican counterpart, as represented by Pusey and others, it is marked by a decided absence of reference to the New Testament conceptions of the Holy Spirit in the individual and the community.

The next movement was Irvingism. This, which sprang from Edward Irving in Scotland and extended to England, created a great stir by its claim to Divine revelations through the Holy Spirit. It developed into a curious blend of what may be called Montanism in relation to the Holy Spirit, and Ecclesiasticism in worship and ministry. But its eclecticism partook too largely of divergent and contradictory elements to permit of its becoming a permanent power.

The third, Plymouth Brethrenism, to use the best-known designation, represented a movement to unite all real Christians in view of divided Christendom in an endeavour to ' keep the unity of the Spirit.' At the outset the Coming of the Lord as the present hope of the Church and the presence of the Holy Ghost as the principle of the unity of God's people were greatly insisted on. The Church as a whole owes much to the testimony of the Brethren on the importance of the Word of God, the judicial standing of the believer in Christ by the Spirit, and the Coming of Christ as the blessed hope of the Church. But, like many other movements, it developed extremes of teaching and discipline, and its undue and unbalanced individualism, with its fissiparous tendency has led to

---

[1] Paterson, *op. cit.* p. 384.

deplorable severances and their consequent weaknesses.
But in so far as the Brethren emphasised the Holy Spirit's
presence in the Church as characteristic of this dispensation,
their witness to primitive truth was as welcome as it was
necessary, and one of their number has rightly said that
' their appreciation of the Holy Spirit's presence, power, and
guidance is the grand and distinctive character of their
theology.'

A period of nearly fifty years, from 1856 to the end of
the century, was marked by three special features, more
particularly in England and America.[1] At first there was
a period of Revival. Evangelistic movements in America,
Ireland, and England created a great impression in 1859
and the following years, with the result that renewed
emphasis was placed on the presence and work of the Holy
Spirit in the hearts and lives of God's people. Then followed Holiness movements, of which the most important
subsequently found its centre at Keswick, wherein the
need and power of the Holy Spirit through faith was
brought into special prominence. Later on the mission
work of D. L. Moody contributed not a little to the insistence on the work of the Spirit of God.

Side by side with these movements came a remarkable
development in the work of Foreign Missions, and both in
America and in England world-wide evangelisation may
be said to have sprung largely from these Revival movements, which led the Church to realise as scarcely ever
before its duty to preach the Gospel to every creature.

The issue of works on the Holy Spirit also characterised
these fifty years in a very remarkable way. From the issue
of Arthur's *Tongue of Fire*, with its powerful appeal to
the Christian, book after book was issued calling attention
to some aspect of the Holy Spirit's presence and work. A
well-known writer, Dr. H. C. Trumbull, has raised the
question whether all this attention given directly to the
Holy Spirit is pure spiritual gain in view of the fact that
the Holy Spirit never glorifies Himself, but Jesus Christ,
and that emphasis on His work tends to a forgetfulness of

---

[1] Erdman, *Princeton Biblical and Theological Studies*, ' Modern
Spiritual Movements,' p. 357.

the supreme place and power of our Lord and Saviour. There is, of course, a decided danger of undue perspective, but as a rule it cannot be said that this has been the practical result of these works, since for the most part there has been an earnest and successful endeavour to keep close to Holy Scripture, and to honour the Son of God in stating the Scriptural view of the Spirit of God.

Reviewing the ferment of thought of the last century, it may perhaps be said that on the whole the emphasis on the Holy Spirit represents clear progress and a decided return towards the full New Testament revelation. It is true that Pneumatology has not received anything like the attention paid during the century to Christology, and it is the opinion of some that, in view of modern researches into the domain of psychology, the time has not yet come for a thorough reasoned statement of the doctrine of the Holy Spirit. This may be so, but it is perhaps equally true that a proper discussion of the doctrine of the Holy Spirit demands something infinitely more and greater than a knowledge of psychology, or even of the ' abysmal deeps ' of personality. It will only be when a real, personal, and corporate experience of the Holy Spirit once again possesses the Christian community that we shall be able to have a thoroughly modern and yet ancient view of the Person and Work of the Blessed Spirit. Philosophy, as represented by Pragmatism and by the names of Eucken and Bergson, seems to be tending more and more towards the reassertion of spiritual realities over everything materialistic, and we may well believe and devoutly hope that through this insistence on the spiritual, God will raise up champions who will declare to all the world the essential, vital, and distinctive truth of the Holy Spirit in the Christian Church.

CHAPTER 16

REVIEW OF THE HISTORY

THE first thing we notice as we look back over the centuries from New Testament times is that there have been two main epochs in the history. The first extended from the Sub-Apostolic age to the Reformation, and was concerned with the Personality and Deity of the Holy Spirit and His relation to the Father and the Son. Almost everything that occupied the attention of the Church during these centuries was connected with the Person of the Spirit. The second took rise at the Reformation, and may be said to reach to the present day. This has been concerned almost wholly with the Work of the Spirit, and no one can doubt the epoch-making character of the Reformation, since its religious attitude revolutionised all that had been held and practised in regard to the relations of the individual and the Church to the Holy Spirit.

' For its development, a division-line is provided simply and solely by the Reformation, and this merely because at that time only was attention intensely directed to the right mode of the application of salvation. Thus were the problems of the specially saving operation of the Holy Spirit, of the manner of His working in the congregation of believers cast into the foreground, and the theological treatment of this doctrine made of ever-increasing importance to the Church of Christ.' [1]

The next thing to be observed in a review of the history is that during the centuries there seem to have been five special dangers besetting the doctrine of the Holy Spirit.

[1] Nösgen, *Geschichte von der Lehre vom heiligen Geiste.* Quoted by B. B. Warfield, Introduction to Kuyper's *The Work of the Holy Spirit*, p. xxxiii, note.

1. *Intellectualism.* This was the weakness of Greek theology in the early ages, and has been the danger of Rationalism ever since, the tendency to sublimate the work of the Holy Spirit into an illuminated mind and a clear perception of the truth.

' Truth or truths about the spiritual life, if they stand alone, are intellectualist, however impressive, or, to use a word fitter in some ways, they are aesthetic, however penetrating. They may produce the certainty of knowledge but not of salvation.' [1]

The Holy Spirit is indeed the ' Spirit of truth,' but truth is at once intellectual and moral.

' Full recognition of the service rendered to religious thought by the Greek genius and by the intellect which the Greek Christian Fathers brought to bear upon Christian problems leaves unaffected the elementary and indisputable historic fact that it was through the Church of the West, and finally through the great Roman Church wherein for centuries the religious life of the West was concentrated, the broad highway of Christendom's future lay.' [2]

2. *Pelagianism.* Under this general title may be combined the various Movements from early days which have tended to ignore and often to set aside the need of Divine grace. Whether we think of Pelagianism proper, or the Semi-Pelagianism of the Middle Ages and of Rome, or the Synergism of the Lutheran Church, or the Arminianism of the Reformed Churches, the essential feature is much the same in its tendency to forget the presence of Him Who is ' the Spirit of Grace.'

3. *Ecclesiasticism* in various forms throughout the ages from the second century onwards. This has been a pressing danger. It is impossible to avoid noticing the various ' heresies' which have sprung up in reference to the relation between the Holy Spirit and the Church. When we mention Montanism, Puritanism, Pietism, Quakerism, Moravianism, Methodism, Irvingism, Brethrenism, and, more recently, Stundism, we observe that all these tendencies have asserted themselves in opposition to what may be generally called Ecclesiasticism. The danger

[1] Forsyth, ' Intellectualism and Faith' *The Hibbert Journal*, January, 1913, p. 322.

[2] H. W. Clark, ' Religious History and the Idea of " Immanence," ' *The Review and Expositor*, January, 1913, p. 9.

of the latter and the significance of each of the former movements, with the particular measure of truth and falsehood in each, constitute one of the most fascinating, important, and also perplexing studies.

' It were well for us to give more heed to the voice of Christian history as related to such questions as these. The rise of " sporadic sects " like the " Quietists," the " Mystics," the " Friends," and the " Brethren," with their emphasis on " the still voice " and " the inward leading," is very suggestive. If we may not go so far as some of these go in the insistence on speaking only as sensibly moved by the Spirit we may be admonished of the hard, artificial, man-made worship which made their protest necessary.' [1]

The tendency of the Church, especially in the West, towards an organisation, and a sacerdotal ministry and rigidity, have tended to rob the individual and the community of that free, direct approach to, and appropriation of the Holy Spirit which are so marked in the New Testament.

4. *Individualism.* Under this term it is intended to include all those Movements which represent pure unbalanced subjectivity, whether of Montanism in the Early Church, or of Mysticism in the Middle Ages, or of Quakerism in later days. The severance of the Holy Spirit from Holy Scripture, and the emphasis on the former to the forgetfulness and exclusion of the latter has often proved disastrous ; sometimes to ethics, and sometimes to truth and devotion.

5. *Idealism.* By this is to be understood that emphasis on philosophical ideals which has tended to sever the soul from dependence on and connection with the Historic Christ. Whatever form this takes, its inevitable result is the denial of distinctive Christianity.

Another feature that stands out from a study of the Christian centuries is the sad but patent fact that the work of the Spirit has been signalised by advancing and receding tides.[2] The question has rightly been asked, how it is that the work of the Spirit ' is marked by so many fluctuations, such apparent irregularity and intermittency in its energies and effects.' It is, of course, possible that ' if our knowledge of all the causes and conditions were

---

[1] A. J. Gordon, *The Ministry of the Spirit*, p. 157, note.
[2] Davison, *The Indwelling Spirit*, ch. ix.

adequate, we could discern a law of periodicity.' But if we may judge from the teaching of our Lord and His Apostles, these ebbs and flows of religious life are not necessary, and are to be deplored in the best interests of the Gospel in the world.

' The restriction does not lie in the Divine power or grace, but in the human capacity, a lack either of power or will on the part of the Church to receive and use the resources ready to her hand. The deficiency may sometimes be the result of ignorance, or it may imply real inability ; but too frequently it springs from carelessness, neglect, unfaithfulness, or actual sin.' [1]

One thing is certain, that the spiritual power of the Church has always been closely associated with the prominence given to the Person and work of the Holy Spirit, and whenever this has been absent, loss has inevitably followed. Purely abstract ideas never existed long, and never exercised great influence. The secret of spiritual blessing has been found in the constant emphasis on the redemptive aspects of the work of the Holy Spirit in relation to Christ, the Saviour of the world.

' All this is countersigned by Christian experience—and that, too, on the highest and widest scale—the experience of all the Christian Church. In all branches of it, the Head has vindicated the honour due to His Holy Spirit—" I believe in the Holy Ghost " has been inscribed on the Creeds of Christendom. Yet the Eastern Church, more than eleven centuries ago, committed herself to the denial of His connection with the Son—a small point, a theological nicety, some would say—but look at the result. In all these centuries that Church has remained an " orthodox fossil," unvisited and unblessed by the Revivals and Reformations of the Spirit. The Romish Church has *filioque* in her Creed, it is true, but in doctrine and practice alike has painfully denied the Spirit, and the result is declension and corruption. Even the Churches of the Reformation have not been all equally faithful. Some of them through their unfortunate Sacramentarianism and Churchliness, leave little room in their teaching for the grace of the Spirit. It is in the Reformed Churches, and especially in those of the Puritan type, that the doctrine of the Spirit has been cherished and most fully illustrated in literature. Does anyone need to be reminded of the practical result, that these Churches have been mainly honoured to extend the Gospel throughout the world, and to manifest the experimental fruits of Christian life and work ? ' [2]

---

[1] Davison, ' The Person and Work of the Holy Spirit,' *London Quarterly Review*, April, 1905, p. 220.

[2] Laidlaw, *Questions of Faith*, pp. 124, 125.

PART III

THE THEOLOGICAL FORMULATION

CHAPTER 17

THE IDEA OF THEOLOGY

THE term ' Theology ' is used for the scientific expression of the truths of Divine revelation. As nature has to be distinguished from science, so has revelation from theology. Science is the technical expression of the laws of nature ; theology is the technical expression of the revelation of God. It is the province of theology to examine all the spiritual facts of revelation, to estimate their value, and to arrange them into a body of teaching. Doctrine thus corresponds with the generalisations of science, and theology, as the science of religion, is concerned with the phenomena of revelation recorded in Holy Scripture.

Special attention has been given of recent years to what is known as Biblical theology, which means theology drawn direct from the Bible and formulated along the lines in which it is there presented. Its value lies in the fact that it stands midway between exegesis and dogmatics. It affords a historical interpretation, and it recognises the progressiveness of revelation. It thus possesses at once variety and unity : variety, because it was not given all at once, but at stages ; unity, because the Bible is held to provide a complete view of theological thought. It is the work of Biblical theology to set forth this variety and unity of truth. The doctrine has to be considered at each stage, the separate facts must be noted, and then the material must be studied as a whole, observing its substantial unity.

From Biblical theology we pass to Dogmatic theology, which may be defined as the systematised statement of truth deduced from the Bible and interpreted by the Christian consciousness through the centuries. It is the intellectual expression in technical language of what is contained in the Word of God, the articulated statement of the Biblical revelation, and the explicit statement of what is implicit in experience. Martensen defines dogmatics as ' the science which presents and proves the Christian doctrines regarded as forming a connected system.' A theological statement of what the Church believes on such a subject as the Holy Spirit is necessary and inevitable.

The source and authority of Dogmatic theology are found in the Biblical revelation, and no theology is to be considered as true which is not derivable from the Biblical data. Then the witness to and confirmation of Dogmatic theology is found in the Christian consciousness of the whole Church. Although a contrast is sometimes made between Biblical theology and Dogmatic theology, Dogmatic theology is not necessarily non-Biblical, and indeed, Biblical theology itself will depend on the standpoint of the writer.

' Now and then we find a man who still gives vent to his dislike of Dogmatic Theology by professing great devotion to Biblical Theology, as though the latter were a protest against the former, and were a little more loyal to the authority of the Bible. It is true that Biblical Theology takes little or no account of ecclesiastical controversies and is silent about the decisions of Councils. Still it must be remembered that Biblical Theology does not consist in grouping the teaching of the Scriptures under certain *loci communes*, such as sin and redemption. That would be a Biblical Dogmatic. The Biblical Theologian seeks to trace the development of doctrine as revealed truth. His subject is the crowning Discipline of Exegesis, but it is an historical Discipline too. It is the task of the Dogmatic Theologian to exhibit the logical unfolding of the Covenant of Grace, but it is the task of the Biblical Theologian to exhibit its chronological unfolding.' [1]

The character and limitations of Dogmatic theology are patent to all. There is, of course, an obvious danger in the attempt at systematising Christian truth, for the human mind seems unable to find a place for every single

[1] Patton, ' Theological Encyclopaedia,' *Princeton Biblical and Theological Studies*, pp. 12, 13.

doctrine, and it is probably wiser to be content with separate though connected truths, or 'articles' with gaps unfilled, than to attempt to include everything within the limits of a system. General lines of Christian truth are safer, and also truer to the growth of thought and experience through the ages. No theological statement which tends to harden teaching into a rigid system of doctrine can ever be true to the genius of New Testament Christianity. But if our statements of theology are regarded as landmarks rather than goals, there will be ample opportunity of growth and development, and as the mind of man will always make the attempt to systematise truth, dogmatic or systematic theology is inevitable.

'The legitimacy of the Systematic Theologian's undertaking cannot be called in question. Even when men have given form to systems foreign to our mode of thought and far away from what we believe to be true it is impossible not to admire and to wonder at the vast constructive power their systems manifest. The first question is, of course, whether or no God has spoken. For if He has spoken, it is certain that He has not said one thing or two. He has said a great many things. And these parts of the Divine message sustain relations to one another. What are these relations ? It is said that God has not given us a Systematic Theology in the Bible. Neither has He given us a ready-made Astronomy nor a ready-made Biology. Linnaeus had to work for his classification. God has not planted nature like a park with studied reference to orders, genera, and species.' [1]

The history of the Christian Church is sufficient justification of the attempt to correlate and combine the truths of the Christian religion into a theological system. The Creeds and controversies of the early Church, the great treatises of the Schoolmen, the works of the Reformers, and the elaborate systems of post-Reformation theologians are proofs, not merely of the necessity of systematic theology, but also, and chiefly, of the vitality of the Christian truth in occupying the minds of the best thinkers in the Christian Church. It means that theology is a reality, possessing a substance and worthy of thorough attention.

'I know that Systematic Theology is discredited in some quarters ; some seem to think that it stands as a barrier to religious

---

[1] Patton, *op. cit.* p. 24.

fervour and practical piety; some tell us that we must get ready for a theological reconstruction and that the time for that reconstruction is at hand. But the only consistent despisers of Systematic Theology are those who in their hearts believe, however slow they may be to confess it, that in the light of history as it is now read, and of philosophy as it is now studied, and of science as it is now proclaimed, there is little or no rational content for Systematic Theology.'[1]

Dogmatic theology is therefore essential and inevitable.

' Theology must be dogmatic, and it is only a choice of the right and wholesome kind of dogmatism. . . . By its nature it is dogmatic, as conscience is, as science is about nature's uniformity, or as society is about marriage. It is not the deduction of a system from an innate principle which Christ brought to the surface, nor is it the analysis of the Christian consciousness, but it is the exposition of what the living conscience of the Church finds in the fact and act of Christ, creative and historic. It is not progressive argument so much as enlarged statement, not the movement of a dialectic but the exposition of a corporate experience. Everything turns on what the soul does, or does not, find in the objective fact of Christ as the self-donation of God to our case. Not otherwise do poetry or science deal with the gift in nature. We are always more sure of the reality than satisfied with the rationality of the matter. Living faith is always more of a moral miracle than a mental sanity. It is a will's mysterious choice and not a mind's lucid flame.'[2]

Dogmatic theology, as expressed in the Christian Creed, is represented chiefly in the threefold form of the Apostles', the Nicene, and the Athanasian. These documents gather out from Scripture, and illustrate by the experience and usage of the early centuries what is germane to the subject, and then present it as an organised whole. The documents of the sixteenth century deliberately express their adherence to these earlier statements, and on the particular subject of the Holy Spirit they only seek to elaborate and apply what is found therein. For the theology of the Holy Spirit we therefore turn naturally to the three Creeds. The Apostles' Creed is a mere statement of belief; the Athanasian Creed is an elaborated form of what is to be understood by the Nicene Creed. It will therefore suffice for our present purpose if we look at the subject primarily

[1] Patton, *op. cit.* p. 30.

[2] Forsyth, ' Intellectualism and Faith,' *The Hibbert Journal,* January, 1913, p. 328.

as it is stated in the last-named document. Combining the formulas of Nicaea and Constantinople, we have the following:

> ' I believe in the Holy Ghost, the Lord and Life-Giver, Who proceedeth from the Father and the Son, Who with the Father and the Son together is worshipped and glorified, Who spake by the prophets.'

This statement will suffice as a starting-point for the consideration of the doctrine of the Holy Spirit under several aspects.

CHAPTER 18

THE SPIRIT OF GOD

THE teaching of the Nicene Creed concerning the relation of the Holy Spirit to the Godhead is found in the words :

'I believe in the Holy Ghost, the Lord and Life-Giver, Who proceedeth from the Father and the Son, Who with the Father and the Son together is worshipped and glorified.'

It is believed that this statement is the explicit expression of what is found implicitly in Scripture. Two questions arise : the Personality and the Deity of the Holy Spirit.

The use of the term ' Person ' in relation to the Godhead calls for special attention. Its theological history is somewhat involved, but on the whole it has been helpfully summarised by various writers.

'The word *persona*, of which Person is the translation, properly signifies a dramatic part, or character ; and was adopted, as Augustine tells us, by the Latins on account of the poverty of their language, which has no word exactly corresponding to the ὑπόστασις of the Greeks, the term employed by the latter to denote each of the three Subjects of the Holy Trinity. The meaning of *persona*, then, must be determined by that of hypostasis. Now this term, as distinguished from essence ʾ(οὐσία), signifies the Divine

---

LITERATURE.—Swete, *The Holy Spirit in the New Testament,* p. 283 ; Smeaton, *The Doctrine of the Holy Spirit,* p. 95 ; Moberly, *Atonement and Personality,* chs. viii., ix. ; Denio, *The Supreme Leader,* p. 196 ; Walker, *The Holy Spirit,* ch. iii. ; Garvie, *The Christian Certainty Amid the Modern Perplexity,* ch. x. ; Martensen, *Christian Dogmatics,* Sections 52-58, 181-184 ; Parker, *The Paraclete,* ch. i. ; Moule, *Veni Creator,* p. 5 ; Downer, *The Mission and Ministration of the Holy Spirit,* ch. i. ; Masterman, ' *I believe in the Holy Ghost,*' ch. vi. ; Elder Cumming, *After the Spirit,* ch. i. ; Bushnell, *The Vicarious Sacrifice,* p. 38 ; J. M. Campbell, *After Pentecost, What ?* ch. iii.

Being when viewed in connection with a particular " Personal property " (Proprietas personalis), that is, the property which compels us to make a distinction between the Persons ; which in the First Person is paternity, in the Second filiation, and in the Third procession ; so that the Father means God considered as begetting, the Son, God considered as begotten, and the Holy Ghost, God considered as proceeding (*essentia divina cum proprietatibus personalibus*).' [1]

Personality with us to-day expresses the fact of a separate individual human being who is rationally self-conscious and distinct from all others. But Personality in God is intended to convey the idea of an inner distinction which exists within the unity of the Divine nature.

' Our popular modern notion of " person "—as signifying a separate individual (human) being—is totally different from what " person " meant or really means when applied theologically to distinctions within the Divine Being.' [2]

' The personal distinction in Godhead is a distinction within, and of, unity : not a distinction which qualifies unity, or usurps the place of it, or destroys it.' [3]

' It is only an extension of principles already implicit in our social existence as human beings when we speak of a true solidarity of life, a spiritual coalescence, between Christ and His people. And if, as Lotze has argued so impressively, personality in us is incomplete, and exists perfectly in God only, we may well conclude that this self-communicating power which we possess only in part will have its perfection and fulness in Him, and therefore also in Christ, Who is God apprehensible by us.' [4]

The facts of Scripture demand from us the acknowledgment of the unity of the Godhead, and also of those interior distinctions between Father, Son, and Spirit which we can only express by our word ' Person.'

' We use the word " Person " from simple poverty of language : to indicate our belief, that is, in the reality of Divine distinctions, not to affirm separate conscious beings, possessed of separate " essences." If it be said that this description of such interior distinctions is negative merely, the comment, however just, is by no means fatal to its validity. Most Christian thinkers are agreed that God is *causa sui*, and that He is omnipresent ; yet when we

---

[1] Litton, *Introduction to Dogmatic Theology*, p. 125. See also Bethune-Baker, *An Introduction to the Early History of Christian Doctrine*, p. 233.

[2] Winstanley, *Spirit in the New Testament*, p. 160.

[3] Moberly, *Atonement and Personality*, p. 155.

[4] Mackintosh, *The Person of Jesus Christ*, p. 339.

look into our own minds, are not these phrases, however necessary, laden with a sense predominantly negative ? When we use them, we are affirming that God owes reality to Himself alone, and that He is nowise limited by space. The conceptions, in other words, can never be positively defined, yet we are obliged to grant their truth.' [1]

Beyschlag is of opinion that the idea of the Holy Spirit as a third Divine Person is ' one of the most disastrous importations into Holy Scripture.' [2] And the Dean of St. Paul's, Dr. Inge, in a sermon preached at St. Paul's Cathedral, on Whitsunday, June 4, 1911, said that

' The Holy Spirit in the Bible was not a " person " in the modern sense ; the Greek language had no word for " person " or " personality." ' [3]

It is, of course, perfectly true that the term ' person ' is used to-day in connection with human life in a way that is quite different from its use in connection with the Godhead. But it is also true that no other term has yet been found adequate to express the essential distinctions in the Godhead.

' The word " Person " has a fulness and totality of meaning of its own, and certainly nothing short of the inclusive completeness of personal being can be predicated, at any moment, of God— whether Father, Son, or Holy Ghost.' [4]

The Holy Spirit is a Person, because He works by personal activities on persons, and with proper safeguards the use of the term is abundantly warranted as that which alone expresses the idea required. This justification is twofold. The facts of Scripture demand it, for, while it is true that many passages suggest the impersonality of the Spirit,[5] there are others that cannot possibly be interpreted in this way. The teaching of Christ about the Paraclete, and the personal references to the Holy Spirit in the Acts and the Epistles necessitate the predication of Personality.

---

[1] Mackintosh, *op. cit.* p. 524.

[2] *New Testament Theology*, Eng. Trans., ii. p. 279.

[3] *The Times*, June 5, 1911. So to the same effect, Garvie, *Expositor*, VIII. 5, p. 46 (January, 1913).

[4] Moberly, *op. cit.* p. 160.

[5] Moberly, *op. cit.* p. 180.

' Spirit means life and power, the saving energy of God within human life ; and it is the uniform teaching of the New Testament that Christ, Who possessed this Spirit in its fulness, has mediated it to all believers. Hence to call the Spirit impersonal must ultimately be meaningless for a religion to which the gracious power of God can never be a mere " thing." Could the love of God be shed abroad in our hearts by the non-personal ? Could a natural force enable men to confess Jesus as Lord ? True, a monotheistic New Testament has nowhere described the Spirit as a " separate personality " ; it is indeed more than questionable whether such a general abstract idea as " personality " had then attained general currency. Yet in the last resort the Spirit of God must be as personal as God Himself. So true is this, that it is only by interior union with the personal Spirit that our proper personality is consummated. To have within us, as the soul's life, the very Spirit that made the inmost being of Jesus, is bestowed by Jesus, and commends Jesus to the heart—this is to be perfected in personal being. By unity with such Spirit man first is fully man.' [1]

The consciousness of the Church bears witness in the same direction. Sabellianism both ancient and modern has always proved impossible in the long run. Modalism even without Successionalism is wholly inadequate to the Scripture testimony.[2] There is scarcely anything more significant in the history of the Church than the recurrence and also the rejection of Sabellianism, for it is at once apparently easy, and soon seen to be utterly impossible to consider the Father, the Son, and the Holy Spirit as mere aspects or manifestations of one God.

' There is one crucial defect about it, a defect which, for us, condemns the language as impossible. For it degrades the Persons of Deity into aspects. Now there can be no mutual relation between aspects. The heat and the light of flame cannot severally contemplate, and be in love with, one another. Whereas real mutuality, —mutuality which involves *on both sides* personal capacities,—is the one thing which we most unflinchingly assert.' [3]

Personal working needs continuity of action, and it has been the experience of the individual Christian and of the Church in all ages that the spiritual renewal needed by the believer and the community requires constant and continuous action, and not a permanent endowment. And so we hold that

[1] Mackintosh, *op. cit.* p. 510.

[2] E. H. Johnson, *The Holy Spirit*, p. 86 ff, criticising W. L. Walker.

[3] Moberly, *op. cit.* p. 165.

' a clear conception of the *personality* of the Holy Spirit is necessary if His living relation to the individual human spirit and to the Spirit-bearing community is to be adequately realised.' [1]

The Deity of the Spirit is a necessary consequence of His Personality, for that which is attributed to His Personality involves His Deity. This belief is based on the facts of Scripture, especially on the revelation of Christ. The allusions to the Holy Spirit are such as cannot possibly be predicated of anyone else than God Himself.

' No one now denies the Divinity of the Holy Spirit. It could be only a freak to interpret the Bible as meaning that the Spirit of God is a creature. And the offices which the Spirit has to fulfil are so clearly personal that His Personality always presses itself into the Christian's conception. There is one God, and yet Father, Son, and Spirit are alike Divine and personal.' [2]

Yet this view is always found in close connection with the unity of the Godhead, and is never associated in the slightest degree with anything polytheistic. None can question the fact that New Testament Theism is inextricably bound up with the Old Testament doctrine of the unity of God. This is fundamental throughout.[3]

The bearing of this on the doctrine of the Holy Trinity is clear and important. It is impossible to question the fact that the New Testament affords clear proofs of distinctions within the Unity.

' The New Testament hardly invites to any discussion of the metaphysics of the Spirit. Of course, it is the Spirit of God, and Divine. It is part of the one Divine causality which—as Father, Son, and Spirit—confronts the sinful world, and works in unison for its redemption. It belongs unmistakably to the sphere of the Divine, not of the human. . . . The New Testament and Christian experience are at one in teaching that the Christian conception of God includes all that is meant by Father, Son, and Spirit ; and as the omission of what is meant by any of these terms leaves the Christian conception unsatisfied, it may fairly be said that the doctrine of the Trinity is the fundamental doctrine of our faith. The Father, the Son, and the Spirit in their unity constitute the God Whom we know as the God of our salvation.' [4]

---

[1] Davison, ' The Person and Work of the Holy Spirit,' *London Quarterly Review*, April, 1905, p. 208.

[2] Johnson, *The Holy Spirit*, p. 43.   [3] Moberly, *op. cit.* p. 154.

[4] Denney, Article, ' Holy Spirit,' *Dictionary of Christ and the Gospels*, p. 744.

' The principle of life and power known as " Holy Spirit " is no one casual factor in perfect religion by the side of others ; it is that to which everything else converges, and apart from which nothing else—not even the revelation of Jesus—could take effect. So the Father disclosed in the Son is imparted in the Spirit. The presence of the Spirit comes but as a higher mode of Christ's transcendent influence, the climax of His work. " Through Him we have access by one Spirit unto the Father " is a great comprehensive Pauline word ; and in such a verse the experience out of which flowed the New Testament faith in a Triune God grows transparent. It is the experience of a differentiated yet single Divine causality in redemption. If then the Spirit belongs to the sphere of the Divine, not of the human even as redeemed, room must be made for it also within the believing thought of God. Its omission leaves that thought incomplete. We speak in the sense of the New Testament, therefore, when we say that " the Father, the Son, and the Spirit in their unity constitute the God Whom we know as the God of our salvation." ' [1]

Yet there is an entire absence of any consciousness of a new revelation, or of any surprise or opposition from the Jews. There is no embarrassment, no difficulty, no hesitation.[2] The New Testament was written by Monotheists who were evidently unconscious of any incongruity or contradiction between their cherished view of the unity of the Godhead and the distinctions which they were teaching and recording. This fact remains one of the most striking problems of New Testament Theism.

The Trinity in the New Testament is primarily revealed in connection with the historic manifestation of Christ.[3] It arises out of the Incarnation : ' if the Incarnation be real the Trinity is true.' Redemption comes from the Father, through the Son, by the Spirit. It is only thus that the facts are explicable. There is no speculation, no argument, only a statement of what is inextricably bound up in Christian experience. Christ is the Divine Saviour, the Spirit is the Spirit of Christ, and so we have a number of passages expressive of the new life of believers (Matt. xxviii. 19 ; Rom. viii. 9-11 ; 1 Cor. ii. 1-5 ; xii. 4-6 ; 2 Cor. xiii. 14 ; Eph. ii. 18). In this association we have the spiritual and experimental foundations of the Trinity.

---

[1] Mackintosh, *op. cit.* pp. 508, 509.

[2] Moberly, *op. cit.* p. 155.

[3] Moberly, *op. cit.* pp. 181-185.

A recent writer has said that ' if Christ did not use the Trinitarian formula, yet the revelation is already present in His teaching.' [1] In support of this, Matthew xi. 25-27 and Luke x. 21, 22 are adduced, which are said to reveal the self-consciousness of Christ, and thus ' demand for its explication the later doctrine.' Further, the ministry of our Lord and the Fourth Gospel are added in support of His doctrine of the Spirit, and in regard to the latter point, the writer remarks : ' I find it impossible to believe that we have here only reflexions of the evangelist, without any basis whatever in his reminiscences of Jesus' teaching.' [2] And thus we come again to the conclusion that ' the doctrine of the Trinity as it is presented in the New Testament is rooted in Christian experience.' [3]

' The whole theological basis of the New Testament is Trinitarian. The following facts appear on almost every page : God is one ; the Father is God, yet distinguishable from the Son and the Spirit ; the Son is God, both in His pre-existent and incarnate states, yet distinguishable from the Father and the Spirit ; the Holy Ghost is God, yet distinguishable from the Father and the Son. Father, Son, and Holy Spirit are all described as personal. We find these facts not only expressed in the direct statements of the sacred writers, but implied in all their teachings, appearing wherever we can perceive the drift and tendency of their theological thought. The redemptive grace of God is ascribed to Father, Son, and Holy Ghost alike. They all appear in the Divine activities by which the work of God's kingdom is carried forward. The Divine attributes are freely attributed to all. In a word, the threefold cord of this great doctrine is everywhere inwoven in the texture of the New Testament.' [4]

This doctrine of a Trinity of manifestation in Christ is necessarily based on the doctrine of a Trinity of essence. It is impossible to account otherwise for the facts of revelation, and equally impossible with these facts to stop short of contemplating the relation of this revelation to the essential nature of God.

' No one to-day will dream of constructing a Trinitarian doctrine *a priori* ; the sufficiency of the syllogism in such a realm has ceased

---

[1] Garvie, *Expositor, ut supra*, p. 37.

[2] Garvie, *Expositor, ut supra*, p. 38.

[3] Garvie, *Expositor, ut supra*, p. 43.

[4] Stearns, *Present Day Theology*, p. 191.

to be obvious : but the clear duty of the Christian thinker—as will be acknowledged once more when the present disparagement of reason has passed by—is to relate Jesus Christ intelligibly to the inmost and eternal life of God. He has no option but to do this ; his instinctive impulse is to do it ; and the impulse is restrained only in obedience to a particular theory of knowledge. Why the effort to translate the initial certitude of faith—which no subsequent speculative procedure can impair—into a luminous conviction of the mind should be flouted as superfluous, or even as an attempt upon the Christian religion, it is not easy to see ; and reason is sure to avenge itself by the gibe that faith, in submission to the unintelligible, is simply indifferent to the truth. There is room in theology for a knowledge that is not so much disinterested as interested purely in its object, and cares enough about God to know Him in His own nature.' [1]

It was impossible to avoid or prevent reflection on the facts of revelation. Theology, as arising out of the facts, was inevitable. The first distinction in the Godhead is that of the Father and of the Son, and implies duality. No one can question the clearness of this in the New Testament. Then comes the more difficult question of the uniqueness and distinctness of the Spirit, which is based on the two grounds of (a) Christ's own testimony to the Spirit ; (b) the works attributed to the Spirit in the New Testament. From the one distinction in the Godhead the mind is naturally led on to the next, because Christ and the Spirit are seen to be parallel manifestations of God and closely related in redemption. And if Christ is *within* the Godhead, it is impossible for the Spirit to be *without*, for this would imply an inferiority of the Spirit which is contradicted by the facts of Scripture and experience.

' With our Lord as a second Person in the Godhead, the theological problem finds no further philosophical difficulty by making the plurality into a trinity. Indeed, for a certain type of speculative mind, the trinity actually helps us to understand the plurality. But the personality of the Holy Spirit is much more than an *easy addition* for the Christian man—it is almost a *necessary addition*.' [2]

It is, of course, true that we have not the same clearness and fulness of revelation in the New Testament in reference to the Deity of the Spirit. It has been suggested that

---

[1] Mackintosh, *op. cit.* p. 522 ; see also p. 513 ; Moberly, *op. cit.* p. 185 ; Denio, *The Supreme Leader*, p. 196.

[2] Curtis, *The Christian Faith*, p. 337.

gradualness was necessary, that, as Christ said, His disciples could not ' carry ' at once everything He had to say. The unity of the Godhead and the Divine redemption naturally came first ; then followed the personal application of redemption and the full revelation to the individual and the community. This would take time, but whether early or late of realisation, it could not be otherwise than a Divine work, so that whatever development we find after New Testament times, is all implicit in the New Testament itself.

' It is not an instance of fundamental addition to the Word of God ; but it is an instance where Christian history and Christian consciousness have rejected certain possible interpretations of biblical data and have resulted in an interpretation which is not satisfactory to any rationalistic scholar. But the rationalistic scholar himself has just as much bias as has the Christian scholar.' [1]

We must assuredly keep the doctrine as close as possible to the facts of religious experience. The Theism of the New Testament is in constant and inevitable connection with the need and provision of redemption. But as reason will continue to play upon experience, we must not be checked by the fear of speculation from attempting to express in thought what is implied in experience.

' We must try to discharge a twofold task, to show how necessary this doctrine is to Christian experience still, and to state the doctrine in such modern categories as will keep it near that experience. Religion cannot rest in pantheism, which removes the distinction between God and man, nor yet in deism, which disturbs the communion of God and man. Religion must have a God both above and near, or in philosophical terms transcendent and immanent. The sense of dependence and submission is as essential as the sense of communion.' [2]

This is the answer to those who decry and denounce all attempts, whether past or present, to express in the best available categories the doctrine of the Trinity.

' In the quiet of the study or the classroom it is easy to speak of banishing metaphysical terms from theology, but in practice it is impossible. To do this would involve not simply the rewriting of our theological systems, but of our hymns, our liturgies, even of the Bible itself. The doctrine of the Trinity in its completeness may be a product of the fourth century, but its beginnings go back

---

[1] Curtis, *op. cit.* p. 339.   [2] Garvie, *Expositor, ut supra,* p. 48.

to the very threshold of Christianity ; and the men who laid its foundations are not Origen and Athanasius, but the Apostle Paul and the fourth evangelist. The Christ of the New Testament is not simply the man of Nazareth, but the pre-incarnate Logos, the Word that lighteth every man that cometh into the world. Either we must be prepared to break with historic Christianity altogether and banish large parts of the New Testament from their place in our public worship, or else we must be able to give some rational account of the presence of the metaphysical element in early Christian theology and of its significance for the present life of the Church.'' [1]

As we have already seen, it is not at all difficult to criticise the use of the word ' person,' but it is exceedingly difficult to suggest any better word. We are compelled to start with the thought of God as personal, for the very idea of human fellowship with God necessitates the conception of personality. When through prayer and trust we meet with God, there is true intercourse and genuine communion, and it is inconceivable that this can come from any but a Personal Being. But the difficulty arising at this point has been well stated.

' If the unity be personal, are the differences within God personal in such sense as the use of the term three persons suggests ? ' [2]

Dr. Garvie admits that he has felt the difficulty so acutely, that until quite recently he preferred to use the terms ' mode ' and ' principle ' instead of ' person,' though he makes the significant admission that in using this language he has always insisted that ' the mode of perfect personality cannot be described as impersonal, but must be conceived as personal.' [3] This is the latest, and in some respects the frankest, admission of the impossibility of finding any better term than ' Person.' The difficulty is, of course, in conceiving of personality as infinite, since our human conception of a person is of someone always finite. But modern thought has been tending more and more towards the view that, while personality is finite in man, this is no necessary proof of finiteness of personality in God. In other words, that personality in the human sense is not the highest of all conceivable realities. Garvie uses the

---

[1] W. Adams Brown, *Christian Theology in Outline*, p. 158.

[2] Garvie, *Expositor, ut supra*, p. 50.

[3] Garvie, *Expositor, ut supra*, p. 51.

illustration of the modern conception of society as organic for the purpose of modifying the conception of personality, and urges us to think of personality ' in the measure of its perfection as transcending individuality in the sense of exclusiveness.' [1] He argues that human personality is only real as it is social, and that the more advanced a society, the more distinct is its corporate consciousness.

' A man is more fully man as he is husband, father, citizen. The intension of personality grows with its extension ; the wider the relations, the fuller the individuality.' [2]

All this tends to show that finiteness is not only not essential to personality, but is rather a limitation or imperfection, since human beings only really become conscious of their own personality through contact with others. Dr. Garvie thereupon draws the obvious conclusion :

' If human persons may transcend their exclusive individuality in such a social unity, real. in, and revealing God as love, may we not conceive God Himself as organic social personality ? May not the one life of the personal God be expressed in the manifold personal life of the Father, Son, and Spirit and the different personal life of Father, or Son, or Spirit be realised in the common life of the personal God ? As individuals in society form an organic unity, so may we conceive Father, Son, and Spirit each as personal, yet one in the personal God.' [3]

To the same effect is the able discussion of the Bishop of Down :

' Personality may be, for human thought, the highest of all categories ; but the existence of certain fundamental antinomies and oppositions, speculative and practical, proves clearly that it is not the ultimate form of being. There is a degree of Reality, a final Unity, higher, more concrete, than Personality. There must be, because a person is, after all, essentially one among many. A person is what he is, not merely because he is inclusive as regards his own experience, but because he is exclusive as regards his neighbours' experience. Personality cannot therefore be a full definition of the Divine nature. God is personal and something more. In His final Unity He is superpersonal, and this superpersonal unity is the ultimate Reality, concrete and universal. Here is exactly the condition demanded by the Christian doctrine of the Trinity. The

[1] Garvie, *Expositor, ut supra*, p. 51.

[2] Garvie, *Expositor, ut supra*, p. 51.

[3] Garvie, *Expositor, ut supra*, pp. 51, 52.

most complete monotheism is compatible with the recognition of a personal multiplicity in the Godhead.' [1]

We return, therefore, to the view that in some way or other we are compelled to contemplate God as a Person, and that in spite of all the difficulties this conception is much nearer the truth than anything else. Such ideas as the love of God, and the Fatherhood of God can only be conceived of in terms of Personality, and we may even go as far as to suggest with Garvie that perhaps this ideal of society as organic, this conception of personality as requiring other personalities for their full revelation and realisation, ' is the earthly shadow of the heavenly substance of the triune God.' [2] It is therefore impossible to avoid coming to the conclusion of a modern theologian, that

' the personality of the Holy Spirit is not a mere question of technical theology, but an article of vital faith for the Christian, and one on which momentous issues depend. The Father is God *over* us, the Son is God *for* us, the Holy Spirit is God *in* us. If He to Whom the administration of redemption is entrusted be not a Person, the very meaning of the phrase is gone. The Unitarian declares that the Trinitarian formula of baptism implies faith in God, a man, and an abstraction. If for the Third Person in the Trinity we substitute, even unconsciously, an abstraction, the living God present in our midst has vanished, we are " orphans " indeed. . . . To ignore the personality of the Holy Spirit is to miss a great theological truth and to fail in apprehending a source of great spiritual power.' [3]

We are thus led still more definitely than ever to the Christian doctrine of the Trinity as that which expresses what God is in Himself quite apart from creation. It means that God is not a solitary individual, abstract and detached from all society. He is rich and full in His nature, manifold in His essential Being, and, as such, the Pattern and Archetype of all society. This is the profound truth that underlies the error of Polytheism, which was the crude and impossible demand of man for society in the

---

[1] D'Arcy, Article ' Trinity,' *Dictionary of Christ and the Gospels*, p. 766.

[2] Garvie, *Expositor, ut supra*, p. 52. See also Moberly, *op. cit.* p. 161.

[3] Davison, *ut supra*, pp. 209, 210.

Deity. On the other hand, Deism with its solitary God represents another essential requirement of the human mind, and the question that faces all Christian theists is whether the essential truth of Polytheism, society in God, and the essential truth of Deism, unity in God, can be reconciled. If, with a modern writer, we may conceive of God as a ' social whole,' we may perhaps regard the word ' social ' as expressive of the essential truth of polytheism, and the word ' whole ' as the essential truth of deism. The threefold distinction in God, which is expressed by the word ' Trinity,' is the attempt of man to conceive and express the meaning of the Infinite God in the terms of Jesus Christ, and we believe that the use of the phrase, ' The Father, the Son, and the Holy Ghost,' is the very best rendering of the mystery that can be given.

' The doctrine of the Trinity stands in truth midway between Agnosticism and Deism. With the former it recognises the impossibility of presenting to our minds the inmost nature of the Supreme One, with the latter it insists upon the absolute necessity of thinking of the Deity in terms of personality. But it keeps closer than either to the facts of the religious consciousness and the needs of humanity, because it builds upon actual experience, the experience which stands central in the history of the race, and it interprets this experience by means of the only perfect Personality known to man.' [1]

The true meaning of Trinitarian doctrine, therefore, is not separate spheres of Divine operation in connection with each Person, but the united and inclusive operations of three Persons in one God. While each Person is (as the pronouns would suggest) self-conscious and self-determining, yet they themselves are never separated from one another. There are three centres of self-consciousness in the one self-consciousness of God.[2] The full statement of truth is, ' *From* and *unto* the Father, *through* the Son, *by* the Spirit. The transcendence in the Deity is expressed by the Father ; the expression of the Deity is represented by the Son ; while the truth of the immanence of the Deity for man's moral and spiritual life is that for which the Holy Spirit stands. And thus the Holy Spirit is at once the personal, energetic life of God and the ' Executive of

[1] D'Arcy, *ut supra*, p. 765. [2] Moberly, *op. cit.* pp. 157-169.

the Godhead' in relation to man. The most serious danger to-day lies in the prevalence of what may be called a practical 'Binitarianism' by the omission of the Holy Spirit from thought and life. But however difficult may be the conception of the Holy Spirit as within the Godhead, it can never be disregarded without spiritual loss. At all costs we must be true to the full New Testament idea of God as Father, Son, and Holy Spirit.

In view, therefore, of all the facts of the case, we are compelled to face the alternatives : the Deity of the Holy Spirit or its denial, for no other standing-ground is possible.[1] But this is in no sense prejudicial to the supreme and final thought of the Divine unity ; rather is it the necessary consequence and expression of the unity. We are compelled by the very nature of the case to insist upon those distinctions in the Godhead which are represented by the doctrine of the Holy Trinity, for they are the application of the essential nature of man as social in his comprehension of the Being of God as social. This conception is our highest and best idea, and receives its supreme expression in the words, The Father, the Son, and the Holy Spirit.

' We cannot but think of Him as eternally being as He expresses and communicates Himself to us. . . . The transcendent God is ours in the *Father*, Whose very Name gives promise of the *immanence* objective in the *Son* as incarnate in Jesus Christ to save man, the consummation of a process of divine revelation which is also redemptive, and the *immanence* subjective in the Holy Spirit, the renewer and perfecter of the soul of man.' [2]

And so, while we emphasise and maintain this distinctness, we also emphasise and maintain the oneness as the fundamental and vital conception of Deity.

' Yet it is in the unity of God as known in Christ that our minds come finally to rest. The triune life is apprehended by us for the sake of its redemptive expression, not 'for the internal analysis of its content. The problem can never be one of ontology mixed with arithmetic. Throughout, our aim is bent on history and its meaning, as we strive to apprehend the one God in His saving manifestation. To this point of view faith is constant. From this

---

[1] Kuyper, *The Work of the Holy Spirit*, p. xi.

[2] Garvie, *Expositor, ut supra*, pp. 49, 50.

point the doctrine must set out only to circle round at last to its fruitful origin. God as Holy Love we name the Father ; this same eternal God, as making the sacrifice of love and appearing in one finite spirit for our redemption, we name the Son ; God filling as new life the hearts to which His Son has become a revelation, we name the Spirit. In this confession we resume the best it has been given us to know of the eternal God our Saviour.' [1]

It is sometimes said that as religion consists in communion with God, God and man are therefore akin, and that human nature is a reflection of the Divine. So that as humanity has three phases : Fatherhood, Motherhood, and Brotherhood, these must have their counterparts in the Godhead. Two are clear : Fatherhood in connection with the Father, and Brotherhood in connection with the Son ; and the attempt is consequently made to associate the Holy Spirit with the remaining one, Motherhood. It is argued that this tendency of all religions would not be lacking in Christianity, and in support of it reference is made to the ' brooding ' of the Spirit in Gen. i. 2 ; the ' birth ' of the Spirit in John iii., and the wording of the original in James i. 18. It may be questioned, however, whether this is a satisfactory basis on which to rest such a conception of the Spirit of God. Nowhere in Scripture is any teaching found which associates the Holy Spirit with Motherhood, and the idea of Motherhood in the Deity (if regarded as necessary to theological thought) can be conceived of and realised without any such definite distinctions as are necessitated by this theory.

---

[1] Mackintosh, *op. cit.* p. 526.

CHAPTER 19

THE SPIRIT OF CHRIST

THE specific and distinctive feature of the New Testament on the present subject is the close and intimate association of the Holy Spirit with Jesus Christ. It is not in His Absolute Being, but as the Spirit of Christ that He is revealed in the New Testament (Acts xvi. 7, R.V.).

' It is only on the basis of the Christian revelation that we can found a doctrine of the Holy Ghost as the Spirit of Truth Who guides the thought of the Christian ages, Who teaches and imparts the mind of Christ, Who takes of Christ and declares it to Christ's people.' [1]

This is the most natural view of the New Testament teaching, and the steps leading up to it call for fresh consideration. As we have already seen, the Holy Spirit in the earlier books of the Old Testament is depicted as the Energy of God for human life, with particular reference to the covenant with Israel. Then gradually the doctrine deepens and widens until the Spirit is seen to be the indwelling life of God in man, and is specially associated with the promises connected with the Messiah (Isa. xi.). In the Synoptic Gospels the Spirit is pre-eminently the

---

[1] D'Arcy, *Idealism and Theology*, p. 256. See also Moberly, *Atonement and Personality*, p. 195, quoted below, p. 145.

LITERATURE.—Swete, *The Holy Spirit in the New Testament*, p. 295 ; Moule, *Veni Creator*, p. 31 ; ch. vi. ; Walker, *The Holy Spirit*, ch. iv. ; Smeaton, *The Doctrine of the Holy Spirit*, p. 116 ; Martensen, *Christian Dogmatics*, p. 322 ; Ridout, *The Person and Work of the Holy Spirit*, ch. vii. ; J. M. Campbell, *After Pentecost, What ?* ch. ii. ; Elder Cumming, *Through the Eternal Spirit*, ch. xiii. ; p. 89 ; Elder Cumming, *After the Spirit*, pp. 62, 231 ; Parker, *The Paraclete*, p. 96.

possession of the Man Christ Jesus, though even there the disciples are bidden to wait for ' the promise of the Father,' while the baptismal formula clearly associates Father, Son, and Holy Spirit in relation to the new work of Christian initiation. In the Fourth Gospel this promise of the Spirit is clearly connected with Christ Himself, His glorification (ch. vii. 39), and His Word (ch. xvi.). The relation of the Spirit to Christ is thus made clear, more particularly in the use of the word ' Paraclete.' [1] Then follows the specific bestowal of the Holy Spirit on the disciples on the day of Christ's resurrection.

' This is not the action of one who, by prayer, would invoke upon them, a Spirit which is not of, or from, Himself : it is the symbolism rather of one who would transfer to them the very Spirit which animates—which may be said to *be*—Himself.' [2]

In the Acts the ' promise of the Father ' is interpreted to mean the promise of the Father to the Son, received at the Ascension and poured out by the Son on the Day of Pentecost (ch. ii. 33).

' It was the promise of the Father—part of Christ's reward for His obedience unto death, even the death of the Cross. The giving of the Spirit was thus the conclusive sign of God's acceptance of Christ's work, and we should not lose this signification of it. Pentecost was won for us at Calvary.' [3]

When we turn to St. Paul we find substantially the same set of ideas. The language about the indwelling of Christ and of the Spirit is practically identical. ' The Lord is that Spirit : and where the Spirit of the Lord is, there is liberty ' (2 Cor. iii. 17). ' Because ye are sons, God hath sent forth the Spirit of His Son into your hearts ' (Gal. iv. 6). Thus, in St. Paul, as also in St. John, the Holy Spirit is the Divine power in a personal form through which the Christian life is realised in the believer, the means by which God makes Himself known to and felt by the Christian man.

As the Spirit of Christ, the Spirit is the Revealer and Bestower of Redemption. Everything we have of and from Christ comes through the Spirit. He is the Spirit

---

[1] Walker, *The Holy Spirit*, p. 128.

[2] Moberly, *op. cit.* p. 197.

[3] Denney, *Studies in Theology*, p. 157.

of Life, of Truth, of Holiness, of Power, of Grace. His work it is to make Christ real, to recall to us the words of Christ, to reveal to us His Person, and to bestow upon us His grace. While the title ' Spirit of God ' expresses the oneness of essence with God, and ' the Holy Spirit ' the nature of His word, ' the Spirit of Christ ' indicates the method of His coming as the Giver of Life, the Revealer of truth, and the Bestower of sanctification. And we believe that God can only become known to us in the historic Jesus, the experience of Whom is mediated to us by the Holy Spirit.

' As He represents the Person and supplies the place of Jesus Christ, so He works and effects whatever the Lord Christ has taken upon Himself to work and effect towards His disciples. Wherefore as the work of the Son was not the Son's own work, but (as He loves to say) the work of the Father Who sent Him, and in Whose Name He performed it, so the work of the Spirit is not the Spirit's own work, but rather the work of the Son by Whom He is sent and in Whose Name He doth accomplish it.' [1]

We are therefore not at all surprised at the variation of the theological expression connected with the Holy Spirit. Sometimes He is regarded as a separate Personality within the Godhead, having a self-consciousness separate from and yet connected with Jesus and the Father. At other times the Spirit is used for the Name of God's own personal activity, as He dwells in the soul of man. But however difficult it may be to express the difference between Christ and the Spirit regarded as within God Himself, no difficulty must allow us to ignore the plain teaching of the New Testament and the personal testimony of Christian consciousness. In our Lord's discourses, while He distinguishes between the relations of the Father and the Spirit with Himself to the disciples, yet there is no essential difference or separation. Whether the Father lives or the Son lives ; whether the Father comes or the Son comes ; whether the Father gives the Spirit or the Son gives Him, the essential relationship is the same. But while closely and intimately connected, Christ and the Spirit are never identical.

' As no Old Testament writer would have used the terms " Spirit of God " and " Angel of the Lord " for each other, so neither can

---

[1] Owen's *Works*, Goold's edition, iii. p. 195.

a confusion of the Word with the Spirit be admitted in any writer of the New. St. Paul says (2 Cor. iii. 17) : " *The Lord is the Spirit.*" But he does not therefore confound the Person of the glorified Saviour with the Holy Ghost. . . . Their parts are perfectly distinct. And they are quite as much so in the work of Pentecost as in that of the Incarnation. The Holy Ghost did not become Christ by producing Him in the Virgin's womb, nor does the Spirit become Jesus by glorifying Him and causing Him to live in us. The Word is the principle of the objective revelation, the Spirit that of the subjective. Jesus is the object to be assimilated, the Spirit is the assimilating power. Without the objective revelation given in Jesus, the Spirit would have nothing to fertilize in us ; without the Spirit, the revelation given in Jesus would remain exterior to us, and resemble a parable which is not understood. Hence it is in one sense true, that when the Spirit comes, it is Jesus Who comes again ; from one without, He becomes one within us.' [1]

It is essential to preserve with care both sides of this truth. Christ and the Spirit are different yet the same, the same yet different. Perhaps the best, expression we can give is that while their Personalities are never identical, their presence always is.

' It is not for an instant that the disciples are to have the presence of the Spirit *instead* of having the presence of the Son. But to have the Spirit *is* to have the Son.' [2]

It is this close association between Christ and the Spirit that gives point to the historical and theological question of the ' Procession ' of the Spirit. The relation between the Father and the Son is usually expressed by ' Generation,' and in order to express at once the unity and yet the distinctness, we are accustomed to speak of the ' Eternal Generation.' But the relation between the Son and the Spirit is described by ' Procession,' and on this there is a historical, and, it would seem, vital difference between the two great sections of the Eastern and Western Church. In the East this ' Procession ' is related only to the time of the Incarnation and the fact of Redemption. The passages in St. John which speak of the Spirit being given by the Son are interpreted in a temporal way. In the West, on the other hand, this ' Procession ' is regarded as an

---

[1] Godet, *Commentary on St. John's Gospel*, Vol. III. pp. 146, 147.

[2] Moberly, *op. cit.* p. 168.

eternal, essential fact of the Deity. Godet thus states the position :

' The divine facts of revelation are based upon the Trinitarian relations, and are, so to speak, their reflections. As the incarnation of the Son is related to His eternal generation, so is the *mission* of the Holy Spirit to His *procession* within the divine essence.—The Latin Church, starting from the words : *I will send*, is not wrong in affirming the *Filioque*, nor the Greek Church, starting from the words : *from the Father*, in maintaining the *per Filium* and the subordination. To harmonize these two views, we must place ourselves at the Christological view-point of St. John's Gospel, according to which the homoousia and the subordination are both at the same time true.' [1]

The question is often raised whether the doctrine itself is justified, and whether it really represents a vital difference between the East and West. A number of modern writers hold very strongly that it is this addition which has given to the West its admitted spiritual superiority over the East. One writer goes so far as to say that the denial of the Procession from the Son

' operated to the deep injury of vital religion in the East. . . . And the Greek Church has become much of a fossil, untouched by any of the reformations or revivals that renovated the Western Church.' [2]

To the same effect is the following :

' The Spirit of the Incarnate is the Spirit of God. But it is not so much the Spirit of God, regarded in His eternal existence, or relation, in the Being of Deity : it is the Spirit of God in Humanity, the Spirit of God become the Spirit of Man in the Person of the Incarnate,—become thenceforward the true interpretation and secret of what true manhood really is,—it is this which is the distinctive revelation of the New Testament, the distinctive significance and life of the Church of Christ. This is the truth, immense in its significance for practical Christianity, which the so-called doctrine of the " Double Procession " directly protects ; and which the denial of that doctrine tends directly to impair. It may be that the removal of the " Filioque " from the Nicene Creed, would not necessarily imply a denial of the doctrine : but there can at least be little doubt, historically speaking, that the " Filioque " has served, to the doctrine, as a bulwark of great importance.' [3]

---

[1] Godet, *op. cit.* p. 175.

[2] Smeaton, *The Doctrine of the Holy Spirit*, p. 291.

[3] Moberly, *op. cit.* p. 195.

Another and very different writer expresses the same opinion :

' As the Spirit of the exalted and glorified Lord, He is not the Third Person of the Trinity in His absolute and metaphysical existence, but that Person as He is mediated through the Son, Who is human as well as Divine. It is on this particular aspect of His being that He diffuses Himself through the members of Christ's body, and abides in them.' [1]

So also, the Bishop of Durham is of opinion that the doctrine is

' no mere phantom of abstract and unlicensed speculation, but a truth of life and love. . . . Such a humble belief is neither an arbitrary and barren demand upon a bewildered or unreflecting assent, nor a thing so sublimated and vanishing as to find no point of contact with life and love. . . . In the light of this belief, every part and detail of the work of the Spirit in connexion with the Person and work of Christ gains indefinitely in our view in respect of closeness and tenderness of contact.' [2]

On the other hand, Dr. Burn believes that all the spiritual results for which these writers contend

' seem to be secure if it is taught that the Holy Spirit proceeds from the Father through the Son.' [3]

Certainly no Western theologian wished for a moment to imply that there were two Sources or Founts of Deity, but only to associate in the closest possible way the Holy Spirit with the Incarnate and Glorified Son, and it must be admitted that in so doing they were keeping very close to the predominant New Testament conception of the Spirit, as the Spirit of Jesus Christ, the Spirit of Jesus, the Spirit of Christ, the Spirit of God's Son. But whether or not we attribute the undoubted spiritual superiority of the West over the East to this cause, the fact itself does not admit of doubt. And so we may say that ' without the Holy Spirit we have practically no Christ,' while, on the other hand, it is equally true that without Christ we have practically no Holy Spirit.[4]

---

[1] Milligan, *The Ascension of our Lord*, p. 189.
[2] *Veni Creator*, pp. 26, 27, 29.
[3] *The Nicene Creed*, p. 91.
[4] Laidlaw, *Questions of Faith*, p. 123.

CHAPTER 20

THE SPIRIT OF TRUTH

THE Nicene Creed expresses a great truth when it associates the Holy Spirit with the Old Testament ; ' Who spake by the prophets ' ; for it implies and involves the entire question of a Divine revelation to man. The various points may first be stated in outline. That such a revelation is possible we infer from the Divine power, and that it is probable we naturally assume from the Divine love. That a revelation is necessary we conclude from the nature of man, as at once limited and sinful. That a revelation has been given we believe from the manifestation of Christ. That a revelation is available in the New Testament we hold from the facts and necessity of the case, since only in some such permanent form can continuity and accuracy of transmission be guaranteed through the centuries.

The need of a revelation, however, calls for further and more special consideration. Man, even as man, needs a

LITERATURE.—Swete, *The Holy Spirit in the New Testament*, pp. 328, 388 ; Moule, *Veni Creator*, pp. 47-55 ; Davison, *The Indwelling Spirit*, ch. xi. ; Welldon, *The Revelation of the Holy Spirit*, p. 302 ; Denio, *The Supreme Leader*, pp. 147, 179 ; Smeaton, *The Doctrine of the Holy Spirit*, p. 137 ; Humphries, *The Holy Spirit in Faith and Experience*, ch. xi. ; Johnson, *The Holy Spirit*, pp. 173, 194, 291 ; Parker, *The Paraclete*, chs. iii., v., vi. ; Elder Cumming, *Through the Eternal Spirit*, ch. iv. ; Masterman, ' *I believe in the Holy Ghost*,' ch. v. ; Robson, *The Holy Spirit the Paraclete*, p. 225 ; A J. Gordon, *The Ministry of the Spirit*, ch. viii. ; Ridout, *The Person and Work of the Holy Spirit*, ch. vi. ; J. M. Campbell, *After Pentecost, What ?* chs. v., ix. ; Tophel, *The Work of the Holy Spirit in Man*, p. 24 ; Swete, Article, ' Holy Spirit,' Hastings' *Bible Dictionary*, p. 407 ; Kuyper, *The Work of the Holy Spirit*, pp. 56, 146, 164.

guide in things spiritual, above, outside, and greater than himself ; someone supernatural, superhuman, Divine. Still more, man as a sinner requires a Divine revelation. Amid the sins and sorrows, the fears and difficulties, the trials and problems of life he needs an authoritative guide concerning the way of salvation, holiness, and glory. Looking away from himself and from his fellows who are in the same position, the cry wells up from the heart of everyone who is concerned about the meaning of life : What is truth ? Where can it be found ? Where is power for life ? How may I obtain it ? Thus as a rational being man needs light ; as a sinful being he needs life. And it is only from God that light and life can come. It is thus that at the foundation of all matters of religious belief and practice lies the great question of authority. The need and value of authority are recognised in every aspect of life and in every branch of knowledge. The child at home, the boy at school, the youth in business, the man in the city, the politician, the scientist, the artist, the soldier, the writer—all in one way or another testify to the fact and power of authority. It is not otherwise when we come to religion ; man needs an authority, and authority in religion has been defined as ' the existence of an ethical standard.' [1] Authority is based on superior knowledge. It is the right to claim the assent of the intellect, the trust of the heart, the control of the conscience, the consent of the will, and the submission of the whole being. Men of all schools and views are practically agreed as to the need of some authority ; they differ only as to the character and place of it. Two things are essential to every man : truth, and an eye to see it. These two, external and in-ternal, are united and inseparable, and meet every conceiv-able situation. Truth alone would not suffice, for in spite of the old saying, ' Truth is mighty and prevails,' it is not mighty and does not prevail unless there is life behind it. The man who needs guidance needs perception to see and power to follow that guidance, and herein lies the close and essential connection between the Word of God and the

[1] M'Pheeters, Article ' Authority in Religion,' *Dictionary of Christ and the Gospels.*

Spirit of God. The one provides the truth, the other gives perception and power. The one bestows the light, the other the life. This is only another way of saying that God is the primary Authority as the Source of all grace and righteousness. Authority is found in the revelation of God to the world, in His presence here, and His action on behalf of man. This revelation is a personal one, personal in source and destination. It is the revelation of a Person to a person, of God to man, and is intended to affect with transforming influence every part of our life. When, therefore, we realise that the Source of Authority is the Divine Person of Christ as expressing and revealing God, the only question that remains is as to where this personal revelation is embodied or recorded. As God is invisible, it is essential to know where and how His personal revelation may become available for life.

It is at this point that we come to understand the truth of the Nicene Creed, when it refers to the Holy Ghost as having spoken by the prophets. This is another way of saying that Holy Scripture preserves for us the revelation of God in its purest available form. Christianity has a historic basis in the Person of Christ, and our one need is the clearest and completest form of that revelation. All that we ask is that the vehicle of transmission shall be certain and assuring. It matters not whether the vehicle is a book, or a man, or an institution, so long as we can be sure of its faithfulness in conveying God's revelation. There is no *a priori* necessity that this revelation should take permanent form in a written word. There are other means of preservation and transmission. Still, there are obvious reasons why written language should best serve the purpose, for it has the valuable and essential marks of durability, catholicity, fixity, and purity, and the testimony of the entire Church through the ages corresponds to the truth of the Creed, that in Holy Scripture God has spoken and has revealed Himself.

But, more precisely, what is the character of revelation, as embodied in Holy Scripture? If we approach the Bible desiring to know what it contains, and if we read it with due attention to its statements, claims and characteristics, what do we find ? (1) We find events recorded which admittedly were not seen by man, and the records must be due either to human speculation or Divine revelation. (2) We find announcements of coming events made ages before their fulfilment, and certainly beyond the possibility of any guess-work or pre-arrangement. (3) We find assertion after assertion of a Divine Speaker uttering words to a human being, who first declares them orally and then records them in writing. (4) We find the history of a people whose relations to God were unique in the records of the world, and whose history testifies to this uniqueness. (5) We find the exquisite picture of a perfect Character, worthily recorded by ordinary men, who have thus accomplished what no literary genius of the world has ever dared to attempt.[1] (6) We find in the latter books definite claims that all preceding writings were due to supernatural power, and that they possessed the authority of a Divine revelation. (7) We find the record of a religion which, starting without any compulsion or material advantage to the adherents, is received on every hand, grows to large proportions, maintains itself for years, overcomes opposition, and blesses and transforms every recipient. Now it is all this that we find in Scripture, and on these grounds we call it a revelation.

At this point the question arises as to its source. Whence is this Book ? We believe it comes from God, through the Spirit. There are three lines of argument. (a) The Old Testament prophets claimed to be the recipients of a revelation that came from God ; such phrases as ' the word of the Lord came,' and ' the Lord spake ' are found almost everywhere. There is no possibility of doubt that the prophets made this claim and believed they were justified in so doing. (b) In harmony with this the New Testament bears witness to the presence and power of the Holy Spirit in the Old Testament. In some passages the Holy Spirit is declared to be the Author or Speaker of Scripture : ' The Holy Ghost saith ' (Heb. iii. 7), and actually the human instrument is not named. In other passages both the Divine and human are mentioned ; ' The Holy Ghost by

---

[1] Bushnell, *The Character of Christ.*

the mouth of David spake' (Acts i. 16). Elsewhere the men who wrote are said to have been 'moved by the Holy Ghost' (2 Pet. i. 21) ; and yet again, their writings are said to have been inspired of God, or 'God-breathed' (2 Tim. iii. 16). (c) When we turn to the New Testament itself, we see the claim to authority and inspiration implicit in the attitude and words of the writers. A claim is made to authority similar to that made by the Old Testament prophet.[1] St. Paul challenges the spiritual man to admit that what he wrote was 'the commandment of the Lord' (1 Cor. xiv. 37).

'The whole of 1 Corinthians ii. is of classic value for the Apostle's view of his own inspiration ; and it certainly does not allow us to think that he regarded himself as groping after great truths, making great guesses, or feeling about at an inchoate stage in the understanding of Christ and His work.'[2]

The New Testament is thus fundamental for Christianity, and, as it has been well said, it is 'not the first stage of the evolution, but the last phase of the revelationary fact and deed.'[3] On these three grounds we believe that Scripture came from God, that it is the work of the Holy Spirit, that the Spirit spake by prophets and apostles.

This position constitutes the uniqueness of Scripture. There is that in Scripture, call it inspiration or give it any other name, which stands out absolutely alone from all else in literature and history. And if we call it inspiration, we mean a special influence, differing not only in degree but in kind from the ordinary spiritual influence of the Holy Spirit. The word 'inspiration' is variously applied. It is used of the communication of knowledge to the natural man (Job. xxxii. 8). It may also be associated with the ordinary work of the Holy Spirit on the heart, as in the Prayer Book : 'Cleanse the thoughts of our hearts by the inspiration of Thy Holy Spirit' (First Collect at Holy Communion) ; and 'By Thy holy inspiration we may think those things that be good' (Collect for the Fifth Sunday after Easter). But by the inspiration of Holy Scripture we understand the communication of Divine

---

[1] Sanday, *Inspiration*, ch. i.

[2] Forsyth, *The Person and Place of Jesus Christ*, p. 164.

[3] Forsyth, *op. cit.* p. 152.

truth in a way unique in degree and kind. The Apostles were evidently inspired to teach orally (John xiv.-xvi.), and it is natural to suppose that they were inspired to teach by writing as well. The New Testament is clear as to the position of the Apostles as founders of the Church. They were unique, and with reference to oral teaching, they had full authority and plenary inspiration. Of the eight writers of the New Testament five were Apostles, and their inspiration could hardly have left them when they began to write. As to the other books, they are written by men who were in special relation to the Apostles, and come to us with apostolic sanction. Inspiration, therefore, means the special influence of the Holy Spirit by which the Apostles and their close companions were enabled to transmit the revelation as they received it. The fundamental ground of our acceptance of the New Testament is our belief, based on adequate evidence, that it came from the apostolic age and from apostolic men who were authorised by the exponents of the Divine will. No one can doubt that the earliest ground of canonicity was apostolicity.

The New Testament dates show the limited period of the unique activity of the Holy Spirit as the Spirit of inspiration. It extended to about fifty years. Just as soon as the facts of redemption were thoroughly announced, the work of transcription began. Then came a chasm which has been rightly described as ' abrupt, sheer, abysmal.' Schaff says no transition has been so radical and sudden and yet so silent. Writers of various schools testify to the remarkable difference between the New Testament and the writings of the second century.

' A phenomenon singular in its kind is the striking difference between the writings of the Apostles and those of the Apostolic Fathers, so nearly their contemporaries. In other instances transitions are wont to be gradual, but in this instance we observe a sudden change. There is no gentle gradation here, but all at once an abrupt transition from one style of language to another—a phenomenon which should lead us to acknowledge the fact of a special agency of the Divine Spirit in the souls of the Apostles and of a new creative element in the first period.' [1]

---

[1] Neander, *Church History*, Vol. II. p. 405.

' When the student of early Christian literature passes from the New Testament to the post-canonical writers, he becomes aware of a loss of both literary and spiritual power. There is no immediate change in the form of the writings ; the earliest remains of the sub-apostolic age consist of letters addressed to Churches or individuals after the model of the Apostolic Epistles. But the note of authority which is heard in the Epistles of St. Peter, St. Paul, and St. John has no place in those of Clement of Rome and Ignatius of Antioch ; and there is little evidence in the latter of the originality or the inspiration by which the leaders of the first generation were distinguished. The spiritual giants of the Apostolic age are succeeded by men of lower stature and poorer capacity. Nor does the fresh power of the first century altogether return to the Church in the years that follow. A higher literary standard is reached in the second century ; the third is adorned by the great name of Origen ; the fourth and fifth centuries can boast of an Athanasius, a Basil, a Gregory Nazianzen, a Chrysostom, an Augustine. But none of these classical authors of Christian antiquity profess to originate or to reveal ; all recognize in the Apostolic writers their masters, and their best work is done in the field of New Testament exposition or in expressing New Testament doctrine in the terms of a later theology.' [1]

' There is no more striking contrast in the whole range of literature than that between the creative energy of the apostolic writers and the imitative poverty of the subapostolic. . . . The difference of canonical and uncanonical, so studiously ignored by some of the literary critics, is not a fiction of some church authority, but a fact which no serious reader can fail to notice. . . . We miss the spiritual depth and the intellectual force and clearness of the New Testament.' [2]

One simple but adequate proof of this is seen by reference to the Epistle to Diognetus, which is a vindication of the superiority of Christianity over heathenism. It is interesting and beautiful, but it is not the New Testament. From this we argue that the very dates of the New Testament books are evidences of a special spiritual activity of the Holy Spirit, and of a limitation of this activity to these dates. The Holy Spirit was active subsequently, but not in the same way, and it is therefore correct to speak of inspiration as a peculiar activity and function of the Holy Spirit, and to distinguish between His inspiration and His illumination. Since the New Testament times the Holy Spirit has illuminated truth, but has not revealed anything new.

[1] Swete, *The Holy Spirit in the Ancient Church*, p. 3.
[2] Gwatkin, *Early Church History*, Vol. I. pp. 98, 99.

The fundamental proof of this unique influence of the Holy Spirit in Scripture is the fact that, as we have seen, Scripture embodies a Divine revelation of redemption in Christ. It is this that gives Scripture its uniqueness. The revelation is the proof of the inspiration, and the inspiration in turn guarantees the revelation. The proof of inspiration is thus to be sought in the record itself, and the record must be tested by its own claims. Faith in the Bible means ultimately faith in God's revelation of Himself, and faith in the revelation will do more than anything else to establish our faith in Scripture. It is Divine revelation that gives substance to Scripture, as it is the Divine purpose that gives unity to Scripture. Both argue a unique presence of the Holy Spirit, for there is no other way in which revelation could be preserved and its reality demonstrated.

' Many current controversies concerning inspiration might be ended, if a clear conception were gained of the unity of the revelation given by the Holy Spirit in history, from those early days in which Israel had some dim conception of His operations, up to the time when revelation culminated in Christ, and some of His followers were inspired to write the records concerning Him so precious to us.' [1]

We conclude, therefore, that the possibility of a Divine authority, and therefore also of the inspiration of the Bible, lie in the fact of our need of an objective standard, and this need is created by the fact and circumstances of Christian experience. We need an authority because we need an ethical standard and a moral dynamic. At first Christ provided these in Person. Then came the Apostles as the revealers and interpreters of Christ by the Spirit. It was their death that really made the Bible necessary, and now the body of truth ' once for all delivered ' takes their place. There are only two ways of perpetuating the presence and authority of Christ through the ages ; the one is by means of Scripture, the other by means of an Institution like the Church.

' If He died to make a Church that Church should continue to be made by some permanent thing from Himself, either by a con-

---

[1] Davison, ' The Person and Work of the Holy Spirit,' *London Quarterly Review*, April, 1905, p. 217.

tinuous Apostolate supernaturally secured in the *charisma veritatis*, as Rome claims, or by a book which should be the real successor of the Apostles, with a real authority on the vital matters of truth and faith. But, we discard the supernatural pope for the supernatural book.' [1]

As therefore the Gospel is essential to the Church, it is natural and necessary for it to be embodied in a written record.

It may seem necessary at this point to go a step further, and enquire as to the theory of inspiration. We are met at once by the fact that no theory is given, and that whatever may be the true one, it is to be derived and deduced from the facts of the case. By Divine revelation we mean the thought of God for the life of man, and as thought needs words for its embodiment it would seem essential to any view of inspiration that the thought should be adequately and accurately expressed in words. St. Paul seems to imply this when he speaks of ' words which the Holy Ghost teacheth ' (1 Cor. ii. 13). And this view has found wide acceptance and endorsement.

' We can in fact speak with good reason of a language of the Holy Ghost. For it lies in the Bible plainly before our eyes, how the Divine Spirit, Who is the agent of revelation, has fashioned for Himself a quite peculiar religious dialect out of the speech of that people which forms its theatre.' [2]

The connection between thoughts and words has been well stated by Bishop Westcott :

' The slightest consideration will shew that words are as essential to intellectual processes as they are to mutual intercourse. For man the purely spiritual and absolute is but an inspiration or a dream. Thoughts are wedded to words as necessarily as soul to body. Language is a condition of our being, determining the conception as well as the communication of ideas. . . . The Book is thus rightly said to be inspired no less than the Prophet. The Book reflects and perpetuates the personal characteristics of the Prophet, but it does not create them. Writing introduces no limitation into the representation of truth which does not already exist in the first conception and expression of it. The isolated writing bears the same relation to the whole work of the Prophet as the Prophet himself to the world from which he is chosen.' [3]

---

[1] Forsyth, *op. cit.* p. 171.   [2] Rothe, *Dogmatics*, p. 238.

[3] *Introduction to the Study of the Gospels*, pp. 14, 15. See also Saphir, *Christ and the Scriptures*, p. 90, and Gaussen, *Theopneustia*.

But if, as the result of this view, we employ the phrase, ' verbal inspiration,' we must be careful to notice that it does not say anything as to the method, only the result of the Holy Spirit's work. It does not tell us *how*, but it does tell us *how far* God has revealed His will. Inspiration is not dictation, and all that is needed is to show that inspiration extends to form as well as substance. The true view of inspiration means such a union of the Divine and human elements that the result is guaranteed to us as the thought of God for the life of man. Such an idea

' combines harmoniously the two terms in that relation of the finite to the infinite which is involved in the very idea of Revelation. It preserves absolute truthfulness with perfect humanity, so that the nature of man is not neutralized, if we may thus speak, by the Divine agency, and the truth of God is not impaired, but exactly expressed in one of its several aspects by the individual mind.' [1]

The Holy Spirit possessed and used the faculties in such a way that without supersession or mechanical compulsion, but working through them, the revelation of God was to come to, through, and for man.[2] The inspiring operation of the Holy Spirit joined with the mental activity of the workers, working through it, determining it, and leading it (1 Cor. xiv. 37). While the process lies beneath our consciousness and we cannot explain the mode, we certainly know the results. No theory of inspiration can satisfy the conditions which allows the human to exclude the Divine at any point, or the Divine to supersede the human.

' For how does Divine inspiration act upon a writer ? In two ways : first by strengthening and intensifying his natural powers, and second, by producing in him what William James has called an uprush of the subconscious. I should prefer to call the last an inrush of the super-conscious. It makes a man a vehicle of deep-lying forces, so that he builds better than he knows. He may think that he is writing for a society, or even for an individual, when he is really writing for future ages, and to meet needs of which he is unconscious.' [3]

---

[1] Westcott, *op. cit.* p. 16.

[2] For passages expressive of the Divine source and the human channel, see Matt. i. 22, ' Spoken of the Lord by the prophet '; Matt. ii. 15 ; Acts i. 16 ; iii. 18 ; iv. 25.

[3] Sanday, ' Cambridge Biblical Essays,' *Journal of Theologica Studies*, January, 1910, p. 417.

This view of inspiration may be justified by several considerations. The Bible is universally employed to-day in the life and work of the Church with an authoritative emphasis on verbal teaching. In all ages scholarly minute exegesis has been prominent, and never more so than to-day. Even the employment of concordances is a testimony in this direction. Then, too, the Bible has always been appealed to in matters of controversy, and the Apostolic Churches undoubtedly held this opinion, believing in an inspiration which was ' supernatural in its source, unerring in its truthfulness, and comprising words as well as subject matter.'[1] The use of the Old Testament by New Testament writers supports this contention with the large number of quotations and the constant use of the phrase, ' It is written.' Our Lord's endorsement of the Old Testament must not be overlooked (John x. 34-36). Nor can we forget the claim of the prophets and other writers to Divine inspiration (Numb. xxiii. 5, 12, 13 ; 2 Sam. xxiii. 2 ; 1 Chron. xxviii. 19 ; Jer. xxx. 2 ; xxxvi. 4-8 ; Luke i. 70 ; 1 Cor. ii. 13 ; xiv. 37).

But this view of inspiration does not mean that every part of Scripture is of equal value or of equal spiritual importance. The idea of inspiration includes several aspects which need to be carefully distinguished. There is, as we have seen, the inspiration of direct communication from God, as claimed by Prophets and Apostles, and as possibly intended by the Apostle's words of ' receiving from the Lord ' (1 Cor. xi. 23). There is also what Canon Liddon rightly called ' the inspiration of selection,' as witnessed by our Gospels (Luke i. 1-4 ; John xx. 30, 31). There is also the inspiration of accurate record, for while at times inspiration guarantees the truth of what is written, at other times it only guarantees the report or record of what is written, which may in substance be untrue. Thus, the speeches of Job's friends, the acts of Jael, the sins of God's people, are all recorded, and in such cases inspiration concerns the accuracy of the report, not the truth of the contents. The fact of recording these sayings and doings does not justify them. Perhaps above all other distinctions

---

[1] Westcott, *op. cit.* Appendix B.

is the important one of the inspiration of progressive revelation. It is obvious that from our present Christian standpoint every part of the Bible cannot possibly be of equal importance, though everything is necessary in its place and for its purpose. Revelation is progressive. While it was adequate and even perfect at each stage for that particular stage, these characteristics do not necessarily extend beyond that time. Its morality must be judged from the standpoint of each stage, and not from ours to-day.

' The Divine teaching, though one, is not uniform. Truth is indeed immutable, but humanity is progressive ; and thus the form in which truth is presented must be examined in relation to the age in which the revelation was made. At one time it is to be sought in the simple relations of the patriarchal household : at another in the more complicated interests of national existence : at another in the still deeper mysteries of individual life : at another in the infinite fulness of the Saviour's work, or in the perplexing difficulties which beset the infant Churches. But each form has its proper and enduring lesson : each record constitutes a link in the golden chain which, to use the Homeric allegory, has again bound the earth with all its varied interests to the throne of God.' [1]

It is such distinctions as these which call for great carefulness in our use of Holy Scripture, and when it is said, ' All Scripture is inspired of God,' it does not in the least mean that every word is true in itself, for the sentiment may be human while the record is Divine. While all is inspired all is not revealed, and for this reason, while we say the Bible *is* inspired, we also say that it *contains* a revelation.

From the uniqueness of Scripture as embodying a Divine revelation, we naturally infer what is called the canonicity of Scripture. What are we to understand by this term ? Scripture, as we have seen, contains a Divine revelation for human life which is to exercise moral and spiritual authority over everything. But the authority does not lie in the volume ; it resides in each book, as it proceeded from an apostolic source, or was sent out by apostolic sanction. Canonicity was the collection of books already authoritative by reason of their source and substance. The Church is described in Article XX. as ' a witness

---

[1] Westcott, *op. cit.* pp. 16, 17.

and keeper of Holy Writ,' but it is never the maker of Scripture. It is not even the judge, for Councils, when they at length assembled, only testified to already existing facts and conditions in the separate Churches. It was not the canonicity which gave the books authority, but the authority which led to their canonicity. As it has been well said, the New Testament is not an authorised collection of books, but a collection of authorised books. The principle on which we receive a book as canonical is the belief, grounded on proper evidence, that the book is an apostolic gift to the Church. This constitutes the possession of canonicity. We accept the books as authoritative because they proceed from apostolic sources, from men uniquely qualified to reveal and record God's will to man. And then the Holy Spirit enables the soul to perceive that these books possess Divine authority. The Holy Spirit does not confer canonicity, but attests it. His witness is evidence to the illuminated and regenerate soul that these books come from God.[1] And thus the ground of canonicity is apostolicity, but the ground of our conviction of canonicity is the witness of the Holy Ghost. The Holy Spirit enables the soul to see the evidences of God's work in the Bible and to realise that it has its origin above. The darkness caused by sin is removed, and the light given illuminates Scripture as a book of Divine origin and authorship. This is something altogether different from the argument from experience. No mere experience can guarantee the Divine character or canonicity of any book, for not only is experience variable and subjective, but it is our own testimony to God, while the work of the Holy Spirit is God's testimony to us. The Holy Spirit Who regenerates and by regenerating illuminates the soul of the believer, enables it to become convinced on proper grounds of evidence that this Book comes from God, has indications of God's work in it, and is thereby authoritative for human life.

It is now necessary to speak of the interpretation of Scripture, for the truth in the Word needs to be applied

[1] C. W. Hodge, ' The Witness of the Holy Spirit to the Bible,' *Princeton Theological Review*, January, 1913, p. 41 (Vol. XI.).

to the heart. Here is the Word ; how are we to use it ?
The Church of Rome says that we must have an interpreter, and in so saying is perfectly right, but when it is
further urged that the Church is the interpreter, Rome is
perfectly wrong. We do indeed need a teacher, an interpreter, and we have it in the Author of the Book, Who
also is its Expounder. This is the work of the Holy Spirit
as the Spirit of Truth. Scripture is full of the thought of
the intellectual and moral darkness caused by sin, the
necessity of spiritual illumination, and the light and leading
bestowed by the Spirit on the repentant and trustful soul.
Our Lord speaks of the new birth to enable us to *see* the
Kingdom of God (John iii. 3). St. Paul speaks of the Holy
Spirit revealing and teaching that which man cannot see
for himself (1 Cor. ii. 14 ff.; 2 Cor. iv. 6). St. John reminds
us of the anointing which teaches us (1 John ii. 27). And
the Apocalypse bids us ' hear what the Spirit saith unto
the Churches ' (Rev. ii. 11). The test of views professing
to come from the Holy Spirit is agreement with the Word.
There is great significance in the parallels referring to the
fulness of the Spirit in Eph. v. 18 and the richness of the
indwelling word in Col. iii. 16. The Spirit enlightens and
the Word attests in regard both to doctrine and duty, word
and work, revelation and morality, character and conduct.
In relation to doctrine, no man speaking by the Holy
Spirit calls Jesus accursed, and no man can say that Jesus
is the Lord, but by the Holy Ghost (1 Cor. xii. 3). And the
unction from the Holy One will enable a Christian to
perceive the true and reject the false (1 John ii. 20, 21).
In relation to morality, the one supreme proof of everything
in Christianity is ethical, and the fruit of the Spirit will
always proceed along this line (Gal. v. 22-25). The
illumination is intended for application, and the more we
have of the one, the more we shall practise of the other.
Illumination will lead to discernment, discernment to
duty, and duty in turn will produce delight in the will of
God.

It is often said to-day that historical criticism has made
it impossible to use the Bible as in former days, and that
it cannot any longer be appealed to as ' an unquestionable

authority, of equal value wherever it is opened.' It should be observed, however, that these two statements are not identical, though they are often confused. The Bible can be appealed to as ' an unquestionable authority ' without being ' of equal value wherever it is opened.' This distinction should be borne in mind when what is generally regarded as the conservative view of Holy Scripture is considered and criticised. But be this as it may, it is said on many hands that Biblical criticism has compelled us to abandon once for all the older views of Biblical inspiration and infallibility. In reply to this, the words of Dr. Denney seem pertinent :

' This depends, of course, on how we define the older views ; but even if it were true, the question would remain whether " Biblical inspiration and infallibility " were not names for something real, and something essential to the effective maintenance of the Christian Church and the Christian religion. Our fathers may have drawn wrong inferences from what they called the inspiration of the Bible, but they did not believe in it for nothing. They may have misconceived the mode or some of the results of that character or virtue of the Bible which they designated by this term, but the term itself designated something real. And so it does still. The inspiration of the Bible is not an outworn dogma, it is the constant experience of the Church. The Bible itself is not merely a record of what God said or was believed to say long ago ; it is an organ through which God speaks perpetually to souls still. Even the modern mind can hear Him speak in it as He speaks nowhere else in the world, and can enter into fellowship with Him through it as through no other voice audible on earth.' [1]

As we have already seen, the uniqueness of Scripture lies in its possession of the record of a Divine revelation of Christ as Redeemer. It is this, and this alone, which is worth emphasising, and apparently it needs emphasising to-day, by reason of the prevalence of an attitude of critical subjectivity which tends to ignore, if not to destroy it.

' Criticism was entitled to some latitude in discrediting false inferences that had been attached to such words as inspiration and infallibility ; but it is time for Christian experience to assert again, even for the modern mind, the truth which these words were intended to express, and to vindicate the authority of the Bible in the Church. That to which the Spirit of God bears witness, by

---

[1] Denney, ' The Preacher and the Bible,' *The British Weekly*, August 22, 1912.

and with the Word, in our hearts, can and will hold its ground as the truth from which there is no appeal.' [1]

What our fathers claimed was that Scripture revealed Christ in the fulness of His Person and Work for Salvation, and herein lies the unique authority and inspiration of Holy Writ.

' Perhaps the old views of inspiration and infallibility—apart from illegitimate inferences—were not so inadequate as is sometimes supposed. . . . A man may have ten thousand questions to answer about the Bible, and yet be as certain, on the ground of the Bible, as he is of his own existence, that a Divine redeeming love has come into the world, and has come for him. The book that can give a sinful soul that certainty is the book of God, and that book is the Bible, and the Bible alone. . . . When a man submits his mind to the Spirit which is in it, it never misleads him about the way of salvation. It brings him infallibly to that knowledge of God, in His judgment and mercy, which is eternal life. . . . The most vital truth about it is covered by the terms inspiration and infallibility, and in virtue of this truth it is indispensable and authoritative to the mind of every age.' [2]

The probable explanation of some modern views on this subject is the absence of any true doctrine of the Holy Spirit. It is significant that amid the multitude of theological works of high value which have proceeded from able writers in Germany, England, Scotland, and America during the last century very few have treated with anything like proper fulness and emphasis the Scripture revelation of the Holy Spirit. Whatever may have been the cause, no one can doubt the fact that both in theology and also in the ordinary life of the Christian Church the place of the Holy Spirit has often been sadly to seek.

' Had a scriptural view of the Person and work of the Holy Ghost been more powerfully prevalent in the Church, not merely in her formularies, but in reality and life, there would never have been so much occasion given to represent the teaching of the Church on the inspiration of Scripture as " mechanical," " converting men into automata," etc. ; and the whole question would not have assumed such a scholastic and metaphysical form. For then the living testimony and the written testimony would appear both as supernatural and Spirit-breathed. The more the supremacy of the Holy Ghost, divine, loving, and present, is acknowledged, the more the *Bible* is fixed in the heart and conscience. But if the ' Book " is viewed as the relic and substitute of a now absent and

---

[1] Denney, *ut supra*.   [2] Denney, *ut supra*.

inactive Spirit, Bibliolatry and Bible-rejection are the necessary results.' [1]

But it is simply impossible to understand a Book which emanates from the Holy Spirit without the Spirit Himself as the Illuminator of our spirit.[2] This is why so much is found in Scripture, as already seen, about the darkness and dulness of the intellect, and the consequent need of spiritual insight, perception, illumination. And when the modern reader on Holy Scripture comes to Christianity with a humble, earnest desire to learn from Scripture what the Holy Spirit has there recorded, he will soon discover the reality and blessedness of its unique power.

' It will teach him also that many of the so-called religious difficulties of the modern mind are the penalty of the excessive intellectualising of religion in the past, and that they are not to be solved on the plane on which they are propounded, but dismissed as irrelevant to the soul's relation to God.' [3]

---

[1] Saphir, *Christ and the Scriptures*, p. 83.

[2] Saphir, *ut supra*, p. 112.

[3] Denney, *ut supra*.

CHAPTER 21

THE HOLY SPIRIT
AND THE INDIVIDUAL

WHEN the Nicene Creed speaks of the Holy Spirit as the
' Life-Giver,' it calls attention to one of the most prominent
features of the New Testament doctrine of the Spirit ; His
relation to the individual Christian. In the Old Testament the predominant characteristic was the fact of the
Holy Spirit as given to special men for special work,
though, as already seen, He was also given to individual
Jewish believers for their ordinary life. Yet the latter
point could not bulk largely by reason of the preparatory character of the Old Testament dispensation, and so
when we come to the New Testament, we see that the
Holy Spirit is intended for each and every believer. ' Such
honour have all His saints.' Indeed, without that Spirit
no man can be regarded as a Christian at all (Rom. viii. 9 ;
1 Cor. xii. 3).

LITERATURE.—Humphries, *The Holy Spirit in Faith and Experi-
ence*, p. 352 ; Walker, *The Holy Spirit*, chs. v.-viii. ; Swete, *The
Holy Spirit in the New Testament*, pp. 340, 352, 390, 391 ; E. H.
Johnson, *The Holy Spirit*, ch. xiii. ; Tophel, *The Work of the Holy
Spirit in Man*, pp. 58, 82 ; A. J. Gordon, *The Ministry of the Spirit*,
pp. 106, 113, 123, ch. x. ; Elder Cumming, *Through the Eternal
Spirit*, chs. x., xiv., xvi., xvii. ; Smeaton, *The Doctrine of the Holy
Spirit*, pp. 162-172, 204-209 ; Hobart, *Our Silent Partner*, Parts
II., IV. ; Denio, *The Supreme Leader*, pp. 128, 147, 205 ; Robson,
The Holy Spirit the Paraclete, p. 123 ; Elder Cumming, *After the
Spirit*, ch. vii., xiv. ; Masterman, ' *I believe in the Holy Ghost*,'
ch. iv. ; J. M. Campbell, *After Pentecost, What ?* chs. vi.-viii.,
x.-xiii. ; Ridout, *The Person and Work of the Holy Spirit*, chs. ii.,
iii., v. ; Parker, *The Paraclete*, chs. ii., xi., xiii., xv., xvi. ; Morris
Stewart, *The Crown of Science*, p. 70 ; Garvie, *The Christian Certainty Amid the Modern Perplexity*, ch. xiv.

There are three special features of Christianity in relation to the individual. The first is Conversion. By this is meant all the initial spiritual experience which includes conviction of sin, forgiveness, regeneration, justification, and adoption. The second is Communion with God. Everything in redemption is intended to lead up to fellowship. Man is saved in order to be united to God and to hold communion with Him. The third is Character. Human life is to be expressed in practical reality, and all grace is given in order to produce this effect. What we are and what we do constitute the supreme criterion of Christianity; without these all else is 'sounding brass and tinkling cymbal.'

Now it is the peculiar province of the Holy Spirit to provide and make real these three essential needs of man. (a) The Holy Spirit convicts of sin, reveals to the penitent soul the mercy and grace of God in Christ, bestows the gift of life, introduces to the presence of God, and assures of acceptance in Christ. In this are included those aspects of His work known as Regeneration, Adoption, Sealing, and Assurance. (b) The Holy Spirit alone makes Communion with God possible and real. The introduction of the soul to God through Justification is the commencement of a life of fellowship. We have 'access by one Spirit unto the Father,' and from that moment our Communion with God begins. The Holy Spirit opens our eyes to see and our ears to hear the Word of God for life. The same Spirit prompts and guides our prayers in response to God's revelation, and enables us to express all our needs, so that whether we think of the private or public 'means of grace' by which the soul comes in contact with God, the Holy Spirit is the medium of communication and the guarantee of blessing. In this are included those aspects of His work known as Indwelling and Anointing, and also His relation to the Word of God and prayer. (c) Then the Holy Spirit alone makes Christian Character possible and real. The Spirit Who has entered for and with the initial blessing of Regeneration abides in the soul for Justification. He produces the 'fruit of the Spirit,'[1]

---

[1] See note J, p. 279.

which is wholly concerned with character (Gal. v. 22, 23), and by constantly revealing, glorifying, and applying Christ to the soul, the believer is ' strengthened with might in the inner man,' and is continually being ' transformed by the Spirit of the Lord.' We live by the Spirit and walk by the Spirit ' unto all pleasing ' (Gal. v. 25 ; Col. i. 10).

There is scarcely anything clearer or more emphatic in Holy Scripture than the full revelation of truth concerning the Holy Spirit in relation to the individual. His action covers the whole life from first to last. He is the Spirit of Life for regeneration (John iii. 5, 8) ; the Spirit of Sonship for adoption (Rom. viii. 15 ; Gal. iv. 6) ; the Spirit of Holiness for sanctification [1] (Rom. viii. 5) ; the Spirit of Glory for transfiguration (2 Cor. iii. 18 ; 1 Pet. iv. 14) ; and the Spirit of Promise for resurrection (Eph. i. 13 ; iv. 30 ; Rom. viii. 11).

This truth of the Spirit in relation to the individual clearly teaches that the power of the Personality of Christ is only really available through the Holy Spirit. It is not what Jesus was when on earth, precious though that is ; it is not what He taught when on earth, wonderful though that is ; it is what He is now as the living exalted Christ, brought near by the Holy Spirit, that guarantees communion with God, and in that communion all that the soul needs and craves. It is for this reason that the Example of Christ or the Teaching of Christ is of no real value when considered alone. *Imitatio Christi* is but a small part of the Christian's relation to Christ. *Repetitio Christi* is nearer the truth,[2] and in the act and fact of revealing Christ as a present living reality to the soul the Holy Spirit as the Paraclete is also thereby the Revealer of the value and the power of human personality. As the Spirit of Truth He reveals God to man and man to himself. He shows what God intends man to be and to have, and thereby shows to man the possibilities of life in the Divine purpose. As the Spirit of Grace He provides man with the needful dynamic for daily life. ' God's biddings are

---

[1] See note K, p. 280.

[2] Tasker, *Spiritual Religion*, pp. 107-112.

enablings.' He never reveals truth without bestowing grace in Christ, and the ideal and the real are both assured.

When it is asked how the Holy Spirit works, we may reply with Denney that Christianity is summed up in the two correlatives of the Holy Spirit and Faith.[1] The Spirit uses the truth of God to reveal Christ to the soul, and to this the soul makes the response of trust. All the avenues of Divine approach to the soul are associated with the Gospel, either preached or written, and the entire attitude of the soul to God is expressed by the idea of trust, involving as it does the three elements of thought, feeling, and volition. But while faith is thus used in connection with the Holy Spirit (Gal. iii. 14), emphasis in the New Testament is rather on the result of faith in the act and experience of ' receiving ' (Gal. iii. 2, 14 ; Acts xix. 2).

' I do not know whether the New Testament ever speaks of believing in the Holy Ghost as the Creed does, and as we all do of believing in the Father and the Son ; but it is more significant still that it constantly speaks of *receiving* Him.' [2]

Every means of grace through which the Holy Spirit comes is associated with faith. Whether the ordinance be private or public, there must be a response of the soul to God, a response which can only be that of faith. Philosophically there may be a theoretical difficulty in conceiving of the relation of the Divine and the human in man,[3] but in practical experience there is no difficulty at all. Personality, as Moberly points out, consists of three prerogatives : freewill, reason, and love. Freewill is defined as

' man's power of becoming a veritable cause to himself, in making personally his own, and being wholly self-identified with, such acts of will as themselves are in perfect accordance with, and are therefore the true experience and development of, the nature which is essentially and properly his own.' [4]

Reason is of course the power of thought and insight. Love is that in which self finds its full realisation. But freewill is the self-realisation of man in perfect dependence. We see at once the need of grace, and we possess that

[1] Article, ' Holy Spirit,' *Dictionary of Christ and the Gospels.*

[2] Denney, *Studies in Theology*, p. 157.

[3] W. Adams Brown, *Christian Theology in Outline*, p. 399.

[4] Moberly, *Atonement and Personality*, p. 225.

grace just exactly in proportion as we are in Christ and the Spirit of Christ is in us.[1] Yet surrender is essential to our highest realisation,[2] and love requires a supreme Object for its full expression. The Holy Spirit uses Christ as the Redeemer of the soul, and in proportion as man yields to Him, the grace of God works on our personality, influencing our freewill, our reason, and our love, and enabling us both ' to will and to do of God's good pleasure.' Nothing is clearer in the New Testament than the reality of Christian experience in and through the Holy Spirit.

' The very word Spirit seems to us a hard one to deal with ; there is something evasive and subtle in it ; its range of meanings is almost incredible, and we hesitate to define it ; but plainly, in the apostolic age, it had a thoroughly *real* meaning. Christian experience was a thing so unique, so entirely apart, so creative, that it could not be overlooked nor confounded with anything else. There had been no time for conciliations, for approximations, for compromises ; that which was Christian possessed all its originality and distinctiveness ; and it was conceived as the gift and work of the Spirit. If we are ever to find the language of the New Testament natural, it must be by a return to that originality and distinctiveness of the Christian life which created the New Testament speech.' [3]

And so, wherever and however we contemplate individual life, we see the constant necessity, definite power, and abundant blessing of the Holy Spirit of God.

' The deep, omnipotent background of all Christian experience is thus declared to be the unresting power of the Holy Spirit. Scriptural insight is tirelessly insistent in the declaration of this fact. It stakes its whole validity on this one ultimate verity.' [4]

---

[1] Moberly, *ut supra*, p. 227. See also p. 233.

[2] Moberly, *ut supra*, p. 242.

[3] Denney, *op. cit.* p. 158.

[4] Warner, *The Psychology of the Christian Life*, p. 271.

CHAPTER 22

THE HOLY SPIRIT AND THE CHURCH

It is a natural and easy transition from the consideration of the Holy Spirit in relation to the individual Christian to that of His relation to the Church, because the Church is nothing less, as it can be nothing more, than the community of individual Christians. Both in the Apostles' and Nicene Creeds the expression of belief in the Holy Ghost is immediately followed by the confession of our faith in the existence of the Church. 'I believe one Catholick and Apostolick Church.' This close connection suggests the truth which is found in Scripture, and which calls for careful attention, the relation of the Holy Spirit to the body of Christian people. Dr. Hort points out, and the matter is one of supreme importance, that the Church in its widest sense as the body of Christ is not the aggregate of particular Churches, but of individuals.

'The One Ecclesia includes all members of all partial Ecclesiae; but its relations to them are all direct, not mediate. It is true that, as we have seen, St. Paul anxiously promoted friendly intercourse and sympathy between the scattered Ecclesiae; but the unity of

LITERATURE.—Swete, *The Holy Spirit in the New Testament*, pp. 306, 317; Welldon, *The Revelation of the Holy Spirit*, p. 338; Smeaton, *The Doctrine of the Holy Spirit*, p. 230; Denio, *The Supreme Leader*, p. 188; Walker, *The Holy Spirit*, chs. x., xi.; A. J. Gordon, *The Ministry of the Spirit*, chs. iv., vii.; Masterman, *'I believe in the Holy Ghost,'* ch. iii.; E. H. Johnson, *The Holy Spirit*, p. 279; Martensen, *Christian Dogmatics*, p. 334; Davison, *The Indwelling Spirit*, ch. xiii.; J. M. Campbell, *After Pentecost, What?* chs. iv., xiv.; Elder Cumming, *Through the Eternal Spirit*, ch. xii.; Elder Cumming, *After the Spirit*, ch. iii.; Ridout, *The Person and Work of the Holy Spirit*, ch. iv.; Tasker, *Spiritual Religion*, p. 143; Hort, *The Christian Ecclesia*.

the universal Ecclesia as he contemplated it does not belong to this region : it is a truth of theology and of religion, not a fact of what we call Ecclesiastical politics.' [1]

And so when we speak of the Holy Spirit in the Church, we refer of necessity to real not to nominal Christians ; to those who are in living union with Christ, the Head of the body. The New Testament reveals various aspects of the Church's life which are definitely and prominently associated with the Holy Spirit.

The Spirit constitutes the Church. It is evident from the record of Acts ii. that the penitent believers received the Holy Spirit, and were thereby added by the Lord to the community of Christian souls. With this agree St. Paul's words : ' By one Spirit are we all baptized into one body ' (1 Cor. xii. 13). As the fundamental idea of baptism is introduction into a new sphere and the designation of the recipient for blessings within that sphere, we can readily understand this reference to the Holy Spirit as introducing us into the body of Christ. It is the Spirit Who unites us to Christ and makes us members of His body, the Church.[2]

The Spirit thereupon abides in the Church. The metaphor of the building is found in the New Testament, implying the union of individual Christians as builded together for a permanent habitation of God through the Spirit ($\kappa\alpha\tau\omega\kappa\eta\tau\acute{\eta}\rho\iota\omega\nu$). With this agree the words of St. Paul, that Christians are the temple of God, and the Spirit of God dwells in them (1 Cor. iii. 16 ; vi. 19).[3]

The Spirit builds up the Church ($\omicron\acute{\iota}\kappa\omicron\delta\omicron\mu\acute{\iota}\alpha$). By adding believer after believer to Christ the building is erected of living stones and becomes a spiritual house, an holy temple. The work is going on continually as one by one men are led to Christ and to each other in Him.

The Spirit administers the Church ($\omicron\acute{\iota}\kappa\omicron\nu\omicron\mu\acute{\iota}\alpha$). He is the ' Executive of the Godhead,' the Representative of Christ, the ' other Comforter,' and in everything that pertains to the life of the Church He is supreme. Worship

---

[1] Hort, *The Christian Ecclesia*, p. 168. Cf. Hort's *Prolegomena to Romans and Ephesians*, p. 130 f.

[2] See Note L, p. 280.   [3] See note M, p. 281.

must be in the Spirit (Phil. iii. 3). Witnessing to Christ must be done in the power of the Spirit (Acts i. 8). Extension of the Church takes place through the Spirit (Acts viii. 29). Missionary work must be undertaken in obedience to the Spirit (Acts xiii. 2). Fellowship is in the Spirit (Phil. ii. 1). Guidance in regard to new undertakings must be given by the Spirit (Acts xvi. 6, 7 ; Rom. viii. 14). Whatever concerns the Church's life and work is to be brought under the control of the Holy Spirit. The Father is the Owner, the Son the Head, but the Holy Spirit is the Administrator of the Church.

The Spirit unifies the Church. The New Testament has much to say on unity, and it is always that of the Spirit. We are to ' endeavour to keep it ' (Eph. iv. 3), implying effort and earnestness. He Who unites each believer to Christ and to his fellow-believers undertakes the work of maintaining those believers and communities united in Christ as the prime secret of blessing and power. It is in proportion as Christians try to understand what this means and requires that the value of unity will be seen.[1]

The teaching of the New Testament regarding the Church, and the relation of the Holy Spirit to it, will do more than anything else to solve the current problems of controversy. It is essential that the term ' Church ' be correctly defined. As the Greek word indicates, it is the community of those who are called (Ecclesia), a body of people who believe in Jesus as the Christ (1 John v. 1), and who confess Him as the Son of God (1 John iv. 15). The metaphors descriptive of the Church as that community which is in vital union with Christ are particularly noteworthy. There are at least seven of them. The Church is a Vine (John xv. 5), a Flock (John x. 16), a Temple (1 Pet. ii. 4), a Bride (Eph. v. 27), a Family (Rom. viii. 29), a Body (Eph. i. 22, 23), a Spirit (1 Cor. vi. 17). It should never be forgotten that the one and only requirement for membership of the Church in its truest sense is vital union with our Lord Jesus Christ.

The fullest teaching concerning the Church and its relation to the Holy Spirit is found in the Epistle to the

---

[1] See p. 259.

Ephesians, and from the aspects there recorded all other views find their source and standard.

'All other meanings of the word "Church" are derived and modified from this, but this must not be modified by them.'[1]

The special interest and importance of Ephesians in regard to the Church is that apart from its companion Epistle to the Colossians it is, after St. Matthew xvi., the next and almost the only place in the New Testament where the Church is regarded absolutely as the one universal Church. In all earlier Epistles, as well as in the Acts, the term seems to be applied to a local Church and a number of local Churches, or else to the one universal Church as represented in the individual Church or local Churches. Out of the 110 places where the word occurs in the New Testament, 86 are in the Epistles of St. Paul, and of these 11 only appear to refer to this idea of an universal Church ; i.e. 9 in Ephesians and 2 in Colossians (Col. i. 18, 24). This does not mean that the idea of the unity of all believers was not in the Apostle's mind and teaching before this time. As a matter of fact it is traceable in earlier Epistles. The principles and duties of unity as based on fellowship with all Christians are already clear (1 Thess. ii. 14 ; 1 Cor. i. 12, 13 ; vi. 9), while St. Paul had also emphasised the essential oneness of Jew and Gentile in Christ (Gal. iii. 28 ; Rom. xi. 17). Thus the idea of all believers being one in Christ is evident from the first, but it is only in the Epistle to the Ephesians that we find it receiving full expression and adequate treatment.

This extension of idea and usage to include all Christians in one great universal Church is characteristic of these two Epistles of the Roman captivity, and for several reasons it is noteworthy and very significant. The time had evidently come for the Christians to receive this fuller teaching as the complement and crown of what they already knew. It was the necessary consequence and completion of the teaching given earlier. Thus the Epistle to the Romans deals mainly and primarily with the relation of the individual to God in Christ. The Epistle to the Ephesians, on the other hand, starts from the corporate

---

[1] Bishop Moule on Ephesians i. 22.

side of Christianity, and views the individual as one of the Body. Further, Romans deals with the great problem of how Jew and Gentile were to be received respectively, and as it were, separately, into fellowship with Christ. Ephesians contemplates them both as already in Christ and making one body in Him. Again, while in 1 and 2 Corinthians St. Paul emphasises and urges unity in the local Church, in Ephesians the thought takes a wider and universal sweep as including all believers of all Churches at all times. We may perhaps also note how the Apostle, writing from Rome, and possibly influenced by the imperial atmosphere, might be led to conceive of the Church of Christ as one vast organism and to emphasise the solidarity of all Christians in Him. It is also noteworthy that this conception of one universal Church was a revelation granted to the Apostle Paul only.

' The full revelation respecting the Gentiles to which St. Paul refers in Ephesians iii. 6 ff. was not obviously involved from the first in the charge to preach the Gospel to all nations. It was to St. Paul himself doubtless that this prophetic illumination came in the first instance.' [1]

The ' mystery' referred to in this Epistle cannot be interpreted to mean simply that the Gentiles were to be brought into blessing in connection with Christ. This was clearly shown even in the Old Testament (Gen. xii. 3 ; xviii. 18), and was no ' mystery' at all (Gal. iii. 8 ; Rom. i. 2 ; iii. 21). The $\mu\nu\sigma\tau\acute{\eta}\rho\iota\nu$ of Ephesians is that a people should be taken out from Jews and Gentiles and should be made a joint body ($\sigma\acute{\nu}\sigma\sigma\omega\mu\alpha$) in Christ (Eph. iii. 2, 9). The various aspects of the teaching need close attention.

1. The Church is regarded as a Body. Up to the writing of Ephesians, St. Paul had used the idea of a body either simply as an illustration (Rom. xii. 3-5), or else with reference to the local Church only (1 Cor. xii. 12, 13, 27). Now, however, he regards all Christians together as the Body of Christ. The following are the main outlines of his teaching on this subject.

(a) Christ is the Head of the Body. ' Head over all things to the Church, which is His body, the fulness of Him that filleth all in all ' (Eph. i. 22 f.). ' The Head, even Christ '

---

[1] Hort, *The Christian Ecclesia*, p. 166.

(ch. iv. 15). ' Christ is the Head of the Church ' (ch. v. 23). As the head to the body, so is Christ to the Church. Head and body are correlatives and organically connected. We are thus taught that the Church is not a fortuitous collection of individuals, but a Society with a Head, an organism and not merely two parts in juxtaposition. This connection between Christ and the Church as illustrated by the metaphor of a Body can be variously applied. (1) There is a connection of life. He is the Source of life to the Church. Apart from Him the Body is dead, for the Church has no life in itself. (2) There is a connection of cause and effect. The thoughts and purposes of the Head are expressed in the activities of the Body. (3) There is a connection of power. All energy in the Body comes from the Head and through union with Him. (4) There is a connection of sympathy. Head and Body are one in feeling, whether of pain or joy. (5) There is a connection of obedience. The Body responds to the orders of the Head, and what the will directs the members carry out. We may say, then, that there is a two-fold need ; that of the Head by the members, and that of the members by the Head. The members need the Head for life, sensation, and volition. The Head needs the members for expression and activity.

' In some mysterious sense the Church is that without which the Christ is not complete, but with which He is or will be complete. That is to say, he [the Apostle] looks upon the Christ as in a sense waiting for completeness, and destined in the purpose of God to find completeness in the Church.' [1]

(b) The Holy Spirit is the Life of the Body. The emphasis laid on the Holy Spirit in Ephesians is very clear and striking, and with the one exception of Romans viii., there is more about the Spirit of God in this short Epistle than in any other of St. Paul's writings. There are at least twelve references to His Divine grace and work in relation to the Body of Christ. From the moment of conversion He is everything to the individual Christian and to the whole Church. It is the Spirit Who seals the believer as belonging to Christ (ch. i. 13 ; iv. 30). By the Spirit we

---

[1] Armitage Robinson, *St. Paul's Epistle to the Ephesians*, p. 42 f.

are introduced to the Father (ch. ii. 18). We are indwelt by the Spirit (ch. ii. 22). We are taught by the Spirit (ch. iii. 5). The Spirit is the secret of inward strength (ch. iii. 16), of outward unity (ch. iv. 3), of inward sensitiveness (ch. iv. 30), and of spiritual fulness (ch. v. 18). The Word of God is described as ' the sword of the Spirit ' (ch. vi. 17), and prayer is to be offered ' in the Spirit ' (ch. vi. 18). Thus in every way, whether we think of the individual or the community, the Spirit of God actuates all.

(c) Each individual Christian is a member of the Body. Believers are viewed first in relation to the purpose of the Father (ch. i. 4-6a), then in relation to the work of the Son (ch. i. 6b-12), and lastly in relation to the grace of the Holy Spirit (ch. i. 13, 14), and thus we are members of His Body (ch. v. 30). To each and every individual member is some grace given ($\dot{\epsilon}\kappa\dot{\alpha}\sigma\tau\omega$, ch. iv. 7), and every one can supply something to the progress and growth of the Body : ' according to the proportional energy of each single part ' (ch. iv. 16). Each individual member is (1) a channel of nourishment to the rest (ch. iv. 16 ; cf. Col. ii. 19) ; (2) a means of unity as a joint and ligament harmoniously fitted and compacted, holding together the framework (ch. iv. 16) ; (3) a condition of growth, all acting as fitted, and so making continual increase (ch. iv. 16 ; cf. Col. ii. 19). Christians are therefore needed by one another for nourishment, growth, progress, fellowship, blessing, and it is a profoundly striking and deeply solemn thought that individual Christians can hinder blessing and growth from coming to the entire Body, hindering the flow of grace and keeping back spiritual power. Thus, while the Church as a whole is the Body, very clear and significant stress is laid on the importance, necessity, and due position of each single member of it. The individuality of single, though not separate, Christians could not be more clearly taught. The importance of this social and corporate aspect of the Christian life is very great, and needs constant emphasis.

' The believer's union to Christ, which is the deepest of all personal things, always involves something social. The call comes to him singly, but seldom solitarily.' [1]

[1] Lindsay, *The Church and the Ministry in the Early Centuries*, p. 7.

We see, therefore, the great value of the Church. It is true that each man is saved solitarily and alone by direct contact as an individual with Christ, but it is equally true that he is sanctified in association with others. It must be constantly borne in mind that the true, full, vigorous, mature Christian life is impossible to any Christian who tries to live a solitary life. Individual Christianity can easily be carried to extremes—and become something very different from the Christianity of the New Testament. The Christian must realise in some way ' the Communion of Saints ' if he is to be a true saint himself. St. Paul prayed that the Christians of Ephesus might comprehend ' with all saints ' the love of Christ (ch. iii. 18), each saint apprehending a little and all together comprehending that which is intended for the whole Church.

(d) Jews and Gentiles go to make up the unity of the Body. It is pointed out by the Apostle that in the atoning death of Christ this oneness of Jew and Gentile was really contemplated, intended, and provided for. ' He is our peace, Who hath made both one ' (ch. ii. 14). ' That He might reconcile both unto God in one body by the cross ' (ch. ii. 16). ' Through Him we both have access by one Spirit unto the Father' (ch. ii. 18). And the fact that there was to be one Body consisting of Jews and Gentiles which, as we have seen, was the special revelation to St. Paul, is stated in very definite and significant terms. The Apostle's language in ch. iii. 3-6 is particularly noteworthy, with its emphasis on σύν- in the words ' joint-heirship,' ' joint-body,' ' joint-partakers.' This truth of Jew and Gentile as one Body in Christ, not as two separate bodies, but a ' joint-body ' of which Christ is the Head, is the magnificent conception of this Epistle, and it is thence that we derive the only true ideas of unity and catholicity.

(e) There are diversities of gifts in the one Body. As ch. iv. 4-6 deal with unity, so verses 7-14 bring before us the diversities of gifts in the one Body.

2. The Church is also considered as a Building. Side by side with the metaphor of a Body and associated with it is the metaphor of a Building. The whole Church is

regarded as a great structure, and several aspects of truth are brought before us by means of this symbol.

First, the foundation. ' Built upon the foundation of the apostles and prophets ' (ch. ii. 20). It would appear that the reference in this phrase is to the New Testament and not to the Old, and concerns the two forms of spiritual ministry by which the Church was commenced and continued (Acts xi. 28 ; xiii. 1 ; xv. 32 ; xxi. 10 ; Eph. iii. 5 ; iv. 11).[1] In speaking of apostles and prophets as a foundation, it is clear that the reference is not to any official position of authority, but simply to the order of the growth of the Church from them and their ministry.[2]

Second, the Corner-stone. ' Jesus Christ Himself being the chief corner-stone ' (ch. ii. 20). In 1 Corinthians iii. 11 our Lord Himself is put as the Foundation (cf. 1 Pet. ii. 6, 7 ; Isa. xxviii. 16). In this passage, however, He is the Corner-stone. It implies that our Lord is essential to the coherence and stability of the structure.

Third, the stones of the Building. By implication individual Christians are regarded as stones, each in his own place contributing his part to the progress and completeness of the whole (ch. ii. 19 f.; cf. 1 Pet. ii. 5, 'living stones '). The individual aspect, however, is not the predominant, or even the prominent point in this Epistle, but the corporate and united effect of the whole.

Fourth, the character of the Building. The Building is to be a Temple (ch. ii. 21). The ναός is the shrine, the actual house, answering to the Holy Place and the Most Holy, the place of the Presence of God, and the Church thus regarded as a shrine is to be the *permanent* abode of God (κατοικήτηριον, ch. ii. 22 ; κατοικεῖν, ch. iii. 17).

Fifth, the progress of the Building. Stress is laid on the gradual upbuilding of this Divine and spiritual structure. The tenses of the verbs are particularly noteworthy in this connection. The Christians have been definitely and once for all placed on the foundation (Aorist, ch. ii. 20).

---

[1] See also Armitage Robinson, and Moule *in loc.*, and Hort, *The Christian Ecclesia*, p. 165.

[2] Hort, *ut supra*, p. 167.

They have been permanently founded (Perfect, ch. iii. 17). They are continually being built together (Present, ch. ii. 22). They are being continuously fitted together harmoniously in the process of building (Present, ch. ii. 21 ; iv. 16). The result is that the whole Building is to be one perfect outcome of a continuous increase and growth (ch. ii. 21 ; iv. 12, 16).

It is noteworthy that we have in this Epistle the blending of the two ideas of the Body and the Building (ch. ii. 21 ; iv. 12, 16 ; cf. iii. 17).

3. The Church is depicted as a Bride. This metaphor is brought before us in ch. v. with reference to the whole Church, though it had already been used in connection with a local Church in 2 Corinthians xi. 2, and also implicitly with reference to individual Christians in Romans vii. 1-4. It is urged by some authorities that as in the metaphor of the Body the Church is a part of Christ, it cannot be intended to represent the Church as His Bride, since the Bride is not a part of the Husband, but separate from Him. It is, however, more likely that we are to regard these metaphors as two aspects of the same relationship between Christ and the Church, the one a relationship of life, the other a relationship of love. This is especially probable in view of the words, ' They twain shall be one flesh,' and also in the light of ch. v. 32, ' This is a great mystery'; as though the Apostle would say, there is more in it than appears. Taking it, therefore, as a separate though connected metaphor we notice several aspects of spiritual teaching in the relationship of the Church as the Bride of Christ.

(a) There is the thought of Union. ' The mystical union betwixt Christ and His Church.' This union is wrought and maintained by the Holy Spirit (ch. i. 13–ii. 18), whereby every believer and all the Church is ' joined to the Lord ' (κολλώμενος, 1 Cor. vi. 17).

(b) There is the thought of Love. Christ loves the Church as the husband is to love his wife, and accordingly our Lord's love is brought before us as proved by the gift of Himself (ch. v. 25). Love in our Lord's case is no sentiment, but a sacrifice, and it does not even cease with

His sacrifice of Himself; it is maintained and continued in service. ' Loving and cherishing it ' (ver. 29).

(c) There is the thought of Duty. Here we see the Bride's part, that of subordination and loyalty. So is it to be with the Church in relation to Christ. The two aspects of wifely duty, submission (ver. 22) and fear (ver. 33), are exactly equivalent to those required of the Church in relation to her Lord.

(d) There is the thought of the Future (ver. 27). Christ's purpose in relation to the Church is that by means of His sacrifice and service on her behalf ' He might present it to Himself a glorious Church, not having spot or wrinkle or any such thing, but that it should be holy and without blemish.' Thus, the glorious future of the Bride, the Church of Christ, is brought before us as ' holy and without blemish.' In like manner in Revelation (chs. xix. and xxi.) we have the picture of the glorious future of the Lamb's Wife in all the eternal glory of heaven.

4. The Church may be regarded as a Brotherhood. Here metaphor is dropped, or at least changed, and the life of the Church is depicted mainly in terms of actuality. At the same time there are the two metaphors of the Household (ch. ii. 19) and the State (ch. ii. 19). The Church is thus brought before us under what may be regarded as the figure of a great Brotherhood having relations to God and to one another.

(a) The Godward attitude of this Brotherhood is emphasised. This is taught under several aspects. God is the Father of our Lord Jesus Christ and our Father in Him (ch. i. 2, 3, 17 ; iii. 14, 15). We are His children in Christ Jesus, adopted into His family (ch. i. 5), beloved (ch. v. 1), children of light (ch. v. 8), and members of His household (ch. ii. 19). We are also citizens of a Divine commonwealth (ch. ii. 19 ; cf. ii. 12 ; Phil. iii. 20). We are also saints, that is, those who belong to God, separated for, consecrated to, and possessed by Him. The prominence given to this aspect of the Christian life in relation to God is very noteworthy (ch. i. 15, 18 ; iii. 8, 18 ; vi. 18). We are also described as faithful (ch. i. 1), which seems to blend the two ideas of trustful and trustworthy. In these various figures, which are strongly expressive of real relationships, we see something of the Church as a Brotherhood. God is our Father, and in Him all Fatherhood and paternal relationships find their source and warrant.

(*b*) The life of this Brotherhood is also taught. This thought is brought before us in relation to the presence and work of the Holy Spirit. All Christians are led to God by Him (ch. ii. 18). He is the bond of peace between believers (ch. iv. 3, 4), and they are sealed by Him in view of the great future when redemption will be completed (ch. i. 13 ; iv. 30).

(*c*) The unity of this Brotherhood is strongly urged. With great fulness and definiteness we are taught the solidarity of the Christian Brotherhood in this Epistle (ch. iii. 15 ; iv. 3, 4). It is a unity based upon love, and the phrase ' in love,' which occurs six times in the Epistle, is applied four times to Christians in relation to one another. None of St. Paul's Epistles are so clear as this as to the unity of Christians as members of the family of God, and a very special feature of the Epistle is the use of the preposition σύν both in connection with our relation to Christ, and also in particular with our relation to one another. In regard to Christ, we have been quickened and raised with Him and are seated with Him (ch. ii. 5, 6). In relation to our fellow-Christians we are being fitted together (ch. ii. 21), builded together (ch. ii. 22), and compacted together (ch. iv. 16). We are fellow-citizens (ch. ii. 19). We have a joint-inheritance, we are a joint-body, and joint-partakers of the promise of Christ (σύν, three times in ch. iii. 6). We are to comprehend the love of Christ ' with all saints ' (ch. iii. 18). We are not to be sharers-together of evil (ch. v. 7), or fellow-partners with the works of darkness (ch. v. 11).

(*d*) The reciprocal duties of this Brotherhood are specially pressed home. In this Epistle to the Ephesians it is most striking to observe how several practical duties are emphasised in direct view of our brotherhood with fellow-Christians. This is all the more remarkable when we compare the companion Epistle to the Colossians, which deals with the same duties from another standpoint, basing them, not on our relation to one another, but on our relation to our Lord.

Reviewing the entire teaching of the Epistle with regard to the Church in this four-fold aspect as a Body, a Building, a Bride, and a Brotherhood, there are several points of immediate and practical importance which arise out of it. The consideration of the one Body of Christ with our Lord as its Head and the Holy Spirit as its Life should dominate all our thinking and action in relation to the various questions connected with the Church to-day. Some of these applications may be fittingly considered as we draw to a close.

We can readily see from the teaching of Ephesians that the primary idea of the Church is that of an organism rather than of an organisation. ' Christianity came into the world as an idea rather than as an institution.' [1] If, instead of ' idea,' we substitute ' the indwelling presence of the Spirit in the hearts of believers,' there is no doubt of the truth of these words and their agreement with the Pauline doctrine. The Church in its true idea is a spiritual fact rather than a visible institution. Such was the case as it was originally constituted on the Day of Pentecost by the indwelling of the Spirit of God, and that which we find recorded in Acts ii. of the birthday of the Church in its present form must necessarily determine its true nature in all ages.

' It is, in its true being and essence, the temple of the Holy Ghost, founded and built up on the doctrine of the Apostles. . . . Its progress was in accordance with this beginning . . . it developed itself from within outwards—not in the reverse direction. . . . Instead of passively receiving a superinduced stamp from without, the Christian society supplied its needs from within, and of itself, that is, the invisible Church preceded the visible. . . . The result is, that when we come to define the Church—when the question relates to its essence, not to its accidents—we must adopt the old explanatory addition of the Article in the Creed, and speak of it as " the communion, or congregation of saints " ; of saints not merely by profession, or external dedication (though this, of course, is included), but in reality and truth.' [2]

---

[1] Newman, *Development*, p. 116.

[2] Litton, *Introduction to Dogmatic Theology*, Second Edition, p. 360 f.

The idea of the universal Church and its gifts as primarily spiritual should therefore dominate all our views of the local and ecclesiastical Church and ministry. When we take up this standpoint and judge everything by this standard, we can see how truly sad, utterly small, and practically futile are many of the controversies about Catholicity, Ministry, and Priesthood, and how dangerous to the true ideas of Church and ministry some of the developments in Church history have been.

It follows from the foregoing that the reference to ' the visible Church ' in Article XIX. of the Church of England is not otiose, but expresses a truth arising out of the Epistle to the Ephesians, a truth, moreover, which is supported by the Prayer Book, and especially by the Creeds. Even allowing that the terms ' visible ' and ' invisible ' represent controversial conditions of the sixteenth century, the truth expressed by them is valid, because the distinction is between a real and an apparent Church, between spiritual reality and outward manifestation, and the point is that the reality is not identical with, or fully expressed by, the manifestation. The New Testament idea of the Church, while not indifferent to visibility or order, nevertheless puts the primary and main stress on spiritual grace, and not on ecclesiastical institution. These two words, ' visible' and 'invisible,' represent the Church in two aspects, according as it is viewed inwardly or outwardly, according to spiritual nature or according to earthly organisation. The Church is visible as to those who compose it, but invisible as to its Divine Head and the Spirit of its life. The two aspects are necessarily connected, but they do not cover exactly the same ground. A man may belong to the Church as visible without belonging to the Church as invisible. He may be united to the outward society of Christians without being spiritually united to Christ. But it is also true according to the New Testament, that a man will not belong to the Church as invisible without belonging to the visible Church. A man in Christ will join himself to other Christians. Christians living and working alone, apart from brethren, are quite unknown to the New Testament. As there depicted, they are all

united in fellowship and included in the Church of Christ,
' the blessed company of all faithful people.' A purely
individualistic Christian life is an utter impossibility.

It is for this reason that we use the words ' I believe '
when we repeat the Creed about the Holy Catholic Church.
We say ' I believe,' not ' I see,' for the essence of the
Church is a matter of faith, not of sight, and lies in its
invisibility to the outward eye and its visibility to the
eye of faith.

' For lack of diligent observing the difference between the Church
of God mystical and visible, the oversights are neither few nor
light that have been committed.' [1]

On this account it is absolutely impossible to identify
' the Holy Catholic Church ' of the Creeds with any existing
institution in the world, and any attempt to refer the
phrase ' Catholic Church ' to any one particular institution
as now organised is of necessity inaccurate and even
disloyal to the Creed.

Not less important in this connection is the consideration
of the relation of the one universal Church to the various
local Churches, and, as Dr. Hort points out, it is certainly
very striking and significant that the units which compose
this one universal Church are not Churches but individuals.
A consideration of this simple fact will always be a safeguard against the erroneous, because inadequate, view
that the one universal Church, which is the Body of Christ,
is necessarily limited to and only coterminous with the
sum total of certain local visible Churches.

' The Church of Christ, which we properly term His body mystical,
can be but one ; neither can that one be sensibly discerned by any
man, inasmuch as the parts thereof are some in heaven already
with Christ, and the rest that are on earth (albeit, their natural
persons be visible) we do not discern under this property, whereby
they are truly and infallibly of that body. Only our minds by
intellectual conceit are able to apprehend that such a real body
there is, a body collective, because it containeth a huge multitude ;
a body mystical, because the mystery of their conjunction is removed
altogether from sense. Whatsoever we read in Scripture concerning the endless love and the saving mercy which God showeth
towards His Church, the only proper subject thereof is this Church.
Concerning this flock it is that our Lord and Saviour hath promised,

[1] Hooker, *Eccles. Pol.* B. III. p. 9.

" I give unto them eternal life, and they shall never perish " (John x. 28). They who are of this society have such marks and notes of distinction from all others as are not object unto our sense ; only unto God, Who seeth their hearts and understandeth all their secret cogitations, unto Him they are clear and manifest.' [1]

This is the Church in which the Holy Spirit dwells as the present, continuous, and permanent life, the Church to which all the promises of God are made, the Church outside which no one can ever be saved, the Church from which no believer can ever be excommunicated, the Church against which the gates of Hades shall never prevail, the Church in which God's presence is continually realised and manifested, the Church through which His grace and glory will be displayed to the spiritual universe throughout the ages of eternity.

---

[1] Hooker, *Eccles. Pol.* B. III.

CHAPTER 23

THE HOLY SPIRIT AND THE WORLD

It is impossible to contemplate the Holy Spirit in relation to the Christian Church without being led naturally and inevitably to the thought of His relation to the world at large. It is obvious that since Christ died for the whole world, and that God is ' not willing that any should perish, but that all should come to repentance,' there must be some definite relationship to humanity on the part of that Spirit Whose work it is to make the redemption of Christ real to mankind. What is this relation ? How is it exercised ? What does it effect ?

The first thing to notice is that in the New Testament there is an entire absence of all cosmical relations of the Holy Spirit such as we find in the Old Testament. This contrast between the two parts of Scripture calls for careful attention. The New Testament revelation of the Holy Spirit is associated solely with redemption, and the wider doctrine of the direct relation of God to the world is expressed by the Logos, the Second Person of the Trinity (John i. 9 ; Col. i. 16, 17 ; Heb. i. 2, 3a). Although most modern writers on the subject of the Holy Spirit speak of

---

LITERATURE.—Humphries, *The Holy Spirit in Faith and Experience*, chs. ix., xii. ; Smeaton, *The Doctrine of the Holy Spirit*, p. 172 ; E. H. Johnson, *The Holy Spirit*, p. 213 ; A. J. Gordon, *The Ministry of the Spirit*, ch. ix. ; Potten, *His Divine Power*, ch. vi. ; Davison, *The Indwelling Spirit*, ch. x. ; Downer, *The Mission and Ministration of the Holy Spirit*, ch. xi. ; Elder Cumming, *Through the Eternal Spirit*, ch. xxiv. ; *After the Spirit*, ch. xi. ; J. M. Campbell, *After Pentecost, What ?* chs. xv., xvi.

the Spirit as related to the world of mankind, nothing is more striking than the simple fact that not a single passage can be discovered in the New Testament which refers to the direct action of the Spirit on the world. On the contrary, St. Paul says quite plainly that ' the natural man receiveth not the things of the Spirit of God, for they are foolishness unto him : neither can he know them, because they are spiritually discerned ' (1 Cor. ii. 14). Even those who favour the view of the Holy Spirit's action on the world fail to adduce definite New Testament evidence for their contention.[1]

But what, it may be asked, are we to understand by the promise of Christ that the Holy Spirit should convict, or convince the world of sin, righteousness, and judgment (John xvi. 8-11) ? The context seems as clear as it is significant. A brief amplification will enable us to appreciate this point. Our Lord was speaking tb His disciples, and addressing them, He said, ' It is expedient for you that I go away : for if I go not away, the Comforter will not come unto you ; but if I depart, I will send Him unto you. And when He is come (that is, unto you), He will (that is, through you) convict the world of sin, and of righteousness, and of judgment.' Is not this the fair and proper interpretation of the passage, and does it not show plainly that the conviction of the world was to come in some way through the Church ? And is not this exactly true both to the teaching of Holy Scripture and to the facts of experience ? When we turn to the preaching of St. Peter on the Day of Pentecost, we notice that what he said produced this very conviction of sin (Acts ii. 37). But it is sometimes forgotten that he proclaimed these very three truths mentioned by our Lord. He declared to the house of Israel their sin in not believing on Jesus Christ. He proclaimed the righteousness of Christ by

---

[1] Humphries, *The Holy Spirit in Faith and Experience*, p. 199 ; Denio, *The Supreme Leader*, p. 120 ; Wood, *The Spirit of God in Biblical Literature*, p. 268 ; Walker, *The Holy Spirit*, p. 23 ; Downer, *The Mission and Ministration of the Holy Spirit*, p. 325 ; Bruce, *St. Paul's Conception of Christianity*, p. 257 ; E. H. Johnson, *The Holy Spirit*, p. 213 ; Curtis, *The Christian Faith*, p. 351 ; Moule, *Veni Creator*, p. 46 ; Hobart, *Our Silent Partner*, ch. i.

reason of God's reception of Him into heaven. And he announced in effect a very definite judgment as he proclaimed the great realities of his message. This is a typical example of what has always taken place as the direct result of proclaiming the Christian truth. The preacher or teacher, either individually, or representing the Church, has been used of God to convince of sin through the proclamation of Divine truth. The same thing is obvious when the history of the Christian religion is considered. No one has ever heard of a conversion to God apart from some human agency, direct or indirect, personal or written. No one has ever been led to Christ in the centre of Africa, or China, or elsewhere by the Holy Spirit apart from some testimony to Christ by life or word ; the latter either spoken or written. Our Lord said distinctly of the Holy Spirit, ' Whom the world cannot receive, because it seeth Him not, neither knoweth Him ' (John xiv. 17).

It seems clear, therefore, that we make a serious mistake in enlarging our conception of the Holy Spirit so as to make Him directly responsible for all the strivings of conscience in the heathen world. There is indeed a moral work going on throughout the human race, and this assuredly comes from God ; but it is better to connect it with the general work of the Logos than with the specific work of the Holy Spirit. Let it be said once again, and surely there must be some meaning in it, that not a single trace can be found in the New Testament to connect the Holy Spirit with the general preparatory work and influence of God on the world. And, indeed, any such attribution would inevitably tend to rob the Church of its responsibility to witness to the world. It was to His disciples that our Lord spoke of the Spirit when He said, ' Ye know Him,' and it is in proportion to our reception and experience of Him that our witness to Christ will be real and effectual. The consciousness that if the world is not convicted of sin, righteousness, and judgment through Christians, it will not be convicted at all is one of the most solemn incentives to holiness, earnestness, and world-wide evangelisation.

This brings us to consider the work of the Church in the

world and the relation of the Spirit thereto.[1] In our Lord's prayer for His disciples in St. John xvii. His four-fold purpose is seen to be : Preservation, Sanctification, Unification, Evangelisation. The preservation was to lead to sanctification, or consecration. This in turn was to produce unity among His followers, and the unity was to bring about world-wide evangelisation ; ' That the world may believe ' (ver. 21) ; ' That the world may know ' (ver. 23). And when this work was about to be commenced, the Holy Spirit was specifically mentioned in connection with it. ' Repentance and remission of sins should be preached in His name . . . but tarry ye . . . until ye be endued with power from on high ' (Luke xxiv. 47-49). ' Ye shall receive power, after that the Holy Ghost is come upon you : and ye shall be witnesses unto Me ' (Acts i. 8). In harmony with these statements the book of Acts emphasises the three essential factors of Christian service : the Spirit as the Power ; the Word as the Message ; and the Man as the Instrument. The combination of these three constitutes the Divine plan for the world's evangelisation. Not the man without the message, not the message without the man, and neither man nor message without the power, but all three united in one forceful testimony to Christ with a view to human redemption. And as the Church proceeds along this line, it will be doing the Master's will in the Master's way for the Master's glory.

Our view of the theological formulation of this article of our faith has clearly taught us that the work of the Holy Spirit is much wider than the dogmatic statements of the Creeds. The Creeds are only landmarks, not goals, and not complete rules of faith. A Creed is a *norma crediti* rather than a *norma credendi*. Modern thought tends to criticise the ancient formularies, but hitherto nothing superior has been found to express the essential truths intended by them. And it is wholly inaccurate to describe the Creeds as Christian truth transformed by philosophy.

[1] For literature on the Holy Spirit in relation to Missions, see Note Y, p. 285.

On the contrary, as Illingworth has said, ' Christianity was not accommodated to philosophy, but philosophy to Christianity.' The Christian consciousness taught by the Holy Spirit will continue to work upon the Divine revelation, and will obtain yet fuller, deeper and richer aspects of the truth found germinally in Holy Scripture as the written record of God's will to man.

PART IV

THE MODERN APPLICATION

CHAPTER 24

THE HOLY SPIRIT
AND THE DIVINE IMMANENCE

EVERY age has its characteristic tendencies and needs, and on this account Christianity has to be adapted constantly and perpetually to human life. The secret of this feature of constant variety and complete adaptation is found in the doctrine of the Holy Spirit. It is impossible in one volume to consider modern life in all its fulness and complexity, but some special applications seem to call for attention, not only because of their own importance, but also as illustrations of the way in which the Holy Spirit's presence in the Christian religion enables the Church to face all the problems of humanity.

Among modern problems connected with this subject, one of the most prominent is that known as Divine Immanence. On every hand we hear to-day of the Immanence of God, and it is at once interesting and curious to observe how ready Christian thought has been to accept it. What

LITERATURE.—W. N. Clarke, *The Christian Doctrine of God*, p. 320 ; *An Outline of Christian Theology*, p. 132 ; W. Adams Brown, *Christian Theology in Outline*, s.v. Immanence ; Illingworth, *Divine Immanence* ; John Caird, *The Fundamental Ideas of Christianity*, Vol. I. ; Garvie, *The Christian Certainty Amid the Modern Perplexity*, ch. ix. ; Davison, *The Indwelling Spirit*, ch. i. ; Bowne, *The Immanence of God* ; Stearns, *Present Day Theology*, p. 206 ; Terry, *Biblical Dogmatics*, p. 508 ; D'Arcy, *Idealism and Theology*, p. 251 ; Walker, *The Holy Spirit*, p. 194 ; Denio, *The Supreme Leader*, p. 120 ; Humphries, *The Holy Spirit in Faith and Experience*, p. 357 ; J. M. Campbell, *After Pentecost, What ?* ch. iii. ; Rowland, Article ' Presence,' *Dictionary of Christ and the Gospels* (with Bibliography) ; H. W. Clark, ' Religious History and the Idea of Immanence,' *Review and Expositor*, Vol. X. p. 3 (January, 1913).

does it mean ? It is said to be the necessary complement of the doctrine of Divine Transcendence, and that together they form the true idea of God.[1]

Let us endeavour to obtain from a competent authority the true meaning of Immanence.

' We mean that God is the omnipresent ground of all finite existence and activity. The world alike of things and spirits is nothing existing and acting on its own account while God is away in some extra-sidereal, but it continually depends upon, and is ever upheld by the ever-living, ever-present, ever-working God.' [2]

To put the matter in a simpler form, Immanence is intended to teach that God is everywhere present and active in nature, ceaselessly at work in history, and spiritually present with and in man.

Now, although differences are made between God's Immanence in nature and in man, it is still a question whether the general idea of Immanence is really clear. Science to-day is teaching an Immanence in the process of nature, a Divine Thought and Purpose immanent in everything. But what about man ? Is God immanent in him ? St. Paul's words are sometimes quoted as bearing on this point, ' In Him we live, and move, and have our being ' (Acts xvii. 28). Yet, apart from the fact that this refers to man's immanence in God, not God's Immanence in man, it surely must be interpreted by the previous words, ' He giveth to all life, and breath, and all things ' (ver. 25). But setting this aside, there still remains the question of sin. Is God in that also ? As Mackintosh well says :

' No one can be so keenly aware of the limits of the Divine Immanence as the sinner, to whom repentance has brought home the divergence of self and God with a vivid realisation which is sharpened and registered by the sense of guilt.' [3]

There is, it is true, a school of Christian philosophy which endeavours to support a doctrine of Divine Immanence, but it may be questioned whether it affords a clear view of it. The way in which Immanence has overthrown an incorrect idea of dualism in nature has been very welcome, and we

---

[1] W. N. Clarke, *Outline of Christian Theology*, p. 132.

[2] Bowne, *The Immanence of God*.

[3] Mackintosh, *The Person of Jesus Christ*, p. 432.

can no longer think of the universe as consisting of two separate and opposed spheres, the natural and the supernatural. The natural is a method by which the supernatural expresses itself. The supernatural works in the realms of history and personal experience, and nature in many respects is the manifestation of divinity. But still the question persists as to where we should stop. Are the souls of men part of this Divine activity? We must preserve moral realities. Immanence must be consistent with Theism, or else it will not be moral. The distinction between the Divine and the human is real. We distinguish ourselves as personal individuals, endowed by God with wills of our own, even though we recognise that we have the basis of our existence in Him, and that by Him all our faculties are bestowed and sustained. Any view that ignores, still more that sets aside this position tends to destroy moral reality, and it is therefore impossible to accept any view of Immanence that does not recognise ethical distinctions.[1]

There are also those who say that God was immanent in the Incarnation, but this does not appear to be an adequate interpretation of the Incarnation in the light of several passages of the New Testament (John i. 14; Rom. viii. 3; 1 Tim. iii. 16). What we can say is, not that God was immanent in Christ, but that Christ is God, that His Person was representative of God, that He was God manifest in the flesh.[2]

It is evidently not intended that we should regard the Divine Immanence as merely a substitute for the old idea of Omnipresence. Immanence means something more, and it is this 'something' that has to be clearly stated and proved. According to one writer, the doctrine of Immanence adds to the doctrine of Omnipresence

'the endeavour to expound the relation between the omnipresent God and the universe with which He is present. It not only affirms that God is present, but attempts to suggest something as to what He effects by virtue of His presence, and how the universe is affected by it. The doctrine of immanence is nothing more than

---

[1] Mackintosh, *op. cit.* p. 432.

[2] Mackintosh, *op. cit.* pp. 433, 434.

an endeavour to interpret the fact of God's universal presence, and tell what that presence signifies, or accomplishes.' [1]

But it may be questioned whether the new idea adds anything material to the old. In the same way, it has been recently said that the Jews taught this doctrine, and that the modern view of Immanence, meaning something more than Omnipresence and suggesting a closer communion between the Creator and His works, was taught centuries ago by the Jewish Rabbis.[2] It is certainly interesting to follow the teaching of the Rabbis on the subject of the Divine Shekinah, or God's presence with His people; of the Ruach, or Holy Spirit; of the Memra, or word of the Targums. But while all this clearly proves, what no one ever denied, that the doctrine of the Divine Omnipresence was held by the Jews notwithstanding the fact that the supreme thought of the Old Testament is the Divine Transcendence, yet it may be seriously questioned whether the writer has succeeded in showing that the Jewish Rabbinical doctrine is one of Immanence in the modern sense.

It is hardly too much to say that there is a good deal of loose thinking on the subject of Immanence, especially when men allow themselves to speak of God's ' incarnation in the race,' which is not only untrue to fact, but also robs the Divine revelation of all thought of redemption from sin, and takes away from Christ His uniqueness as the Incarnate Son of God. Neither in the past nor in the present can we speak of God's incarnation in this way. On the contrary,

' the loose and confused notion of " incarnation in the race," which has been offered as a profounder substitute for the Christian view, is out of harmony with concrete fact. Any attractiveness it may seem to possess is in reality owing to a crude obliteration of moral distinctions, resting on the mistaken assumption that the relations of God and man are completely interpretable in physical and logical categories.' [3]

It is clear, therefore, that while Immanence is a useful term, it may be ' the parent of a nest of fallacies.' The

[1] W. N. Clarke, *The Christian Doctrine of God*, pp. 329, 330.

[2] Abelson, *The Immanence of God in Rabbinical Literature*.

[3] Mackintosh, *op. cit.* p. 436.

only true Immanence of God is the presence of Christ by the Holy Spirit in the heart and life of the believer (John xiv. 17, 21; 1 Cor. iii. 17; vi. 19). Converted lives have been well said to be the best proof and the truest safeguard of Divine Immanence, since they involve the entrance of a new Divine power into life. An able writer in vindication of Modernism has expressed surprise that the Church should think it necessary to combat the view of Divine Immanence held by the Modernists, which he says is as old as religion itself and is wholly in keeping with the doctrine of the outpouring of the Spirit. But this is just where the doctrine of Divine Immanence robs Christianity of its distinctiveness by a quasi-pantheistic conception of God's presence in the world. The New Testament, as we observed, never associates the Holy Spirit with God's action in nature, but only with the redemptive work of Christ for and in man. The sphere of the Spirit is definitely spiritual, and His activities are spiritual also. There may be analogy, but there is certainly no identity between the presence of God in nature and the Holy Spirit of God in the believer. This is all we can say, but it does not carry us where the Modernists would have us go. Indeed, Modernism in this respect is the very antithesis of the Christian position. It robs Christianity of everything characteristic of redemption; it endangers man by emphasising his spiritual possibilities without reminding him of his sinfulness; above all, it makes Christ a Teacher rather than a Redeemer, and sums up man's greatest need as revelation rather than redemption; knowledge rather than salvation. But this, whatever else it is, is not New Testament Christianity. The Incarnation of Christ and the gift of the Spirit were unique, both in their manifestation and destination, and the only Immanence of which we can speak with truth and safety is the presence of God in Christ by the Spirit in the hearts and lives of the people of God. Ethical indwelling is one thing, natural causality is quite another.[1]

It is in relation to the Holy Spirit that the Christian doctrine of God meets the deepest human need. Man's

---

[1] Mackintosh, *op. cit.* p. 439.

prevailing desire has always been for the presence of God. This is the essential truth underlying pantheism.

' The doctrine of the Holy Spirit represents the truth of pantheism. The infinite Power that is everywhere present, the reality of which the energy and life of nature are the manifestation, is the Spirit of God. He is the substratum of the human spirit, the light of our intellectual seeing, the source of all that is pure and holy in us. Moreover, by the Incarnation God has become immanent in the world in a peculiar and wondrous way for our redemption. The Word has become flesh, the Father has come to us through the Son.' [1]

But an impersonal doctrine of Immanence is utterly insufficient to satisfy this need. A mere ' stream of tendency ' is impossible. The logical outcome of a belief in Divine Immanence in the modern sense is seen in a recent article entitled ' The Little Rag of Faith that is Left.' [2] It is said that the orthodox conceptions of Christian worship have disappeared, that the religion of nature is taking their place, and that even the conception of God as the Heavenly Father introduced by Jesus Christ is only a metaphor expressive of kinship with the Eternal. The article goes on to call attention to ' the remarkable extent to which within the last generation especially, the conception of Divine Immanence has found favour both in and beyond the Church.' This conception is declared to be ' a prominent form of, and a great stepping-stone towards the Impersonality of the Divine Nature.' This apparently is what is meant by the title, ' The Little Rag of Faith that is Left,' and it is said to constitute the problem of Christian philosophy to-day. But the view stands condemned by the writer's own admission that Divine Impersonality ' can never be a really popular thought for the bulk of the religious world,' even though it is said to be constantly becoming more certain, and ' for the higher and more trained minds the natural and final resting place.' A religion which can never be popular and is only occupied with a metaphor will never meet the deepest needs of mankind. Personality in God is essential if human personalities are to be satisfied, and it is here that Christianity

---

[1] Stearns, *Present Day Theology*, p. 206.

[2] *Westminster Review*, January, 1913.

steps in with its distinctive message. It is easy to say that the principle of Immanence has for ever destroyed the deistic conception of God, but it is sometimes forgotten that for all practical purposes the two ideas come to the same thing. If God is apart from the world, or is identified with the world, it is obvious that He cannot come into essential relationships with the human beings who crave for fellowship with the Divine. ' A uniform world with God locked in is exactly equivalent to a uniform world with God locked out.' [1] It is only in the Holy Spirit that man finds the truth suggested by pantheism, that of a definite offer, guarantee, and realisation of the presence of God.

' All the longing of pious mysticism, and the affinity for pantheistic union with the Eternal Existence which have shown themselves in millions of the religious peoples of the earth may find deepest satisfaction in this doctrine of the Spirit. The human soul cries out for a God that is personally present, and not afar off ; an abiding Comforter, whom the world cannot receive nor cast out. The Spirit of truth reveals Himself with all this blessed assurance to them that worship in spirit and in truth. Herein we recognise the blessed reality which was from the beginning but has been sadly overlooked at times—the reality of the vital, everlasting Immanence of God.' [2]

But the distinctness between the Divine Spirit and the human is always maintained. Sanday and Headlam point out that

' the very ease with which St. Paul changes and inverts his metaphors shows that the Divine immanence with him nowhere means Buddhistic or Pantheistic absorption.' [3]

It is easy for Christians to sing :

> ' Till in the ocean of Thy love
> We lose ourselves in heaven above.'

But we do well to remind ourselves that this is not strictly correct, that it is only a poetic expression of an anticipated satisfaction, and that it would be infinitely truer (in the double sense) to say :

> ' Till in the ocean of Thy love
> We *find* ourselves in heaven above.'

---

[1] Mullins, *Freedom and Authority in Religion*, p. 243. See also pp. 241-244.

[2] Terry, *Biblical Dogmatics*, p. 508.

[3] *Inter. Crit. Com.* on Romans viii. 9.

Even in the future there will be no absorption, though withal the most complete satisfaction. It is in this way that we are safeguarded against a false Mysticism due to an equally false Monism, which ignores the fact of moral evil, and therefore sets aside the redemptive element in Christianity. No doubt the problem is one of great difficulty. It has always been one of the profoundest questions, how we can conceive of an all-embracing Mind, and yet find room for free independent beings of limited knowledge. If in order to avoid Deism we endeavour to prevent the infinite and the finite from remaining in isolation, we are in danger of Pantheism, and on this theory Personality inevitably disappears and with it all distinctiveness of human nature. But every philosophical attempt to reconcile the two great realities—the Divine Immanence and the Divine Transcendence, has utterly failed, and invariably led to forms of Monism which have not only obliterated human personalities, but have underestimated and even ignored the universal consciousness of moral evil. Say what we will, human life is not normal, and the abnormality is due to what the Bible calls sin.

' The recognition of something divine in man and the recognition of something inconsistent with and contrary to that divine element in man always start up side by side. . . . Recognition of that which is of God in man, and recognition of something in man that is not of God, are always in the New Testament, the two close-lying planks in the platform of thought. . . . It is an impaired Immanence, therefore, with which the New Testament has to deal. . . . An impaired Immanence can be repaired only by and out of Transcendence.' [1]

Any view which ignores or denies this is false from the outset to the most patent and potent realities of life. And it is just here that the Christian doctrine of the Godhead enters with vital, uplifting, transforming, and satisfying power. Its attitude to sin is four-fold : it reveals, rebukes, redeems, and restores. When this is seen, we understand the statement that Immanence in the New Testament is the goal to which all else in Christianity leads up, and that the New Testament is eminently concerned with the means

[1] H. W. Clark, ' Religious History and the Idea of " Immanence," ' *Review and Expositor*, pp. 7, 8 (January, 1913).

and method of reaching that goal.[1] And so the problem of the New Testament is the entrance of God into man's life for the purpose of removing that which is wrong and bestowing that which is right. Immanence, or, rather, Fellowship, is the end, and Redemption is the means.[2] ' God was in Christ, reconciling the world to Himself,' and this reconciliation is applied to the soul by the Holy Spirit. Everything in belief and practice, in doctrine and duty, is intended to lead up to and bring about the indwelling of God in the believer. ' Christ in you the hope of glory ' is the centre of Christianity. His earthly Life, His atoning Death, His Resurrection, His Ascension, His gift of the Spirit—are all for the purpose of accomplishing this, and the great New Testament words, like Faith and Justification, which express man's attitude to God, are all so many ways of indicating our appropriation of this indwelling Christ in order to bring God into our life. Christ for us, our Atoning Sacrifice, is intended to lead up to Christ in us as our living power.[3]

And so while from one point of view we agree with Phillips Brooks that the doctrine of the Holy Spirit is a continual protest against every constantly recurring tendency to separate God from the current world, it is equally true that the doctrine of the Holy Spirit is a continual protest against every constantly recurring tendency to identify God with the world. Dr. Forsyth lately had an article on Schlatter, in which he says of that great theologian :

' He distrusts the mysticism of a natural and rationalist spirituality, of mere warm intimacy apart from a positive and creative content in the final act of God in Christ. He is, of course, a Christian mystic, as everyone must be whose citizenship is in heaven, and whose life is hid with Christ in God.' [4]

And he quotes Schlatter, who speaks of

' the central, given point of history ; to what Christ's disciples said at first ; to the fact that He is Lord. The whole theme and

---

[1] H. W. Clark, *ut supra*, p. 5.   [2] H. W. Clark, *ut supra*, p. 9.

[3] H. W. Clark, *ut supra*, pp. 27, 28.

[4] Forsyth, ' The Religious Strength of Theological Reserve,' *British Weekly*, Feb. 13, 1913.

motive of my Christology is that here a human life issued from God, lived in His service, and was hallowed to be the instrument whereby God's grace reached us unmaimed and complete.' [1]

In the Holy Spirit as the Applier of Divine Redemption which emanated from the Father, and was wrought out by the Son, we have the only and adequate safeguard against all extremes of theistic speculation, and the only and adequate guarantee of a theistic doctrine which is vital to the life of mankind.

---

[1] Forsyth, *ut supra*.

CHAPTER 25

THE HOLY SPIRIT
AND THE CHRIST OF HISTORY

THE doctrine of Divine Immanence leads naturally and inevitably to the modern problem, as it is sometimes stated, of the connection between the Jesus of History and the Christ of Experience. The greatest need of mankind is a moral dynamic. Ideas and ideals, however excellent, fail when the attempt is made to realise them. The only possibility is that of some inner power which will provide man with the secret of realising his ideals and of ' possessing his possessions ' (Obad. 17). It is the glory of Christianity that this is provided in the redemptive Person and Work of Jesus Christ. If there is one word more than another that sums up what Christianity can do for man, it is the word δύναμις, and Christ is revealed to us as the δύναμις of God (1 Cor. i. 24), and His Gospel is said to be the δύναμις of God unto salvation (Rom. i. 16). But the pressing problem is how to come in contact with the historical yet exalted Divine Person Who was revealed on earth eighteen centuries ago. It is a far cry from the life and needs of to-day to the Palestine of the first century. How can an event in time ages ago become efficacious

LITERATURE.—Mackintosh, *The Person of Jesus Christ*; Forsyth, *The Person and Place of Jesus Christ*; Denney, *Jesus and the Gospels*; Fairbairn, *The Place of Christ in Modern Theology*; Forrest, *The Christ of History and Experience*; Garvie, *Studies in the Inner Life of Jesus*; Forsyth, *The Principle of Authority*, ch. vi.; Mullins, *Freedom and Authority in Religion*, ch. ii.; Denney, *Expositor*, Eighth Series, Vol. V. p. 12, ' Christianity and the Historical Christ.' See also Bibliography in the present author's *Christianity is Christ*.

for man to-day ? Is the influence of Christ anything more than that of other commanding personalities who have left this earth ? Is His a case merely of posthumous influence ? [1] One way of answering this question is to refer us back to the Historical Christ of the Gospels in order to discover the essential features of the inner life of Jesus as the standard of our life to-day. This is the meaning of the well-known phrase, ' Back to Christ.' But we need something more than a Christ of the past. However beautiful it may be, a picture of centuries ago will not be adequate for human needs to-day. We must have a Christ for the present, and be told how the Christ of Palestine can touch, meet, and satisfy our sinful life to-day.

' If by your scholarship you so make to live again the classic scenes in which the Nazarene moved and taught that I am made painfully conscious of the long centuries that intervening divide Him from me : then all the more, if you would secure the abiding of my faith in Him, you must let me see how He can still reach *me*, and stand for *me*, the wings of His affluent personality outstretched to cover *me*.' [2]

Besides, there is an equally serious matter facing us if we attempt to realise afresh the Historical Jesus.

' Even if you got back to Christ ever so surely, it would be no gain ; you would be face to face with something which had its value and significance for its own place and time, no doubt, but something which, like all things historical, has not more than a relative and transient importance, and cannot therefore supply the basis and rule of religion which you crave.' [3]

From other quarters comes the suggestion that there is no need to concern ourselves with personality, that ideas are sufficient, and that we should concentrate our attention on them ; Love, Pity, Righteousness, Sympathy, and the like. But here again we enquire whether this really meets the need. It may suit the thinker—though even this may be doubted—but will it satisfy the average man ? If there is one thing writ large upon modern life

---

[1] In the treatment of this subject some material from the author's *Christianity is Christ* is utilised, pp. 112-120.

[2] Johnston Ross, *The Universality of Jesus*, p. 15 ff.

[3] Denney, ' Christianity and the Historical Christ,' *Expositor*, Eighth Series, Vol. V. p. 14 (January, 1913).

it is that ideas are powerless apart from Personality, and we know that the ideas of Christ were the expression of Himself, so that we must have some power of transmuting ideas into reality. It cannot be too often or too definitely emphasised that ' an ideal may charm the intellect, but it cannot satisfy the heart.' [1]

' It is in vain, however, that we seek to escape the intellectualism of Jesus the doctrinaire by the impression of Jesus the hero or saint. Ethical magnetism will not deliver us from the bondage to mere knowledge, nor from the cult of the religious genius and his illumination. The choice between Jesus the prophet and Christ the Redeemer is in the long run imperative and sharp.' [2]

Others again endeavour to solve the problem by laying all stress on personal experience as something quite independent of historical fact and criticism. It is argued that even if we knew little or nothing about the life of Christ on earth, we should still be able to experience His grace as Saviour and Friend. Now, while there is profound truth in this argument from experience, yet experience as the sole foundation of life is a very different matter, and even those who take this line are compelled to predicate some knowledge, however slight, of the Jesus of History. Experience, to be of any use, must be experience of something, and it is therefore impossible to be independent of history, or to rest content in some vague sentiment. No modern writer has put the matter more clearly than Dr. Forsyth in his emphasis upon the importance of experience and his equal insistence on its proper position and real limitations.

' We do not believe things *because* of an experience, but we do *in* an experience. They are true not *by* the experience, but *for* it.' [3]

' The great matter therefore is not *that* I feel, but *what* I feel. If I believe in Christ it is not because I *feel* Him, but because I feel *Him*.' [4]

' The real ground of our certitude, therefore, is the nature of the thing of which we are sure, rather than the nature of the experience in which we are sure.' [5]

---

[1] Quoted in Streatfeild, *The Self-Interpretation of Jesus Christ*, p. 41.

[2] Forsyth, ' Intellectualism and Faith,' *The Hibbert Journal*, Vol. XI. p. 326 (January, 1913). Also Denney, *ut supra*, p. 15.

[3] Forsyth, *The Principle of Authority*, p. 30.

[4] Forsyth, *op. cit.* p. 34. [5] Forsyth, *op. cit.* p. 58.

This shows, as Forsyth says, that experience is the medium not the canon, the sphere not the source of knowledge and certainty.[1] Our life must therefore be based upon something far more and other than experience, or else we shall be the prey of variableness of knowledge and constant flukes of conviction.

' It is not so much peace we crave, not comfort. That may be but an experience. What we crave is strength, power, confidence, a stand-by (παράκλητος)—One Who is our peace. To grasp that is faith ; and by that we live, and not by our experience as such. We live not by experience, but by something experienced, not by knowing but by being known.' [2]

' The deepest thing in human experience does not rise out of the depths of the soul, though it rises within the soul's area, but it descends from the depths of God.' [3]

The fact is that we cannot sunder the Christ of Experience from the Jesus of History without losing both, and when this is the result, our uncertainty is greater than ever.

' Nothing produces more uncertainty than a constant reference to subjective experience alone. It is detaching the Spirit from the Word, and the hour from its history. Some of the experiential Churches seem almost as much bewildered with Modernism as the authoritative Churches, when one gets below the surface. . . . In various ways religious uncertainty dogs the steps of an excessive subjectivity, such as marks an age that has just discovered the value of experience and can think of nothing else.' [4]

What, then, is the true solution of this problem ? There is vital truth in all the suggestions we have contemplated, but none of them alone is the whole truth. The solution is only found in taking all three and uniting them by means of that which gives vitality and force to them all, namely, that which is the unique feature of Christianity as a Divine revelation. In a word, the answer to our question is found in the Holy Spirit. ' He shall glorify Me.' Some time ago a thoughtful French pastor expressed to the writer great perplexity in the face of the fact that while scholars often spent years in arriving at adequate conclusions about the Jesus of the Gospels, unlettered Christian

---

[1] Forsyth, *op. cit.* pp. 66, 83.

[2] Forsyth, *op. cit.* p. 89.

[3] Forsyth, *op. cit.* p. 172. See also pp. 182, 201, 237.

[4] Forsyth, *op. cit.* p. 393.

people became convinced of the reality of Jesus Christ through experience, with scarcely any difficulty. He could not understand the reason for these very different results. ' May it not be due,' he was asked, ' to the Holy Spirit ' ? ' How so ? ' he replied, ' the Holy Spirit does not witness to a man's heart that Jesus was born in Bethlehem, lived at Nazareth, worked in Capernaum, and died in Jerusalem.' ' No,' was the answer, ' but the Holy Spirit is admittedly the Spirit of *Truth*, and the fact that He does witness to Jesus and does make Him real to the soul, and that He does *not* do this in regard to Mohammed, or Buddha, or Plato, is surely a proof that the facts about Jesus are *true*, or the Holy Spirit would not witness to them.' ' I never thought of that,' he said ; ' I believe this will resolve my difficulty.' There must be some philosophical explanation why the intuitions of faith should be capable of receiving support from the historical events of Christ's Death, Burial, and Resurrection. In a recent review in the *Times* the matter was thus summed up :

' If faith can use the facts recorded in the Gospels to justify belief in the divinity of the Person of Whom they are recorded, those facts must have a peculiar significance. There must be something in them which makes them different from other facts of history. The evangelists show this in their record of the miraculous works of the Gospel. Those works are something more than wonders. They are congruous to the character of the Worker, and signs of Divine Power existing in Him. Whatever we think about Christ, He is what He is. Faith does not create, it apprehends. It does not feed on itself ; it goes out to One Who can meet its demands and respond to its energies. But when Faith has once taken this Person as its full satisfaction, it must strive to " account " for Him.' [1]

The Holy Spirit applies Christ's redemption to the soul. He reveals the Lord Jesus in His three-fold office as Prophet, Priest, and King : Prophet to reveal ; Priest to redeem ; King to rule. This is the true solution of the relation of facts to faith. The Atonement of Christ, to which His Divine Personality gave abiding efficacy, becomes ours by the work of the Holy Spirit. It is He Who transforms the God of one time into the God for all time as He makes Him real to the receptive heart.

[1] Review of J. M. Thompson's *Through Fact to Faith*.

It is impossible to rest in any vague idea of a general Divine influence.

' The action of the Holy Spirit, an action different from the general spiritual presence of the Creator in His universe, inseparably bound up with the historic act of Jesus Christ, and differentiating that act from every other that has taken place in history, as the pointed outcrop of the Moral Act which is the soul and sustenance of things. Apart from the Holy Ghost, with His individualising and time-destroying action, there is no means of making the past present in the Christian sense.' [1]

A mere ' cosmic principle ' is wholly insufficient. While we believe and rejoice in the doctrine of the Divine Logos as the Light that ' lightens every man coming into the world,' something much more than this is required for human life. Indeed, even the Logos is mainly redemptive in Christianity, and if man is to face the facts of sin he must possess some specific spiritual power which can only come from a redemptive Divine Personality. Christ is at once Saviour, Lord, and God, and in order ' to do justice to all the phenomena with which we have to deal,' we must

' lay equal emphasis on the historical Jesus and on His exaltation into eternal life, and His perpetual presence with us through His Spirit in the very character which His history reveals.' [2]

This necessity of the Divine redemptive Personality calls for the strongest emphasis to-day. Justification and Sanctification come through the truth, apprehended and appropriated by faith, but truth is only ' as in Jesus ' (Eph. iv. 21), Who is ' the Truth ' (John xiv. 6). And faith loses its power if it be not constantly grounded on the historical fact of a Person.

' The prominent thing in Christianity is not a seer's eternal truth but a Person's eternal deed and gift. It is not the doctrine but the Cross. In the beginning was the endless Act. And the Cross is here taken not as the closing incident of the martyr life of Jesus, but, first, as the supreme action of the Son of God, and the supreme crisis of man's fate, and, second, as the eternal act of a Person thus present with us still.' [3]

---

[1] Forsyth, *op. cit.* p. 129.

[2] Denney, *op. cit.* p. 28.

[3] Forsyth, ' Intellectualism and Faith,' *The Hibbert Journal*, Vol. XI. p. 325 (January, 1913).

A spiritual life unrelated to historical Christianity is doomed to failure, and no number of references to ' the Eternal Christ ' can ever make up for the possession of the Christ of the Gospels.

' The shadowy Jesus of the new Idealism, with the Absolute Life of the Spirit in the background, as a philosophical substitute for the living God, is not likely to prove a Captain of Salvation for a sinning and perishing world. The Christ of the New Testament is a living Lord, the same yesterday, to-day, and for ever, and " this is the victory that overcometh the world, even our faith." ' [1]

We must continually return to, and rest on the facts of our faith, and for this we shall need the presence and power of the Holy Spirit Who glorifies Christ and makes Him real to the heart. Any philosophy or mysticism which endeavours to dispense with the historic Christ, and any humanitarianism which would have us rest satisfied with the human Christ, stand condemned as untrue to the New Testament revelation, and unsatisfying to the deepest needs of humanity.

One of the most striking illustrations of this is found in a well-known book, *Communion with God*, by Herrmann, who, perhaps more than any other writer of his theological school, has impressed himself by his intense devoutness on the minds and hearts of many thinkers. Yet when tested by the simple, but all-sufficient criterion of the New Testament, the presence and power of the Holy Spirit of God in human life, the inadequacy and insufficiency of Herrmann become manifest, so that even his greatest admirers are compelled to acknowledge that he falls short of the full New Testament revelation.

' I do not think Herrmann's noble and vivid picture of the action on us of the inner life of Jesus really lifts us above profound moral impressionism ; it does not give the regeneration.' [2]

Herrmann fails because he stops short with the portrait of Jesus given in the Gospels, and would have us believe that God acts upon us exactly as if Christ were now alive and acting as He did on His earliest disciples. The inadequacy of this is patent to all readers of the New Testament.

---

[1] Davison, ' Eucken on Christianity,' *London Quarterly Review*, April, 1912, p. 225.

[2] Forsyth, *op. cit.* p. 326, note.

' Herrmann seeks in vain to combine the idea that grace comes only through a person, with the contradictory idea that grace comes through a portrait. Personalized grace is the New Testament teaching everywhere.' [1]

It is only in the presence of the living Christ, mediated by the knowledge of His earthly life of redemption through the constant action of the Holy Spirit, that all the needs of mankind are met and satisfied.

' Faith is not dependent upon a bare historical judgment ; yet the historical judgment is indispensable to faith. . . . We must have the revelation of God in Christ in order to the experience. The living experience and not the historical judgment is the sphere in which the momentous issues are finally settled. Without the living experience the historical judgment would not convince. But this would not be due to lack of evidence, but to the character of the objects to which the evidence refers.' [2]

And it is the unique presence of the Spirit in His work of revealing Christ to the soul that constitutes the essential difference between Christianity and all other religions.

---

[1] Mullins, *Freedom and Authority in Religion*, p. 313.

[2] Mullins, *op. cit.* pp. 362, 363.

CHAPTER 26

THE HOLY SPIRIT
AND DEVELOPMENT

THE doctrine of an uniquely-inspired and therefore authoritative Scripture, produced and guaranteed by the Holy Spirit, has several modern bearings of great importance. One of these is concerned with the doctrine of Development. As the true view of Scripture is to regard it as embodying an unique Divine revelation of God in Christ, mediated by the Holy Spirit, it is not surprising that in St. Jude's Epistle we read of ' the faith once for all delivered ' (ver. 3), and in St. Paul of ' the deposit,' which Christians are to guard by the Holy Ghost (1 Tim. vi. 20 ; 2 Tim. i. 14). There was a definite deposit at a definite time in history, a revelation and bestowal of Christian truth from Christ to His Apostles, and then to the whole body of believers. This apostolic deposit of doctrine is now enshrined for us in the New Testament.

' The Holy Spirit that made them Apostles could but go on in the Church to open up their Word ; there was no idea of a later and parallel revelation, to say nothing of a superior, by which their Gospel could be judged and outgrown. . . . There was a close of strict Revelation, a specific revelationary period, outside which the Word revelation takes another sense, inferior and expository. . . . The New Testament, taken as a whole, is perpetually and exclusively canonical for conscience, sanctity, guilt, and grace. It does not form just the first stage of patristic literature, and of the whole classic literature projected from Christianity, but it is the authentic revelation of revelation, and projected with it as its penumbra from God. It is the revelation as truth of that revelation which appeared in Christ as historic fact and personal power. The whole issue of the Reformation is bound up with the view that there we have deposited with us an authentic but indirect interpretation from Christ Himself of the revelation direct in Him, and one final, though germinal and not statutory.' [1]

To this deposit there can be no additions, for it was ' once for all ' given. Fuller and richer interpretations there may and will be, but they will be interpretations of already-existing truth. Astronomy is continually learning of new bodies, but these have been in the heavens all through the ages. Music cannot add one single note to the scale, for the octave is the final measure of all possible tones. There can be new combinations and new melodies, but they will be produced from the existing tones. In the same way, we believe with John Robinson of Leyden that ' the Lord hath yet more light and truth to break forth from His Holy Word ' ; but it will be ' from His Holy Word,' from the already-existing embodiment of the faith once delivered. Theology, History, Philosophy can present new combinations, fresh interpretations, and additional applications, but they cannot produce new additions. Inspiration, in the unique sense of the Holy Spirit conveying a Divine revelation, ceased when the last uniquely-qualified medium delivered his last contribution to the faith of Christ. After and since then, we have illumination, but not inspiration. The New Testament is therefore unique as enshrining the absolute, final truth of Christianity once for all delivered by the Spirit to the saints.

This ' faith ' as a ' deposit ' of truth needs to be guarded, because, as then, so now, dangers imperil the integrity and reality of the deposit. One peril is that associated with the doctrine of Development, now so well known in connection with the name of Newman. His theory was set forth in support of the distinctive positions of Rome, which he claimed were the legitimate development and outcome of apostolic teaching. He laid down certain general principles by means of which development was to be tested. His requirements are seven :

1. Preservation of Type. 2. Continuity of Principle. 3. Power of Assimilation. 4. Logical Sequence. 5. Anti-

---

[1] Forsyth, *The Principle of Authority*, pp. 156, 157.

cipation of the Future. 6. Conservative action in the Past. 7. Chronic Vigour.[1]

These are all as true as they are admirable, but everything depends upon their application. We readily admit the truth of development of doctrine, whether we use the figure of an oak developing from an acorn, or the simile of a case unpacked as needed, though the former is probably more correct. But all true development will bear at least two marks : (a) Continuity, (b) Progress. There will be a clear continuity from the original germs, and an equally clear progress in harmony with those germs, and if we test the distinctive doctrines developed in Roman Catholicism by the principles laid down by Newman, it would not be difficult to see the entire baselessness of the Roman position. There is in fact a real danger of confusing between legitimate development and growth by accretion. Development from apostolic germs is as undeniable as it is necessary, but the result must bear a true relation to the germs without any admixture of foreign elements.[2] Anything else would mean growth from alien germs, planted side by side with the apostolic deposit, and this is really parasitic in tendency and inevitably means the destruction of the original germs. Herein lies the danger of the theory of Newman, as applied to Roman Catholicism, for it represents a development which is not legitimate and involves the peril of changing the apostolic deposit by addition. If we take any distinctive doctrine of Roman Catholicism, and compare it with the corresponding germinal doctrine in the New Testament, we see that the apostolic deposit has become so overlaid with erroneous additions that it has lost its true character. We can compare the teaching of Scripture with that of Rome on such subjects as the Church, the Ministry, the Sacraments, and the Mother of our Lord in order to see the vital and fundamental differences. To take two instances only : a ministry to-day which finds its essence in a sacerdotal priesthood cannot possibly be derived from an apostolic ministry which never uses the term ' priest,' and never prescribes any essentially

---

[1] *Doctrine of Development*, ch. v.

[2] Orr, *Progress of Dogma*, ch. i.

priestly functions. So a religion which speaks of the
Mother of our Lord as ' the Queen of Heaven,' addresses
her in prayer, and pleads for her interposition with her Son,
cannot find its origin in the simple statements of the New
Testament concerning the Virgin Mary. The fact is that
in the Church of Rome Scripture is no longer the sole fount
of truth and the supreme authority, but, as the Bishop
of Oxford (Dr. Gore) has said, it has become ' merged in
a miscellaneous mass of authorities.' [1]

This question of the relation of Holy Scripture to the
Church and of the Church to Scripture is of supreme
importance. We fully believe that it is impossible to
ignore Christian history and to start our consideration of
doctrine *de novo*.[2] But we also believe in the essential
identity between the product of to-day and the germ of the
first days, our criterion of this being the *litera scripta* of
the New Testament. We believe that Holy Scripture, as
therein found, constitutes the title-deeds of the Church,
the law of the Church's life, the test of its purity, the source
of its strength, and the spring of its progress.

But it may be said, How can this be when the Church
existed many years before a line of the New Testament was
written ? This is historically true. But if we are intended
to learn from it the supremacy of the Church, the conclusion does not necessarily follow. At any rate we must
examine the position somewhat carefully. It is assumed
that the Church had no Bible in the Apostolic Age, and
that the Bible came historically after the Church, authorised
by the Church. But the Church had a Bible from the
outset, the Old Testament Scriptures, and such was their
power that St. Paul could say that with the single but
significant addition of ' faith in Christ Jesus ' these Old
Testament Scriptures were ' able to make wise unto
salvation ' (2 Tim. iii. 15).

' It is sometimes said, and an important truth lies concealed
under the phrase, that the Church existed before the Bible. But
a Christian of the earliest days, if you had used such words to him,
would have stared at you in undisguised amazement. He would

---

[1] Gore, *The Body of Christ*, p. 223.
[2] Swete, *The Holy Spirit in the Ancient Church*, p. 4.

have explained to you that in the Law and the Prophets and the Psalms the Christian possessed all the Scriptures he could want, for they all spoke of Christ.' [1]

But leaving this aside, the argument that because the Church was before Scripture, therefore it is above Scripture, is really fallacious. It is perfectly true that the Church existed before the *written* Word of the New Testament, but we must remember that first of all there was the *spoken* Word of God through Christ and His inspired Apostles. On the Day of Pentecost the Word of God was spoken, the revelation of God in Christ was proclaimed, and on the acceptance of that Word the Church came into existence. The Word was proclaimed, the Word was accepted, and so the Church was formed on the Word of God. As long as the Apostles were at hand the spoken Word sufficed, but as time went on and the Apostles travelled and afterwards died, there sprang up the need of a permanent embodiment of the Divine Revelation, and this was given in the written Word. From that time forward, in all ages, the written Word has been the equivalent of the original spoken Word. The Church was created by the Word of God received through faith. The Word created the Church, not the Church the Word.

We see the very same process in the mission field. There was a Church in most places through the spoken Word long before the written Word could be given, but now the written Word is at once the foundation and guarantee of the Church's existence and progress.

' In the history of the world the unwritten Word of God must of course be before the Church. For what is a Church (in the wider sense of the word) but a group of believers in God's Word? And before the Word is spoken, how can there be believers in it? "Faith cometh by hearing, and hearing by the Word of God." Therefore the Word of God must be before faith. It is only of the Bible, or written volume of God's oracles, assuredly not of God's spoken Word, that we assert it to have been brought into existence later than the Church.' [2]

---

[1] C. H. Turner, *The Journal of Theological Studies*, October, 1908, p. 14.

[2] Goulburn, *Holy Catholic Church* ; quoted in *Four Foundation Truths*, p. 13.

The Apostles may be regarded as representatives of Christ or as members of the Church. It was in the former, not the latter aspect that they conveyed first the spoken Word, and then the written Word of God which has ever been the source of all Christian life.

'Our authority is not the Church of the first century, but the apostles who were its authority. The Church does not rest on its inchoate stages (which would poise it on its apex) but on its eternal foundation—a Christ Who, in His apostolic Self-Revelation, is the same deep Redeemer always.' [1]

'We have a variety of opinions and sections in the first *Church*, but I am speaking of *the representative apostles*, and of the New Testament as their register and index. The Church of the ages was not founded by the Church of the first century, but by the apostles as the organs of Christ. We are in the apostolic succession rather than in the ecclesiastic. It is not the first Church that is canonical for us Protestants, but the apostolic New Testament.' [2]

The function of a Rule of Faith is the conveyance of the Divine authority to men, and this Rule of Faith existed in the mind of Christ and His Apostles long before it existed as a written work. Accordingly it precedes and conditions the existence of the Church. The Church is to the Word a witness and a keeper. The Church bears testimony to what Scripture is, and at the same time preserves Scripture among Christian people from age to age.

But though the Church is a 'witness and keeper,' it is not the *author* or *maker* of Scripture, and the reasoning employed in support of the latter contention is fallacious. It seems to be as follows :

'The Apostles were the authors of Holy Scripture.'
'But all Apostles are members of the Church of Christ.'
'Therefore, the Church of Christ is the author of Scripture.'

This has been well compared to the following :

'Mr. Balfour wrote a book on *The Foundations of Belief.*
'Mr. Balfour is a member of the Privy Council.'
'Therefore, the Privy Council is the author of the book called *The Foundations of Belief.*' [3]

The mistake of course lies in attributing to a body in its collective capacity certain acts of individual members

---

[1] Forsyth, *op. cit.* p. 96.

[2] Forsyth, *op. cit.* p. 142. See also pp. 146-155.

[3] Rev. C. H. Waller, D.D.

of the body. The Church is not, and never was, the author of Scripture. The Scriptures are the law of God for the Church, delivered to her by the Apostles and Prophets. We must ever distinguish between the *record* of God's revelation in the Bible and the *witness* to that revelation as seen in the fact and history of the Church of Christ. The function of the Christian Church as the ' witness and keeper of Holy Writ ' is exactly parallel to that of the Jewish Church in relation to the Old Testament. The Prophets who were raised up from time to time as the messengers and mouthpieces of Divine Revelation delivered their writings of the Old Testament to the Jews, who thereupon preserved them, and thenceforward bore their constant testimony to the reality and authority of the Divine Revelation embodied in the books.

And so the Church of Christ, whether regarded in her corporate capacity or in connection with individual members, is not the author of Holy Scripture. The Church received the Scriptures from the Lord Jesus Christ by the Holy Spirit through His Apostles and Prophets, and now the function of the Church is to witness to the fact that these are the Scriptures of the Apostles and Prophets which she has received and of which she is also the keeper and their preserver through the ages for use by the people of God. We could not wish for anything clearer than the statement of the Anglican Article XX. as to the relation of the Bible and the Church.

It will help our thought if we ever keep in view that strictly speaking it is the Lord Jesus Christ Who is our Authority, and that we accept the Bible because it enshrines the purest, clearest form of our Lord's Divine Revelation. What we mean is that the Church is not our highest authority because it is not our highest authority for the revelation of Christ. And we say the Bible is our supreme authority, because it is our highest authority for the historic revelation of Christ. If Christ is the Source of our religious knowledge, then the condition of our knowing Him centuries after His historical appearance is that we must know *of* Him, and for this perpetuation and transmission we must have an objective body of historical testimony. The superiority of the Bible is due to the fact that it gives this fixed, objective, final revelation of Christ. This is the sum and substance of the Gospel, the Person of Christ. The great outstanding objective fact of history is the supernatural, superhuman, unique, Divine Figure of Christ, and this Figure is enshrined for us in the written word. We cling to Scripture ultimately on this ground alone. Take away Christ from the Bible and it ceases to be an unique Book and our authority in religion. In view of the history of the Church, it is impossible to maintain that the authority of the Church can ever be identified with Christ's. We can identify Christ's authority with God's, but not the Church's with Christ's, and it is nothing less than a Divine authority that we need for life.

This question of the Bible and the Church has a special application in regard to what is known as Church Tradition. The Church of Rome puts Tradition, that is, Church beliefs, customs, usages, on a level with Scripture as the Rule of Faith. But the Church of England, while valuing such testimony in its proper place, refuses to co-ordinate the two. The moral authority of the universal Church is of course weighty and powerful, and when the whole Church through the ages testifies to doctrines like the Godhead of Christ, no individual Christian can lightly reject them. But this after all is only the work of a witness to an ultimate and original authority. We put the Bible high above all else as our supreme authority in things essential, and as the Bishop of Birmingham (now of Oxford) said at the Bristol Church Congress (1903), ' the Word of God in the Bible is the only final testing-ground of doctrine.'

The Anglican Article XX. tells us that the Church has ' power to decree rites or ceremonies, and authority in Controversies of Faith.' The word ' power ' (Latin, *jus*), implies full legal right to appoint and order any ceremonies or methods of worship that may be regarded as fitting and appropriate, so long as nothing is ordained contrary to Holy Scripture. In Controversies of Faith, however, it is to be noticed that the Church has not this full legal right, but only ' authority ' (Latin, *auctoritas*), which means the moral authority arising out of the testimony of the Church as a whole throughout the ages. The ultimate court of appeal must of necessity be the spiritually enlightened judgment of the individual Christian with reference to any and every matter of truth and conscience. This is the inalienable right of the individual, whether like the Protestant he exercises it continually and directly from the Bible, or whether like the Roman Catholic he exercises it once for all in deciding to submit himself to an external organisation which he believes to be an infallible guide. But the individual judgment of a believer must continually be checked and safeguarded by the continuous consensus of Christian opinion and practice, and it is part of our Christian discipline to combine properly the spiritual right of the individual believer and the moral authority of the Christian community. For all practical purposes very little difficulty will be found in this connection.

This position of the supreme authority of the Bible over Tradition is the assertion of the historic basis of Christianity. Sabatier truly says :

' It is a historic law that every tradition not fixed in writing changes in the process of development.' [1]

The Bishop of Oxford points this out in connection with the history of the Jews.[2] He shows that the lesson we ought to learn from the Jewish Church is that a real religious authority can be so seriously misused as to become misleading. Further, that this failure in the old covenant ought to have been a warning to those in authority in Christianity. They ought to have been more thoroughly on their guard against anything that would tend to detract from the constant appeal to Scripture and the supreme and unique model of Christian truth.[3] Dr. Gore believes that the ancient Church did on the whole faithfully recur to Scripture in this way, but that everything became changed in the mediaeval Church.

' The specific appeal to the Scriptures of the New Testament to verify or correct current tendencies is gone. . . . The safeguard has vanished.' [4]

---

[1] Sabatier, *The Religions of Authority and the Religion of the Spirit*, p. 40.

[2] Gore, *The Body of Christ*, p. 220.

[3] Gore, *op. cit.* p. 222.   [4] Gore, *op. cit.* p. 223.

There is perhaps nothing more patent or certain in the progress of history, whether secular or sacred, than the untrustworthiness of Tradition without some historic and literary safeguard.

' Tradition is utterly unsafe. The Roman Catholic doctrine of tradition is the concrete proof of the assertion. Unwritten tradition is always coloured and transformed by the medium through which it passes. An unwritten Gospel would be subject to all the fluctuations of the spiritual life of man and most likely to gravitate downward from the spiritual to the carnal and formal. Institutions may symbolize or embody truth, but without a written standard they always tend to become external means of grace, or sacraments. They are ladders on which we may climb up or down. Without a corrective it is usually down.' [1]

This position of the supremacy of the Bible is the charter of spiritual freedom. It would seem as though some believe that the function of the Church is to settle definitely every question of difficulty as it arises, but no trace is found of any such view, whether in Scripture or in the Creeds, or in early Church history. It would have been perfectly easy for the Church to summon a Council when any dispute arose and settle the question by a majority, but no hint of such action can be found. On the contrary, we know that after the Council of Nicaea, a struggle went on for many years before the decisions of that Assembly were thoroughly accepted. The great authority of the first four General Councils is acknowledged by all, and their doctrinal standards are the heritage of the Christian Church to-day. Yet even their decisions were accepted only because they immediately and readily commended themselves to the judgment of the whole Church as in accordance with Divine revelation. It cannot be questioned that it was not the simple decision of a Council, but its subsequent endorsement by the whole Christian world, that constituted the real test of universality. Besides, the Councils were not so much intended to settle what belief ought to be, as what it had been from the beginning. The Councils were landmarks rather than goals. It is along this line that the Church of England accepts the authority of General Councils, for ' things ordained by them as

---

[1] Mullins, *Freedom and Authority in Religion*, p. 349.

necessary to salvation have neither strength nor authority, unless it may be declared that they be taken out of Holy Scripture.' General Councils, however, have expressed themselves on a few matters only, and do not offer any help on the many problems of life on which the soul needs guidance. It is hardly realised how little we should know for certain, if we were strictly limited to these Conciliar judgments. Consequently, the final decision must be made by the spiritually illuminated Christian consciousness guided by the Word of God, and advised by every possible channel of knowledge available.

While, therefore, we cannot for a moment co-ordinate tradition with Scripture, we do not hesitate to appeal to it whenever possible and necessary. The testimony of the primitive Church is in many ways valuable, but there is a wide difference between the Roman Catholic and the Protestant appeals to tradition.

' Leibnitz, at the end of the seventeenth century, asked if the Catholic dogma of tradition rested on the notion of a complete revelation of truth, exceeding what was in Scripture and was conveyed to the apostolic age, or upon the hypothesis of a continuous inspiration of the Church in regard to such Scripture truth. In the latter case he said it would be very hard to define the features required in such an infallible organ of tradition ; in the former case all the traditions of the Church could not be traced to an apostolic authority. Tradition is either an exposition of apostolic doctrine or an addition to it. If an exposition, how is it to be shown that the Reformation branch *of the Church* was wrong ; if an addition, what becomes of the claim for the apostolicity of all Catholic doctrine ? Since the time of Leibnitz papal infallibility has been defined indeed ; but in the forty years since 1870 it has never been exercised. It is an invention that is specified and patented, but does not work.' [1]

Rome appeals to tradition for official sanction ; we appeal for information on questions of fact. Rome appeals to tradition as to a judge for authoritative decisions on questions which the individual is unable or unwilling to decide for himself ; we appeal to tradition as to a witness for evidence which is regarded as credible and which we can weigh for ourselves. Rome asks for the opinion of the Church in order to make it hers ; we seek for information

---

[1] Forsyth, *op. cit.* p. 320.

from which to form our own opinion. It is evident, there-fore, that to accept decision without weighing it is really to surrender our judgment, while to require evidence is to assert our judgment. We are always grateful if we can obtain the consensus of Church opinion, but its use is as historical evidence, and not as that which settles the matter apart from consideration.

When this is clearly realised it removes all objections to what is often scornfully described as ' private judgment.' It *is* this, but it is very much more. It is the decision of the judgment, the conscience, and the will of the man who desires to know and follow the truth, who finds the source and embodiment of truth in the Scripture, and bows in submission to it. He does not separate himself from or set himself above the corporate Christian consciousness of his own and previous ages, so far as he can determine what that corporate consciousness teaches, but while welcoming and weighing truth from all sides, he feels that Scripture is the supreme and final authority for his life.

' As a matter of fact, the unlimited right of private judgment is not a fruit of the Reformation but of the Renaissance and of the Revolution with their wild individualism. It is Socinian and rationalist, it is not Protestant. The Reformation certainly made religion personal, but it did not make it individualist. The Reforma-tion, if it destroyed the hierarchy of the Church, did not destroy the hierarchy of competency, spiritual or intellectual. In a political democracy we speak of one vote, one value ; but in the intellectual and spiritual region all opinions are not of equal worth ; nor have they all an equal right to attention. What the Reformation said was that the layman with his Bible in his hand had at his side the same Holy Spirit as the minister. Each had the testimony of the Spirit as the supreme religious Expositor of Scripture.' [1]

This position is abundantly justified on several grounds. It comes to us with the example of our Lord, Who constantly appealed to the Scriptures as the touchstone of truth. It is that which is the most consonant with the nature of our personality and its responsibility to God. It is the assertion of our indefeasible right to be in direct personal relation to God, while welcoming all possible light from every available quarter as helping us to decide for ourselves

---

[1] Forsyth, *op. cit.* p. 320.

under the guidance of God's Word and Spirit. This position has also ever been productive of the finest characters, and the noblest and truest examples of individual and corporate Christian life. We have only to compare those countries like South America and Spain, where the opposite principle of Church authority and supremacy has had undisputed sway for centuries, to see the truth of this statement.

Once again let it be said that we do wisely and well in giving to the universal voice and testimony of the Church (wherever and in so far as it can be discovered), the utmost possible weight, for no individual will lightly set aside such united and universal belief ; but the last and final authority must be the Word of God illuminating, influencing, and controlling the human conscience and reason through the presence and power of the Spirit of God.

The warrant for regarding this authority as sufficient is that we base it, first, on the claim of Scripture itself. The Old Testament could not of course claim finality for itself as a whole, because of its gradual growth from separate authors, but we can see throughout the process the claim of the prophets to authority and inspiration, and the New Testament certainly sets its seal retrospectively on the finality of the Old Testament. Similarly the New Testament could not claim final authority for itself as a whole, but we can see clearly from the words of Christ and His Apostles that they claimed this for themselves. Indeed, the finality of the New Testament is implicit throughout in its whole matter and manner. The general tone and attitude of a parent are much more effective for authority than any number of specific reminders by *verbal* assertions. No one can doubt the claim of Scripture to finality by its whole attitude to man's life.

We base it, next, on the testimony of Church History. The general tenor of Patristic Testimony is in this direction.

' The ancient Church did faithfully and continually recur to this pattern, and faithfully recognised the limitation of its function. It is evident how constant is the effect of the scriptural pattern, on which they are mainly occupied in commenting, in moulding and restraining the teaching of Origen and Chrysostom and Augustine. The appeal to Scripture is explicit and constant. These fathers knew that they existed simply to maintain a once-given teaching, and that the justification of any dogma was simply the necessity for guarding the faith once for all delivered and recorded. There can be no doubt of their point of view.' [1]

Every heresy in the early Church claimed to be based on Scripture. The most severe attacks of opponents were always directed against Scripture. The ancient liturgies are saturated with Scripture. Indeed, the whole history of the Church tells the same story. If there is one fact plainer than another in Christian history it is that Christ does not fully reveal Himself apart from and independent of knowledge and study of Holy Scripture. Whenever the Bible has been neglected, the reality of Christ's presence has been obscured, and as often as men have come back to Scripture, Christ has again become real. It is sometimes said that Protestantism substituted the idea of an infallible Book for the older Roman dogma of an infallible Church. But the antithesis though clever is fallacious. The idea of Scripture is, as we have already seen, not younger, but older than Romanism. It is not a late invention of Protestantism, but the original idea which is found in Scripture itself, and which was acted on by the Church from the first. As a body of Divinely authoritative writings the books of the Old and the New Testaments were accepted by the post-apostolic age, and the writings of the early Fathers are full of examples of the way in which they used these writings as the ultimate authority on the matters of which they speak.

It is incorrect, therefore, to say that we are shut up to the Roman Catholic view of supreme authority, or to pure subjectivity.[2] On the contrary, we believe that there is a real and constant authority in Scripture to which Christian men can make an appeal.[3] The effects of Scripture on human life are ample proofs of this contention. There is nothing required for the spiritual life of all men, at all times, in all places which is not found in Scripture. There is enough in Scripture to guide every honest soul from time to eternity. There is an answer in Scripture to every vital and essential question of the soul regarding salvation,

---

[1] Gore, *op. cit.* pp. 222, 223. [2] Mullins, *op. cit.* pp. 31, 41.
[3] Mullins, *op. cit.* pp. 370-375.

holiness, and immortality.   Even its accessibility can
be adduced in evidence.   Here is a Book, easily obtained,
quickly read, and adequate to every conceivable circumstance, and to the soul that receives it, it affords its own
blessed and satisfying proofs.   Surely there is something
remarkable in the simple fact that the soul needs nothing
that is not derived thence for spiritual life and power.
We say, therefore, that the Bible is adequate as a spiritual
authority ; that it is neither insufficient nor obscure ; that
it is not necessary to go to the early Church to clear it of
obscurity, or to supplement its inadequacy.   It is not to
be supplanted by any organisation or personage, and is
not to be supplemented by tradition, whether primitive
or current.

It might seem at first sight that this discussion of the
relations between the Church and the Bible has very little
to do with our present subject of the Holy Spirit.   But
in reality the two questions bear directly on each other
and are inextricably bound up together.   This consideration of the supreme place of the Bible presupposes and
demands the presence and power of the Holy Spirit as the
Author of God's revelation for human life.   In the light
of what has been said [1] of the special and unique work
of the Holy Spirit in the provision of Scripture as the
inspired Word of God, it is clear that the Bible constitutes
the primary, fundamental and constant test of all development which claims to be Christian.   If the Holy Spirit
so inspired the writers of the Bible as to give for all ages
an unique expression of the will of God, it necessarily
follows that the Divine will embodied in Holy Scripture
is the final court of appeal and rules out everything that
is regarded by any Church as ' requisite or necessary to
salvation ' if it is ' not read therein nor may be proved
thereby ' (Anglican Article VI.).   In every aspect of
Church life, either of thought or of practice, which may
be considered as vital and essential, the Scripture inspired
by the Spirit is supreme, and it is therefore the constant
remembrance of the unique work of the Holy Spirit in
inspiration that alone can prove an adequate protection

---

[1] Ch. xx. *The Spirit of Truth*, p. 147.

and safeguard against the errors and dangers connected with ecclesiastical and all other forms of development. As we shall see still more clearly in the next chapter, on an allied subject, the root of many of our troubles is the practical severance of the Holy Spirit from the Scriptures, and the virtual ignoring of the presence and power of the Spirit as the Revealer and Interpreter of spiritual truth. When the two are kept together, the Spirit using the Word and speaking through It, the result is assured and authoritative for all Christian life. This great truth of the supremacy and sufficiency of Holy Scripture may be summed up in the words of the Apostle Paul, who, speaking of the Old Testament (though the words are still truer of the New Testament books), says 'All Scripture is given by inspiration of God (*lit.* God-breathed), and is profitable for doctrine, for reproof, for correction, for instruction in righteousness ; that the man of God may be perfect, throughly furnished unto all good works' (2 Tim. iii. 16f.).

CHAPTER 27

THE HOLY SPIRIT AND MODERNISM

THE relation of the doctrine of Development to Christianity can be seen still more definitely in the way in which the movement known as Modernism has at once adopted and departed from Newman's theory. What Newman used for ecclesiastical purposes against Protestantism, Modernists apply all round to justify their position of continuance in the Roman Catholic Church while claiming freedom in regard to its distinctive doctrines. Modernism began by the realisation on the part of certain Roman Catholic scholars that in the critical knowledge of Holy Scripture and even in questions of history and philosophy, the Church of Rome was far behind the scholarship of the day, and was still relying upon the philosophy and history of past ages, With a splendid courage and an evident confidence in the fundamental truths of their Church's position, these scholars determined to learn from their opponents. They realised that the traditional method of apologetics was no longer sufficient, that it was in their judgment useless to continue to assert that the Roman Catholic religion was developed logically from a ' deposit ' of the faith committed by Jesus Christ to His immediate followers, because modern scholarship was held to be proving by the evidence of history and archaeology that the characteristic features of Christianity were derived from many sources in the course of

LITERATURE.—Garvie, *The Christian Certainty amid the Modern Perplexity*, ch. xvi., ' Modernism.' Tyrrell, *Through Scylla and Charybdis* ; *Christianity at the Cross-Roads*. *The Programme of Modernism*.

the Christian centuries. It was thus that men like Loisy attempted to defend the position of Roman Catholicism against German scholarship as represented by Harnack. The result was soon seen in a view of Christianity which was dominated entirely by the theory of evolution. The original ideas of the New Testament were said to have become modified in the course of time, and the Jesus of history had been developed into the glorified Christ of faith, as the germinal idea assimilated materials from every side wherever the religion spread. This, it was pointed out, had gone on through the centuries, till at length, by the end of the thirteenth century, the Church found itself safely protected by the citadel built by the great Schoolmen. Modernism now holds that this scholastic philosophy, based on Aristotle, has served its purpose and must be left behind or set aside in the onward march of thought ; and that Christianity, if it is to live, must continue to become modified and to adjust itself to every changing environment.

This is the position, and the leaven is at work everywhere in the Roman Catholic Church. On one side Modernism stands for a religious democracy. Father Tyrrell puts this with his accustomed clearness :

'One thing, at least, is certain, that democracy has come to stay ; that to the generations of the near future any other conception of authority will be simply unthinkable ; that if the authority of Popes, Councils, and Bishops cannot be reinterpreted in that sense, it is as irrevocably doomed as the theologies of man's childhood. The receptivity of the general mind is a fact that priesthoods have to reckon with, and always do reckon with in the long run. They cease to say, nay, they cease to believe, that to which the general ear has become permanently deaf. They would fain seem to lead, but, in fact, they follow the spirit in its developments ; for it is there, and there only, that truth is worked out.' [1]

On the other hand, Modernism claims to have a definite relation to Roman Catholic dogma. It desires to think with absolute freedom, and yet to deny nothing which Rome teaches. But the story of Tyrrell's life shows that such a position is really untenable. To have freedom of thought and yet to accept what Rome teaches is to draw a

---

[1] *Through Scylla and Charybdis*, p. 381.

distinction between religious and historical truth which is impossible. Suppose, for example, a Modernist scholar were ready to accept the New Testament teaching of the Lord's Supper as an institution commemorative of the death of Jesus Christ ; would it be possible for such a one to hold the distinctive Roman Catholic doctrine of transubstantiation ? Or suppose the same scholar were to accept the New Testament account of the Virgin Mary in its simplicity, would it be a logical and inevitable result that he should teach and practise the adoration of the Queen of Heaven ? As a matter of fact, leading Modernists distinguish between the Historical Christ and the Mystical Christ ; the Christ of Reason and the Christ of Faith ; between the mortal life of Christ in the Gospels, and His spiritual life in the faithful. The following proofs from *The Programme of Modernism* could easily be increased.

' The results of Biblical and historical criticism . . . have necessitated a distinction between the outward history and the inward history, between the historical Christ and the mystical Christ, the Christ of reason and the Christ of faith ' (p. 25). ' The Gospel story is the result of two opposite tendencies—one toward the material truth of fact, the other toward a higher order of truth than that of historical exactitude ' (p. 75). ' Faith-truth is not always historical truth, but often only historical fiction. And, therefore, since it is faith-truth that governs the Gospels from beginning to end, we must not expect to find historical truth as well. It is found in different measures in different Gospels ; most of all in Mark, least of all in John ' (p. 76).

' The mortal life of Christ, as evident to the senses, is an object of history. His spiritual life in the faithful and in the Church can only be known by means of the experiences of faith. But this second kind of life can be at least represented under a historical form ; and this gives rise not only to a distinction but to a separation between the historical Christ and the Christ of faith. The supernatural life of Christ in the Church has expressed itself outwardly in conformity with outward circumstances, and has thus gradually given birth to permanent ecclesiastical institutions. Now the Evangelists, in order better to signify the dependence of these institutions on the Spirit of Christ, have thrown their origin back into the very history of the mortal life of Jesus. . . . And, therefore, criticism does well to distinguish between what is history proper and what is merely a historical form of representing those supernatural facts which the Church's faith has brought forth ' (pp. 81, 82). ' The title " Son of God," which in Hebrew was synonymous with the Messiah, once transferred to Greek soil, where parentage between gods and heroes was a common belief, opened the road to the notion of a unique relation between Christ and the Father ' (p. 99).

And the same distinction is drawn in the case of almost every characteristic doctrine of Christianity. Thus one of the English interpreters of the Modernist Movement puts the matter as follows :

' The dogma of the Personality of God may not add to our speculative knowledge of the nature of God ; but it serves to direct that practical knowledge of Him which is the only knowledge that religion is concerned with. It says in effect to us : " Conduct yourselves in your relations with God as you would in your relations with a human person." In the same way, the dogma of the Resurrection of Jesus does not add to our knowledge of the new life which Jesus lived after death or to the manner of the transformation of the old life into the new. But it says to us : " Let your relations to Him now be what they would have been before His death, or what they are to your own contemporaries." And, again, the dogma of the Real Presence conveys to us no knowledge of the modality of that presence. But it enjoins upon us the necessity of preserving in the presence of the consecrated Host such an attitude of spirit as we should feel in the presence of Jesus Himself if He were visible to us.' [1]

It ought to be obvious that this method of interpretation cannot possibly be accepted by any natural, we will not say orthodox, view of the New Testament. The truth is that Modernism is a philosophy based on critical theories, which the upholders endeavour in vain to harmonise with the Christianity of the New Testament, or with the dogmas of the Roman Church. When Tyrrell speaks of ' Catholicism ' as ' Divine with the Divinity of a natural process ' we can easily see the drift and tendency of the movement. If the conception of evolution is to be applied without limit, it is hard to see where any place can be found either for the Fall or for the Incarnation. The distinction between the Christ of Fact and the Christ of Faith is utterly impossible if we would retain a Christ that is historical, or indeed, any Christianity at all. To illustrate once again from *The Programme of Modernism* :

' It matters little to faith whether or no criticism can prove the virgin-birth of Christ, His more striking miracles, or even His resurrection ; whether or no it sanctions the attribution to Christ of certain dogmas or of the direct institution of the Church. As

---

[1] Lilley, *Modernism.*

ultra-phenomenal, these former facts evade the grasp of experimental and historical criticism, while of the latter it finds, as a fact, no proof. But both these and those possess a reality for faith superior to that of physical and historical facts.'

It ought to be evident that such a position is not congruous with the primitive Christianity of the New Testament. It is impossible to find the real worth of Christianity in what it is now rather than in what it was at first, or to think that the essential truth lies in to-day's view rather than in apostolic teaching. The present age is no more infallible, and has no more promise of finality than those which have preceded it, and there must be some criterion of truth to which we can appeal. Revelation is a reality in history and not a mere evolution of opinion. Christianity is bound by its past, and while there is, and must be, development, the later stages must not contradict the earlier.

' The fascinating movement known as Modernism, which engages the very *élite* of the Roman Church, is drawn almost entirely to the rationalist, the illuminationist, the Socinian side of Protestantism, which in all matters of criticism and thought has influenced it very greatly. But it seems not only uninfluenced by the great evangelical theologians or discussions, old or new, it seems quite ignorant of them—almost as ignorant of them as its enemy, Curialism, is of rationalism. And in so far as it knows them, it dislikes them. . . . Some of the most able and genial writing of the Modernist School goes back with a clear somersault over the Reformation to the mediaeval idea of mystic love, as if the evangelical idea of faith were but a negligible aberration, justification a juridical fiction, and the Protestant movement the black sheep of the Christian family which it was charity to wrap in silence.' [1]

Besides, the essence of the Modernist position is intellectual rather than spiritual, a question of ideas rather than of experience, of thought rather than of redemption.

' Modernism, dropping much even of the teaching of Jesus, and almost indifferent to His history, seeks to keep the Church alive on its dogmas taken as ideas, on truth emptied of the person yet treated as the power. But, however modern, that theology is simply exchanging old lamps, old clothes, old views for new. For it is a case of views or truths either way, new or old, narrow or broad ; and it is not a case of act and deed in the heart of universal reality.' [2]

---

[1] Forsyth, *The Principle of Authority*, pp. 78, 79.

[2] Forsyth, ' Intellectualism and Faith,' *The Hibbert Journal*, p. 323 (January, 1913).

But to say this is to record the futility of Modernism for ordinary human life. Critical scholarship is one thing, human redemption is another, and the attempt to sublimate Christianity into a set of ideas suited to the naturalistic tendencies of to-day will not minister to the deepest needs of the human race. It cannot be too strongly emphasised that Modernism

' can never permanently capture or hold the western mind ; it is too far away from obvious facts, reaches such unity as it possesses merely by shutting its eyes to what declines to be included, and leaves no sufficient scope for that palpitating activity and that legitimate delight in responsibility from which true manhood declines even in supreme concerns (or rather, most of all in supreme concerns) to be severed.' [1]

It is not difficult to see that granted the Modernist premisses the inevitable conclusion will be something far removed, not merely from Roman Catholicism, but from Christianity itself. A careful reading of Tyrrell's *Autobiography and Life* seems to show that his latest views would not have been his last if his life had been prolonged. The acceptance of the evolutionary theory, when pressed with Tyrrell's remorseless logic, cannot end without the removal of the most distinctive, supernatural elements of Christianity. If there is one truth more than another ' writ large ' on Tyrrell's *Life*, it is that not Christianity, but George Tyrrell was ' at the Cross Roads.'

The serious fact in most, if not all discussions is the absence of any real reference to the Holy Spirit in relation to the deposit of faith. It is essential to notice how seldom His work is mentioned ; indeed, there are few more significant facts than the relative neglect of the Holy Spirit in the system of the Roman Catholic Church. And yet if we recall His place in the provision of the deposit, it ought not to be difficult to notice three things that He is constantly doing for that deposit. (*a*) It is the province of the Holy Spirit to preserve the deposit in its pristine purity. Tradition, as we have already seen, is notoriously uncertain and inaccurate, and tends inevitably to impurity, but the Holy Spirit, working on and with Scripture, will keep

[1] H. W. Clark, ' Religious History and the Idea of " Immanence," ' *Review and Expositor*, p. 25 (January, 1913).

Christianity pure. (b) The Holy Spirit guarantees the proper continuity of Christianity. It is inevitable that the mind will think and explore, but there may be an assimilation of alien ideas which only the Holy Spirit, using and applying Scripture, can prevent. (c) The Holy Spirit effects and guides the legitimate development of Christianity. Christian doctrine, to be kept true, must not be evolved merely by the ordinary processes of human thought and experience. The true test of all development is harmony with the apostolic deposit. The Vincentian canon, *id quod ubique, quod semper, quod ab omnibus*, is only applicable in part, because of the impossibility of arriving at what was actually believed, ' *ubique semper et ab omnibus.*' We believe the original deposit was at once the germ and ' the compressed totality ' of all true Christian doctrine. But we do not on this account believe that *all* the ideas of later ages are ' the natural outcome ' of the teaching of Christ and His Apostles. These ideas need to be constantly checked and tested by reference to the original deposit. While we hold that everything that is true in Christianity to-day was ' latent in the original teaching,' we do not believe that it was only awaiting any Conciliar or Papal announcement to bring it forth. On the contrary, we believe that the whole Church, when full of the Holy Spirit, brings forth from the treasure house of truth things new and old, and by the superintendence of the same Spirit will be preserved from the perils of addition or modification. We welcome all the helps that modern life can give, but we believe that these will only be interpretative and illuminative, not creative. While we claim the fullest possible freedom for the human mind to work, yet it is a freedom to be continually associated with the original deposit of truth and the indwelling presence of the Spirit of God.

' The effect of a real authority upon personality is the most kindling and educative influence it can know. In the interior of the soul authority and freedom go hand in hand.' [1]

The Church cannot be separated from the Gospel which Christ revealed and wrought, and the authority of the

---

[1] Forsyth, *The Principle of Authority*, p. 322.

Church is only of value in so far as it declares and adheres to that Gospel in its purity and fulness.[1] We believe in the Holy Spirit as Christ's representative on earth, the sole Applier of His redemption.[2] It is only in Him that Christ is made real to the soul and to the Church. When this becomes a definite spiritual experience ; when the soul surrenders to Christ, and the Spirit makes Christ known, then, and then only, do we begin to realise and enjoy the essential verities and Divine grace of the Gospel of Christ.

---

[1] Forsyth, *op. cit.* p. 329. [2] Forsyth, *op. cit.* p. 328.

CHAPTER 28

THE HOLY SPIRIT AND MYSTICISM

THE New Testament doctrine of the Holy Spirit has a definite bearing on various modern movements to which is given the general designation of Mysticism. What does this mean? If we interpret it in the New Testament sense of personal fellowship with God, the direct contact of the soul with God in Christ, it of course represents an essential and profound truth of Christianity. The very heart of the Pauline Gospel is found in the truth of the indwelling Christ, and the identification of Christ with the believer. 'I am crucified with Christ: nevertheless I live; yet not I, but Christ liveth in me: and the life which I now live in the flesh I live by the faith of the Son of God, Who loved me, and gave Himself for me' (Gal. ii. 20). 'Christ in you, the hope of glory' (Col. i. 27.) 'Strengthened with might by His Spirit in the inner man; that Christ may dwell in your hearts by faith' (Eph. iii. 16, 17). But it is, to say the least, unfortunate, that the term 'Mysticism,' which has so many other uses, should be employed to express this essential feature of the true Christian life.[1] Assuming for the moment that this is what is meant by the word, we are able to see not merely its reality as an

---

[1] Garvie, *The Christian Certainty amid the Modern Perplexity*, p. 177.

LITERATURE.—Davison, *The Indwelling Spirit*, chs. xv., xvi.; Garvie, *The Christian Certainty amid the Modern Perplexity*, chs. xi., xiii., xiv., xvii.; Hodgkin, *The Trial of our Faith*, ch. x. 'George Fox'; Grubb, *Authority and the Light Within*; Forsyth, *Faith, Freedom, and the Future*, chs. i.-vi.; Fleming, *Mysticism in Christianity*.

integral and essential part of Christianity, but its practical value in more than one direction. In relation to doctrine, it tends to preserve the life from pure intellectualism, theological severity, and dogmatic rigidity. The mellowing power of a consciousness of Christ's presence in the soul is a preservative against any mere intellectual orthodoxy which stops short of personal experience. Then again, the same idea of Mysticism is a constant safeguard against the over-activity which is only too apt to characterise the Christian life of to-day. If ' Solitude is the mother-country of the strong,' then there must be time for devotional contemplation and personal adoration, and these can only be derived from a consciousness of the nearness and indwelling presence of God in Christ. So that whether against doctrinal severity or practical superficiality the necessity of the New Testament idea of fellowship with God in Christ is obvious and constant.

But most unfortunately the term ' Mysticism ' has to do duty for three different ideas, and herein lies its dangers.

The word evangelical has, even within the Church, fallen into discredit, for various reasons, some better and some worse. And its place has been taken by such a word as mystical. Shrewd publishers welcome the one word in a title and frown at the other. This may be a straw, but there is a current beneath it. It means at bottom the same thing as the aversion from the name Protestant, with its victory of power and faith, and the culture of the word Catholic, with its comfort of taste and love.' [1]

In the minds of some Mysticism stands for an attitude which tends to dispense with Christ altogether and to seek union with God apart from Him. By a very general use of the idea and term ' Inspiration,' it is urged that God has not confined His inspiration to Bible times, that the men of to-day are equally inspired to give messages for our age, and that while in times past Christians found authority in a Book, or in a Church, to-day man finds in his own self his greatest discovery, and that when he is true to himself he realises to the full what salvation is intended to mean. But it is evident that in all this there is nothing necessarily Christian ; and indeed, in certain applications the idea

---

[1] Forsyth, *The Principle of Authority*, p. 463.

of Mysticism is utterly opposed to everything distinctively true of the New Testament.

'It is most unfortunate that the spiritual in Christianity has been so often described as the mystical; and men have advocated mysticism when they were really pleading for spirituality. Mysticism, as represented by Neo-Platonism or Vedantism is the religion of pantheism; its aim is to transcend the distinction in consciousness of self and God, and to realise the identity of the Divine and the human. Even in its modified mediaeval form, where Christ was substituted for the Absolute, mysticism tended to a pantheism in which the historical Jesus as the mediator of the life in God was left behind, and an immediate union of the soul to God was claimed; or to an *erotism*, in which spiritual ecstasy was scarcely distinguishable from sexual passion.' [1]

Or to put it in another way :

'The mysticism which is essential to religion is not therefore a glow sent through a natural *a priori*, the transfiguration of a human postulate by a divine current, the elevation of a latent religiosity in us to high and ruling place.' [2]

The word ' Mysticism,' however, is also used in connection with something quite different, which claims to be distinctively Christian. In the Mysticism of the Quakers we find the tendency to emphasise the doctrine of the ' inner light ' as something either independent of, or superior to the written Word. This position is set forth by Barclay, the leading theologian of the Society of Friends.

' " We may not call them (the Scriptures) the principal fountain of all truth and knowledge, nor yet the first adequate rule of faith and manners, because the principal fountain of truth must be the truth itself; *i.e.* that whose authority and certainty depends not upon another." Again, " God hath committed and given unto every man a measure of light of His own Son—a measure of grace, or a measure of the Spirit. This, as it is received, and not resisted, works the salvation of all, even of those who are ignorant of the death and sufferings of Christ." ' [3]

Now it is necessary and important to recognise the truth underlying the Quaker position. There is a sense in which Jesus Christ, as the Divine Logos, ' lightens every man.' Call it what we will, light of reason, or of conscience; there is that in every man which answers to the truth

---

[1] Garvie, *op. cit.* p. 177.

[2] Forsyth, *op. cit.* p. 181. See also p. 183.

[3] Barclay, *Apologia.*

enshrined in this great saying of the Apostle. But it is not true to say that every man, as such, has the Spirit of God, nor can we call the same thing 'light,' 'reason,' 'grace,' 'the Spirit,' 'the Word of God,' 'Christ within,' and 'God in us.' Such a procedure would create untold confusion and lead to almost endless trouble. George Fox once had a discussion with a doctor, arguing that everyone possessed this light, and he appealed to an Indian who was present, in regard to his sense of right and wrong. But, as a Quaker scholar, Dr. Hodgkin, allows, Fox was therein confusing conscience with strictly religious illumination.[1] The Spirit of God, according to the New Testament, is given to believers as their light and life, but always together with an objective standard as a safeguard. This standard is the historic and redemptive Person of Christ, recorded in the New Testament, and mediated by the Spirit.

' Is the true badge of spirituality what the Anabaptists who would have wrecked the Reformation thought it to be—a *lex insita*, an inner light, mystic individualism, and quietist piety, which is co-equated with the historic Word, and moves in socialist sympathies to anarchic demagogy ? Or is it historic faith, founded on fact, energising in love, and working by constitutional progress ? Which is the way of the Spirit—subjective illuminism with its shifting lights, or objective revelation in an ever-fresh and growing experience ? Is it to-day's vagrant insight or yesterday's apostolic inspiration, good for to-day and for ever ? '[2]

' We are not at the mercy of the inward light alone. The Church was not created by the inward light. It was not created by the Spirit of God alone. It was created by the Holy Spirit through an apostolic Word of Jesus Christ crucified ; it was created by the redeeming Lord as the Spirit.'[3]

According to the early Quakers a man of their time might be as truly inspired of God as were the Prophets and Apostles of the Bible. Against the imposition of dogma by authority George Fox said that ' though he read of Christ and God,' he knew them only through a like spirit in his own soul.' And to refer to Barclay again, he taught that ' God hath placed His Spirit in every man, to inform him of his duty and to enable him to do it.' Coming to

---

[1] Hodgkin, *The Trial of our Faith*, p. 260.

[2] Forsyth, *op. cit.* p. 272.

[3] Forsyth, *op. cit.* p. 282.

our own day, the poet Whittier wrote in his last years, ' I have an unshaken faith in the one distinctive doctrine of Quakerism—the light within—the Immanence of the Divine Spirit.' But, as a leading member of the Society of Friends has well said, this doctrine has never been

' adequately harmonised, either with a sound conception of Authority, or with the Divine revelation which they, in common with more orthodox Christians, found in the Christ of history.' [1]

It is a great satisfaction, however, to know that there are many among the Friends to-day who hold faithfully to the supremacy of the written word and to the need of that in association with the Holy Spirit as the foundation of spiritual authority. To speak of this ' inner light ' as an ' immediate revelation ' of God to the individual is to allege what is not warranted by anything we know of primitive Christian truth, while it confuses between revelation and illumination. The weakness of the theory is seen in the fact that it involves something like a claim to individual infallibility and the denial of any objective authority, whether in the Bible or in the united Christian consciousness of the centuries. No Mysticism, or ' inner light ' can be safe which tends to dispense with, or ignore the historic Christ or the New Testament.

' Mystical experiences are an unquestionable fact in man's life. The weakness of mysticism is that it is subjective, emotional, and indeterminate. Christ made it objective by grounding it in a personal God, and He made it cognitive as well as emotional by the specific character which He assigned to God as Father, and He made it determinate and practical by prescribing an ethical task. Jesus was a mystic of the most pronounced type if we define mysticism as fellowship with God. But Jesus was no mystic at all if mysticism be regarded as an indeterminate emotional communion with the infinite without specific theological meaning and apart from the moral life.' [2]

The danger lies in the occupation of the soul with what is thought to be fellowship with the exalted Christ, and in letting the historic Jesus fall into the background. But this will not happen if we honour and make prominent the

[1] Grubb, *Authority and the Light Within*, p. 6. See also pp. 39, 83.

[2] Mullins, *Freedom and Authority in Religion*, p. 233.

Holy Spirit, and allow Him to do His work. He will witness to the redemptive, mediatorial work of Christ in Whom alone salvation is made possible. Redemption is by the truth (2 Thess. ii. 13), and truth is only embodied in the Personal Christ. Faith to be real must have a foundation, and it inevitably fails if it is not constantly based on historic fact. The Holy Spirit is no vague impersonal influence or principle, but a Divine Indwelling Person Who glorifies Christ as Redeemer, Life, and Lord (1 Cor. xii. 3).

' To measure truly the Christianity of an age we must ask how far it grasps God's true gift, and not how eagerly or finely it seeks it. What is its conception of salvation ? What is it that makes it religious ? What is the object of its religion ? Do not ask, What is its dream ? or, What is its programme or its piety ? but, What is its Gospel ? Do not ask, What is its experience ? Ask what emerges in its experience ? It is not the lack of religiosity that ails the Church, it is the lack of a Gospel and a 'faith, the lack of a spiritual authority and a response to it. For the leaders of the Reformation the gift was not an institution, nor was it vaguely a Christian spirit, but the Holy Spirit as personal life. It was direct and personal communion with a gracious and saving God in Jesus Christ.' [1]

While, therefore, we are thankful for all that Quakerism has done in its initial protest against a rigid ecclesiasticism, its emphasis on inward and spiritual religion, and its insistence upon social, moral, national, and international obligations,[2] we are compelled to call attention to the vital danger of a doctrine of the inner light which tends to separate the Spirit from the Word, and to open the door to tendencies which are far removed from the simplicity and soberness, balance and beauty of New Testament truth.[3]

From an entirely different quarter the same tendency, to which also is given the name of Mysticism, appears in

---

[1] Forsyth, *The Person and Place of Jesus Christ*, p. 23. See also Mullins, *op. cit.* p. 318.

[2] Forsyth, *Faith, Freedom, and the Future*, pp. 42, 43.

[3] Forsyth, *Faith, Freedom, and the Future*, p. 211. See also ch. i., and the entire book for the relation of the Reformation to Quakerism through Anabaptism.

the exaggerated emphasis on Christian experience, which finds its best expression in Dale's *The Living Christ and the Four Gospels.* This argues that even though the Gospels were disproved as historical documents, we should still be enabled to rest upon the experience of Christ in the heart. By some this position is accepted as a refuge from modern critical problems and disturbances. It is thought that the intellectual unsettlement and uncertainty due to Biblical Criticism can be practically nullified by the protection of a personal experience of Jesus Christ. But such a position really overlooks the fact that absolute independence of the Gospels is utterly impossible, because this necessarily predicates an imaginary Christ of Whom we know nothing.[1] Besides, it is in reality a confession of intellectual defeat and cowardice which cannot satisfy the minds of men. The true attitude of the soul is surely the determination to face its doubts and gather strength by recurring again to Scripture, and by seeking the solution of the problems of criticism in the only right way of a deeper historic insight and a fuller experience of the Holy Spirit in relation to the truth. It is the bounden duty of every man to use his reason to the utmost in all these questions of criticism, and yet to remember the need of his reason being illuminated by the Word and the Spirit. Whatever may be said about the Bible as a whole, it is absolutely certain that we still possess, as Forsyth says, ' the infallible and historic Gospel ' in it and ' the infallible and present Spirit.' In this ' lies our standard and control,' [2] and this is the irreducible minimum which Christendom cannot remove or explain away.

The peril of these forms of Mysticism, whether represented by Quakerism or by the emphasis on Christian experience, lies in the severance of the Word and the Spirit. The Christian doctrine of an immediate communion of the soul with God is only possible through the union of the Divine Word and the Divine Spirit. For guidance and inspiration we must have truth. For purity we must have holiness. For consolation we must have grace. And

---

[1] Garvie, *op. cit.* p. 381 ff.

[2] Forsyth, *Faith, Freedom, and the Future,* pp. 210, 211.

these are only available through the Word of God and the Spirit of God.

'We need more mystic souls and mystic hours. But the true mysticism is not raptly dwelling in the mystery of God, it is really living on His miracle. It is not prolonged elation but sure salvation. And the only mysticism with a lease of life is that which surrounds the moral miracle which makes Christianity in the end evangelical or nothing. It is the mysticism of the Cross.' [1]

It is the association of the Word and the Spirit which constitutes vital Christianity, preserving us on the one hand from a dry orthodoxy, and on the other from a mere pietistic sentimentality. We must hold with all possible tenacity to the immediate action of the Spirit on the believing soul, but it is always through the Word of the Truth of the Gospel.

'The action of the Spirit is immediate to the soul yet not unmediated by the Word. The Spirit when He had set the Word down in history did not abdicate for it and its rich posthumous effects. He is always there, personally with and over it. But in bringing it to our experience He does not come to it from the outside, nor simply work alongside. He is immanent always to the Word (for this Word is a perpetual act); He imbues it, flushes it, brings it, carries it home from within for the individual soul.' [2]

We therefore insist on both elements, never the one without the other. The Spirit without the Word will result in intellectual vagueness; the Word without the Spirit in spiritual dryness.

'Spiritualism, left to itself, does mean the dissolution of the Churches and of Christianity. But then evangelism left to itself, the mere re-echo of the Word without the vitality of the Spirit, is no less fatal. If the one pulverise the Church the other petrifies it.' [3]

The Christian consciousness can never be the seat of authority, because it necessarily differs with different men.[4] The only absolute standard and test of truth is the Divine revelation of God in Christ, and this is to be found in Scripture alone. As we approximate towards the truth

---

[1] Forsyth, *The Principle of Authority*, p. 465.

[2] Forsyth, *Faith, Freedom, and the Future*, p. 29.

[3] Forsyth, *Faith, Freedom, and the Future*, p. 42. See also Elder Cumming, *Through the Eternal Spirit*, p. 371.

[4] Mullins, *op. cit.* pp. 53, 298.

revealed there, we shall have safety, certainty, and enjoyment, but in so far as we allow ourselves to be ruled by subjective criteria, we must never be surprised at the recurrence and persistence of intellectual uncertainty and lack of spiritual conviction. When the Word and the Spirit are blended and brought to bear on the believing soul they correct, steady, balance, and protect it under all circumstances.

' Christian mysticism therefore reposes, not on the depths of subliminal being, which give no footing for any authority that royalises life, but upon the miracle of the forgiven conscience of the world and its holy redemption.' [1]

It is no doubt true that the recent rapid increase of Mysticism is one of the most significant signs of the times, yet, it must be said again, no religion of direct personal experience will ever suffice to meet the problems raised by philosophy, socialism, criticism and ecclesiasticism. The dangers of institutionalism, of the corporate idea, of pantheistic thought are real and pressing, but they will not be met by a faith which has no authority but its own conceptions, intuitions and desires. The objective authority of the Word of God and the Spirit of God can alone suffice for human life. And so, while we can welcome every movement that tends towards direct intercourse with God and a definite spiritual experience of God in the soul, we must not forget the truth of Saphir's words that, though every Christian is a mystic, not every mystic is a Christian.

---

[1] Forsyth, *The Principle of Authority*, p. 470.

CHAPTER 29

THE HOLY SPIRIT
AND INTELLECTUALISM

ANOTHER modern movement calls for attention because of
the important bearing that the doctrine of the Holy Spirit
has upon it. It may perhaps be described as Intellectualism, and is represented by such names as Martineau and
August Sabatier. In some respects the most vital question
of modern days is as to the seat of authority. The view of
Martineau and Sabatier is that it is found in the human
reason and conscience. This is the general line taken in
Martineau's *Seat of Authority in Religion,* and more recently
in Sabatier's *The Religions of Authority and the Religion of
the Spirit.* In this latter book it is said that there have
been two religions of authority, the authority of the Church
in Romanism and the authority of the Bible in Protestantism. Sabatier first subjects the claims of Rome to a close
and thorough examination, and repudiates them in a series
of arguments of remarkable force. Then he subjects the
Authority of the Bible to an equally severe test and
repudiates that with equal definiteness. Finally, he puts
forth his own view of the supremacy of reason, which he
calls the Religion of the Spirit. His main contention is
that the mind is autonomous and finds the supreme rule of

LITERATURE.—Sabatier, *The Religions of Authority and the Reli-
gion of the Spirit ;* Orr, *The Christian View of God and the World ;*
Garvie, *The Christian Certainty amid the Modern Perplexity,* ch. vii. ;
Oman, *The Problem of Faith and Freedom ; Vision and Authority ;*
Forsyth, *Positive Preaching and the Modern Mind ; The Principle
of Authority ;* Grubb, *Authority and the Light Within ;* Mullins,
Freedom and Authority in Religion ; Stanton, *The Place of Authority
in Religious Belief.*

its standard and ideas within itself, that is, within its own constitution and not outside. To quote his words : ' The consent of the mind to itself is the prime condition and foundation of all certitude.' According to this view truth seems to be simply a matter of opinion, for as a man thinketh a thing is, so it is—to him. To the same effect, M. Reville, a colleague of Sabatier, says, ' An authority only exists for us in the measure in which we recognise it as such.'

Now while Sabatier's protest undoubtedly contains important elements of truth, it involves a false antithesis to speak of his own subjective view of religion as the Religion of the Spirit. In reality his position is that of an illuminated rationalism, with which the Spirit, as revealed in the New Testament, has very little to do. It is indeed the old, yet ever new question of the place of reason in religion, whether it is or is not the supreme authority. Let us be quite clear on this point. Reason is both valuable and necessary as one of the means of distinguishing the claims of authority, and also as a recipient of the truth of revelation. Long ago Butler taught us that reason is the only faculty for judging anything, even revelation. No authority can be legitimate which subverts or stultifies reason. The right of verification is the inalienable prerogative of every man, and no external compulsion can ever set aside the necessity and duty of proving all things as well as of holding fast that which is good. But while we thus insist on the right and duty of reason to judge and verify, it is quite another thing to claim for it the seat of authority itself. After all, reason is only one of several human faculties, and Divine revelation is intended to apply to them all. Then, too, reason has been affected by sin, has become biassed, darkened, and distorted, so that it cannot be regarded as reliable as the seat of authority in religion. Besides, there is such a thing as reality independent of our mind, and if there be no authority except that which our mind recognises, then such facts as, for instance, the existence of God must depend solely on our recognition of them, which is absurd. The consent of the mind cannot be ·the foundation of truth. Our certitude is only the result of our acceptance and

experience of reality outside ourselves. It is our testimony
to an already existing fact. Knowledge and certitude
come through the apprehension and acceptance of objective
truth based on adequate evidence. To regard reason as
autonomous is to deny the existence of objective reality.
Reason is not originative, but only receptive ; not a source,
but a channel ; it is not creative, but only weighs and then
appropriates the data offered to us. The true idea is of
the authority which is not against reason but in accordance
with it.

' It is not a test, so that we can act critically on Revelation. Nor
is it a germ whose innate resources Revelation develops. But it is
a recognising power, a receptivity.' [1]

Sabatier never seems to contemplate the possibility that
the Holy Spirit may conceivably have been at work behind
and even through the two forms of religion which he
rejects. But what is still more important, he does not
seem to be conscious of the fact that ' objective ' and
' external ' are not identical terms ; and that ' authority '
and ' Spirit ' are not necessarily antithetical and contradictory. Divine revelation as expressed in the redemptive
Person and Work of Christ can be at once objective and
internal.

' All absolute authority must reveal itself in a way of miracle.
It does not rise out of human nature by any development, but
descends on it with an intervention, a revelation, a redemption. It
does not evolve from human nature, it invades it. An authority,
which has its source in ourselves, is no authority. In us authority
can have but its sphere and its echo, never its charter.' [2]
' A large part of the reaction against authority is due to its
externality being treated in this abstract and almost literal way,
instead of being realised as within the nature of the spirit or will
itself. Externality here means otherness, and not outwardness or
foreignness.' [3]

We therefore believe that the seat of authority is the
Divine revelation in Christ, as embodied for us in the Bible.
We hold this because the New Testament preserves for
us the revelation of Christ in its purest available form.

[1] Forsyth, *The Principle of Authority*, p. 176. See also pp. 187,
189, 193, 196.
[2] Forsyth, *op. cit.* p. 339.　　　　[3] Forsyth, *op. cit.* p. 371.

Christianity has a historic basis in the Person of Christ, and what we need is the clearest and completest form of that revelation. The books of the New Testament being the product of the apostolic age give and guarantee this. All that we require is that the vehicle of transmission be certain and assuring, whether it be a Book, or an Institution, or a Man. But just as we have seen that it would be impossible to guard the purity of Christ's revelation against corruption by embodiment in an institution, so we are equally certain that human reason is no preservative against impurity and corruption. Reason is human, Scripture though human in form has Divine elements which no criticism can touch. As such, Scripture is the light of reason, the informant of the mind, and the guide of all religious thought. To speak, therefore, of reason or conscience as our supreme authority is to incur grave danger of misconception, since, as we well know, neither reason nor conscience is creative but only receptive, not a source of truth but only a medium. And although modern thought with its doctrine of evolution has rightly abandoned the deistical idea of natural religion, many writers still argue as if conscience and reason were independent and sufficient authorities ; as if they were not only the receptive but even the originative organs of religious principles. Reason is not the origin but the organ of truth. Revelation does not dishonour reason, but honours it by appealing to it with evidence. To the spiritual, enlightened moral reason the Scriptures make constant appeal. Indeed, the human reason has a vital duty to perform. It must judge of man's need of Divine revelation. It must examine the credentials of revelation, and it must understand and interpret the meaning of revelation. The place of reason has been well illustrated by a simple fact of life. The warden of a prison receives from the proper judicial officers the warrant for the execution of a murderer. It is his duty to examine the document so as to satisfy himself as to its genuineness, authenticity, etc. He carefully scrutinises the seal, signature, and other marks of identification. But he has no right to tamper with the contents of the death-warrant. He dare not change the form of execution nor alter the date. His duty is to obey its order. It is similar with the reason. Men may examine the credentials of revelation ; nay, they must do so. But having done this, reason necessarily yields to the superior authority of Divine revelation accepted by faith. The mind of man may not add or omit one jot or tittle of Divine revelation.

The tendency to-day to fix the seat of authority within ourselves is doubtless due to the reaction from the pure externalism of an authoritative Church, or of an authoritative Book, considered apart from internal reception and experience. We have rightly come to realise that the authoritative religion is inward and spiritual, and that nothing can become genuinely authoritative for us without exercising moral and spiritual control over heart and conscience. But we must beware of going to the other extreme and precipitating ourselves into the error of pure subjectivity. That authority must be inward does not in the least mean that our ideas and prejudices are the measure of truth. There is an element of objectivity in all our knowledge, and so there is an objective authority in religion. The idea that ' objective ' and ' external ' are identical, and that this means a purely mechanical authority leads to untold mischief. Since the ultimate authority in the Christian religion is Christ Himself we see at once that even when Christ is within us He is not identical with us. Although He speaks in the innermost sanctuary of our being yet He speaks as One Who is not a Christ of our own invention. He is the Divine revelation given to us, mediated to us through Holy Scripture, so that if Christ is to be an authority at all He must be primarily objective.

' Many earnest and forward people to-day are concerned with the repudiation of an external authority. Some are as passionate about it as only those can be who do not gauge, or even grasp, the situation. Often they are more concerned to repudiate the externality than to own the authority. They are not always quite clear what externality means. An authority must be external, in some real sense, or it is none. It must be external to us. It must be something not ourselves, descending on us in a grand paradox. We might well for a little relax our recalcitrant animus against the externality of the authority and bestow more anxious pains upon the reality of it.' [1]

---

[1] Forsyth, *op. cit.* p. 306. See also, p. 356.

It is the revelation of the Person of our Lord which is our supreme authority, and this revelation is at the outset entirely external to man though subsequently coming within him. It is the historical fact of His Divine Person, prior and external to us and primarily independent of us, that forms our final authority in religion. To regard reason as the supreme authority is really to transfer to it the infallibility which we have denied to the Church and the Bible, and at the same time to ignore utterly its variableness and the entire absence of any confirmatory proof of its decisions. If it should be said that reason is superior to all because it testifies to and approves of revelation, it must never be forgotten that reason itself needs to be purified and developed before it can give a proper answer to and verification of religion. This itself shows that reason cannot be primary and superior. This need of cleansing and enlightenment is a reminder that man's deepest need is not illumination but redemption.[1] Christ ' restores the sight to which He presents the light,' and while reason and conscience, as they are at present, may apprehend just sufficient to warrant faith in Christ, the full vindication of His claims is only made possible to a conscience and reason transformed by Divine grace. And when revelation is thus apprehended, it is at once accepted and submitted to, thereby proving the supremacy of revelation over reason.

It is worth while saying again that the Lord Jesus Christ is our authority and that we accept the Bible because it enshrines the Divine revelation in the purest, clearest, and most available form. All that we desire is the highest and best knowledge of Christ. The seat of authority cannot be the consciousness of Christ, to which we have no access, but only the record of that consciousness which we find in the New Testament. And we hold Scripture, as we have already seen, to be not merely the record of the spiritual experience of the first Christian generation, but the Divinely provided and Divinely inspired record of the consciousness of Christ as the Redeemer of men. As such it is the touchstone of experience, which is genuine only as it corresponds

[1] Forsyth, *op. cit.* p. 424.

with Christ's revelation in Scripture. Then by this correspondence experience becomes a witness to Scripture. As a French writer well puts it :

' Christianity is the Person of Jesus Christ. Still we must enter into relations with this Person. In order that two moral subjects should communicate with one another there must needs be manifestations between them. A person manifests himself clearly to us only by his acts and his words ; and he has value for us only as we form for ourselves a certain idea of him. Christianity is, therefore, essentially, above all, a person : but on pain of reducing it to a magic, which would no longer possess any ethical and, consequently, no longer possess any religious quality, we must needs grant that Christianity, precisely because it is *essentially* a Person, is *also* a body of facts and of ideas.'

' For the contemporaries of Jesus Christ, who could see and hear Him, the teaching that fell from His lips and the deeds performed by Him, constituted this necessary middle term between Jesus Christ and them. For us, with no wish, certainly, to deny the personal, present, and living relations of Jesus Christ with the soul of the redeemed, we cannot, without opening the door to the most dangerous mysticism, reduce Christianity to these relations, in derogation of the acts and revelations of the historical Christ, which we have neither seen nor heard, but which have been transmitted to us by tradition, by the Bible : this would be equivalent to cutting down the tree at its roots under pretext of being thus better able to gather its fruit.' [1]

There is always grave danger in rationalistic subjectivity,[2] and Sabatier's position, which is so often and so widely accepted to-day, tends to make Christianity little or nothing more than a set of intellectual conceptions of truth which vary with each holder, *quot homines tot sententiae*. Dr. Sanday, in a lecture delivered a few years ago, on ' The Place of Dogma in Religion,' made a very apt and acute criticism of Sabatier's position, when he protested against the assumption that small minorities must be right.

' It almost appears as though (in M. Sabatier's view) the larger aggregations of men might be assumed to be always in the wrong, while the self-confident dogmatism of an individual might be trusted to be in the right. One looks in vain for any safeguard against mere religious subjectivity.'

But this view is not the Christianity of the New Testament, mediated by the Holy Spirit, and applied to every

---

[1] Bois, *Le Dogme Grec*, p. 107.

[2] Mullins, *Freedom and Authority in Religion*, pp. 59, 182, 323.

part of man's nature. Let it be said again that reason is important and essential, but is one of several faculties, all affected by sin. It needs cleansing and illumination if it is to do proper service. In its province of testing the credentials of revelation it is a vital part of our being, but it is equally vital to its duty to bow to those credentials when it has tested them satisfactorily. While, therefore, we value every opportunity we can obtain of examination, enquiry, and consideration, we must never forget that

' in the last resort the only religious authority must be some action of God's creative self-revelation, and not simply an outside witness to it.' [1]

And while, of course, we must necessarily experience this Divine authority, we must also remember that it is not the experience but the authority which is supreme.[2] No real Christianity is possible which is not derived from the New Testament as the purest source of our knowledge of Christ, Who is God's authority for life revealed by the Holy Spirit.

' In religious knowledge the object is God ; it is not the world, it is not man. And that object differs from every other in being for us far more than an object of knowledge. He is the absolute subject of it. He is not something that we approach, with the initiative on our side. He takes the initiative and approaches us. Our knowledge is the result of His revelation. We find Him because He first finds us. That is to say, *the main thing, the unique thing, in religion is not a God Whom we know but a God Who knows us.*' [3]

In the movements that we have been considering one feature emerges as common to them all ; the tendency to ignore the primitive revelation and to forget that the Source of that revelation is still its Safeguard and Illuminator. All error, intellectual and fanatical, comes in this way. Contrariwise, the only guarantee of preserving Christianity in its purity and fulness will be the insistence on the supremacy of Divine revelation in Scripture, and the necessity of the Holy Spirit as its guard and guide. Any movement which severs the Word from the Spirit tends inevitably to deny both ; whether it be Development in Roman Catholicism,

---

[1] Forsyth, *op. cit.* p. 23.   [2] Forsyth, *op. cit.* p. 55.
[3] Forsyth, *op. cit.* p. 167 ; see also pp. 356, 373, 377 ; Mullins, *op. cit.* pp. 43, 45.

Evolution in Modernism, Mysticism in Quakerism, or Intellectualism in Rationalism. Primitive, full, pure Christianity will only be assured as we rest everything upon the supreme authority of the Divine revelation in Holy Scripture, illuminated, guarded, and developed by the Holy Spirit. When these two are thus united and made our supreme standard, we know the truth and the truth makes us free ; we love the truth, and the truth makes us safe ; we follow the truth, and the truth makes us strong, sure, satisfied, for then we become united to Him Who is the Truth ; we are His disciples indeed, and are led by the Spirit of truth.[1]

---

[1] Forsyth, *Faith, Freedom, and the Future*, ch. i.

CHAPTER 30

THE HOLY SPIRIT
AND PERSONAL QUESTIONS

THE value and power of the Bible doctrine of the Holy
Spirit in relation to individual life is seen in the fact that it
is the solution of several modern problems and the safeguard
against several perils that concern the soul.

There is the problem of Spiritual Uncertainty. Scarcely
anything presses more heavily and seriously on life to-day
than the problem of spiritual certitude. 'Who will show
us any good?' is the cry heard all around. Dr. Forsyth
once said that the prophets in their definiteness and fear-
lessness of position said without hesitation, 'Here am I,'
while to-day men are groping in the twilight, and amidst
moral uncertainty are asking, 'Where am I'? The
constant and persistent pressure of the problems raised
by science, philosophy, and criticism has shaken the
foundations of life for many, and people know not where
to turn for satisfaction. It is particularly striking that
the age which has been most hopeful and expectant in
regard to science, because always on the verge of fresh
discoveries, has shown itself the most hopeless in reference
to religion. So much so, that a leading scientist of our day
coined the word 'agnostic' to express his attitude towards
some of the deepest things in life.

And yet the New Testament is clear: 'That thou
mightest know the certainty of those things wherein thou
hast been instructed' (Luke i. 4). St. Paul says, 'I know
Whom I have believed' (2 Tim. i. 12); 'I am persuaded'
(Rom. viii. 38). And he speaks of 'boldness and access
with confidence' (Eph. iii. 12). To the same effect, St.

John writes his Epistle for the express purpose of giving moral and spiritual certitude. ' These things have I written unto you . . . that ye may know ' (I John v. 13). What, then, are we to do in the face of all these clear considerations ? There is only one answer. ' The Christian certainty amid the modern perplexity ' is found by reverting to the Gospel of God in Christ :

' The base and condition of all independent certainty was the experience in the Holy Ghost of the apostolic Gospel.' [1]

It is in the realm of grace, ministered by the Holy Spirit, that we shall lose our fears, resolve our doubts, and get rid of our hesitation. All efforts to arrive at certainty in connection with the Church, or philosophy, or reason, will fail. There is only one secret of certitude, the personal acceptance of the Divine Gospel of redemption, mediated by the Holy Spirit. We are thankful for knowledge ; we are grateful for the results of enquiry ; we are prepared to accept every absolutely assured result of criticism ; we rejoice in all philosophical justification of our position ; we glory in the historical vindication of Christianity. But beneath, behind, and above all, we have the presence and power of the Holy Spirit witnessing to Christ, and assuring us of ' Safety, Certainty, and Enjoyment.' There is such a thing as Grace, or rather, there is such a reality as the presence of God in Christ, a presence that guarantees grace through the Holy Spirit, and the possession of and experience of this is the foundation and spring of all certitude. This is the essential meaning and vital power of the doctrine known as ' The Witness of the Spirit.' ' The Spirit itself beareth witness with our spirit, that we are the children of God ' (Rom. viii. 16). This testimony, resting on and connected with the redemptive Gospel of Christ, is the secret of assurance and the guarantee of satisfaction. But it does not involve any reversion to the subjectivity which makes certitude depend on the Christian consciousness. While it *is* within, it is not *from* within, Christian consciousness is of immense value in relation to the religious life, but it cannot possibly be made the ground of certainty in religion.

---

[1] Forsyth, *The Principle of Authority*, p. 153.

' A real authority, we have seen, is indeed *within* experience, but it is not the authority *of* experience, it is an authority *for* experience, it is an authority experienced. All certainty is necessarily subjective so far as concerns the area where it emerges and the terms in which it comes home. The court is subjective but the bench is not. Reality must, of course, be real for me. It must speak the language of my consciousness. But it makes much difference whether it have its *source* in my consciousness as well as its *sphere*.' [1]

There is also the danger of Modern Pessimism. Nothing could be more disheartening and hopeless than much modern thought in science and literature. The laws of causation and heredity are being pressed in certain quarters to exclude all possibility of right living, while the law of determinism tends to destroy all sense of moral responsibility. Scientists like Huxley and Haeckel, authors like Hardy and Ibsen, and even earlier writers like George Eliot and Hawthorne teach the nemesis of broken law and the utter impossibility of escape and recovery. The note of pessimism in modern fiction is one of the most significant and even startling phenomena of to-day.

In opposition to this comes the message of the Gospel of grace, administered by the Holy Spirit. It tells of sin, but also of pardon ; it speaks of failure, but also of recovery ; it emphasises weakness, but also power ; it declares law, but also grace.

' If we have not a Gospel against heredity it is very doubtful if we have any Gospel at all.' [2]

Dr. Forsyth [3] has pointed out that three things are ignored by pessimism : Sin, Redemption, Personality. The idea of sin in much modern writing is very largely associated with its physical and moral consequences, not with its lawlessness and guilt in the sight of God. And as to Redemption, modern thought has nothing whatever to say, its one idea being punishment and destruction. But the Gospel of Jesus Christ, while emphasising sin to the utmost and preaching without qualification or reserve,

---

[1] Forsyth, *op. cit.* p. 83 ; see also p. 89 ; Mullins, *Freedom and Authority in Religion,* pp. 296-299.

[2] Rendel Harris, *Communion with God,* p. 263.

[3] Forsyth, ' The Pessimism of Mr. Thomas Hardy,' *London Quarterly Review* (October, 1912).

' Be sure your sin will find you out,' nevertheless proclaims redemption from the condemnation and guilt of sin, and deliverance from its power in the Person of the Divine Christ, Who died on Calvary and lives for evermore. So that, as Forsyth remarks, we arrive at the great fundamental and eternal principle :

' Pessimism cannot be the final reading of the world and life, because holiness is a greater interest than happiness, sin is blacker than misery, and guilt is only revealed by grace. No experience of life shows a world so bad, black, perverse and hopeless as it is shown by the revelation of its holy salvation.' [1]

This redemption is made real to the soul by the Holy Spirit, and when we make much of the Holy Spirit it is impossible to be pessimistic. Not that we shall be optimistic in the modern sense of a cheap, superficial consideration of human ills without any serious regard to their reality and removal, but we shall be possessed by an optimism which in spite of, and indeed in face of the deepest and most potent results of sin fearlessly declares that ' the blood of Jesus Christ His Son cleanseth us from all sin ; (1 John i. 7). ' There is therefore now no condemnation to them which are in Christ Jesus. . . . For the law of the Spirit of life in Christ Jesus hath made me free from the law of sin and death ' (Rom. viii. 1, 2). The man who has received into his life the inestimable benefits of the redemption that is in Christ Jesus knows for a surety that all is well for time and eternity, and he cannot possibly be pessimistic because ' the joy of the Lord is his strength ' (Neh. viii. 10). [2]

There is also the danger of regarding Christianity merely as a system of Ethics, depicting a moral ideal which cannot be realised. The practical result of such a position is an aspect of the modern hopelessness already considered. Christianity has a system of ethics and a moral ideal, but first and foremost it is and has a dynamic. From time to time young men are exhorted to follow the advice of Emerson, and ' hitch their wagon to a star.' But nothing in Emerson, or those who use him, tells how this is to be

---

[1] Forsyth, *ut supra*, p. 210.

[2] Morris Stewart, *The Crown of Science*, p. 74 ; Forsyth, *The Principle of Authority*, ch. iv.

done. Yonder is the star, here is the human wagon ; but how are they to become connected ? Christianity not only tells men to hitch their wagon to the star, but provides that which connects the wagon below with the star above. The 'dynamic' of the Gospel is the prominent feature of the Pauline theology, and its constant theme may be expressed in two statements of the Apostle :

'God is faithful . . . that ye may be able ' (1 Cor. x. 13).   'God is able . . . that ye may (be faithful) ' (1 Cor. ix. 8).

' The Holy Spirit is the real dynamic of the Christian religion. Surely there are historic facts and mental conceptions which the Holy Spirit utilises, but these facts and conceptions are but useful pivots of power and not the power itself. The power itself is the energising will of the Holy Spirit. Without Him, the Christian religion would be, at the most, but an empty intention to rescue men. The rationalists, some of the extreme ones, are wont to say that we need more truth, that truth will lift men out of all their failure. We do need truth, more and more of it ; but under all that need is the paramount need of a vitalised moral personality.' [1]

It is at this point that the work of the Holy Spirit is particularly noteworthy. By dwelling in the soul and revealing Christ to it, all human needs are met ; the warfare of the flesh is overcome (Gal. v. 17, R.V.) ; the fruit of the Spirit is produced (Gal. v. 22, 23) ; and victory over the devil and the world is accomplished.

' The objective dynamic of Christian Ethics is the Holy Spirit, or God exerting moral creative power. The Holy Spirit is not simply the immanent Spirit of God, as that is generally viewed. Its character is revealed and its power acts through Jesus. A great moral activity of God has been manifested in the earthly life of Jesus, consummated in His death, and exhibited as completed in His resurrection, which makes the beginning of specific ethical Christian experience possible. Hence Christianity is a Gospel of God (even as an ethical system), not the product of man's working or thinking, but an offer of life impinging on man for acceptance. Christian moral experience, then, takes for granted the Holy Spirit of God uniting His help to our weakness (Rom. viii. 26).' [2]

---

[1] Curtis, *The Christian Faith*, p. 117 ; see also J. M. Campbell, *After Pentecost, What?* p. 243 ; Morris Stewart, *The Crown of Science*, p. 72 ; Walker, *The Holy Spirit*, p. 52.

[2] Mackenzie, Article ' Ethics and Morality (Christian),' *Encyclopaedia of Religion and Ethics*, Vol. V. p. 469.

In this close union between the Holy Spirit and the believing soul all that is necessary is made absolutely secure (John xiv. 17 ; Rom. viii. 9, 11 ; 1 Cor. iii. 16 ; vi. 17 ; Jas. iv. 5).

Not the least pressing of modern dangers is that of a merely intellectual conception of Christianity. This peril is particularly urgent because ideas are so widespread and tend to dominate human life. But ideas alone cannot save. If they could, the disciples would not have been powerless until the descent of the Holy Spirit on the Day of Pentecost. It is the province of the Holy Spirit to make the Christian ideas real and vital in their informing and inspiring force for human life. Man's true motto is *Sancte et Sapienter*,[1] and both the *Sancte* and the *Sapienter* are made possible by the Spirit of Holiness and the Spirit of Truth.

' " Arouse man," Schelling once said, " to the consciousness of what he *is*, and he will soon learn to be what he *ought*." This is about half true, true in its appreciation of the worth of full self-consciousness, false in its lack of appreciation of the significance of personal freedom. You cannot make any man right by intensifying his self-consciousness. But it is true, and momentously true, that no man can have a profound moral life until he has a profound personal life. And the Holy Spirit does give a profounder personal life.' [2]

---

[1] The motto of King's College, London.

[2] Curtis, *op. cit.* p. 118.

CHAPTER 31

THE HOLY SPIRIT
AND CHURCH PROBLEMS

IT is apt to be overlooked that the truth about the Holy Spirit has an intimate connection with some of the burning ecclesiastical questions of to-day.[1] Indeed, it may be said that if this doctrine had been more carefully attended to and more closely adhered to, those questions would never have come into existence, or at least would have occupied only a very secondary place in the thought and life of the Church. The emphasis on the Holy Spirit in the Church is really our safeguard against many ecclesiastical dangers that are rife to-day and have been so through the ages.

There is the danger of erroneous ideas of Unity. We can see from two passages in St. Paul a clear distinction drawn between ' the unity of the Spirit ' as a present fact, and ' the unity of the faith and of the knowledge of the Son of God ' as an ideal for the future (Eph. iv. 3, 13). A recollection of this distinction would save us from many a danger. We *have*, and must therefore ' *keep* the unity of the Spirit,' but we are travelling towards the unity of ' faith and knowledge.' Unity is often confused with a unit of organisation, but this has never existed since the first congregation of Christians met at Jerusalem. Indeed, it is an absolute impossibility in view of differences and difficulties of time, distance, nationality, and races. In the Eastern Churches to-day there is no such unit, for all those bodies are federated as a collection and combination of individual Churches. In the Anglican Church there is no

---

[1] See also chap. xxii., p. 169.

such unit, since the diocese, or at most the province, is the highest form of organisation. And it goes without saying that there is no unit of organisation in the other Protestant Churches. It only exists in Roman Catholicism under the unit of the Papacy, and we know that this is far removed from ' the unity of the Spirit.' It would offer one of the most striking studies in Church History to observe the way in which the Holy Spirit has been set aside in the practical working of the Roman Church.

Unity has also sometimes been confused with unanimity of doctrine. But here again, unanimity on fundamentals has been found compatible with remarkable variety in non-essentials without any breach of unity. Unanimity of opinion on every point is as impossible as it would be intolerable and unnecessary, and yet essential unity can exist under a great deal of doctrinal variety.

Unity has also been identified with uniformity of cere- monial, but, once more, the two are not necessarily one and the same thing. The existence of the great liturgies and the remarkable variety of ritual in all ages show that unity is possible apart from all such outward oneness of ceremonial.

The unity of the Spirit is a unity of life and love in Christ. It springs from unity with Christ, and consists of living unity in Him through the Spirit. The Church is a con- gregation not an aggregation ; a community of those who have Christ for their Centre and Source of life. Our Lord distinguishes between the unity of the fold and the unity of the flock (John x. 16), and makes the latter the more important. If we follow His example, we shall be most thoroughly in harmony with the New Testament teaching on the unity of the Spirit. The trouble has been caused by the endeavour to identify the Body of Christ with a visible organisation, but this is opposed to the very first principles of Christianity as found in the New Testament. The truth taught above [1] is often overlooked, that the Church in the Creed is associated with faith, not with sight, and this simple but significant fact shows that the unity, holiness, catholicity, and apostolicity in which we express our confidence are therefore matters of faith,

---

[1] See ch. xxii., p. 183.

not of sight. We believe that there is one Church, though we do not see it ; we believe that the Church is in this sense holy, or ' consecrated ' to God even though this holiness is very partially realised by any visible community ; we believe that the Church is universal even though there are many visible communities of those who ' profess and call themselves Christians.' The Church as the Body of Christ embraces all times, all places, and all people, and the claim to the sole use of the term by any one body of Christians involves a contradiction and in reality is an utter impossibility. The Church Catholic is the Church Universal, not any one Church or combination of Churches with a merely partial following. We believe that the Church is Apostolic, because it is built on the foundation of the Apostles and Prophets. The succession is that of truth, and the Church founded by the Apostles is still guided by them in their writings as found in the New Testament. So that any Apostolic Succession cannot be personal, because as Apostles the men were unique and had no successors. But there can be Apostolic Succession by adherence to Apostolic doctrine and life. The Church is therefore Apostolic, Catholic, and Holy, and One, because it is in Christ. Everything is based on life, and life is based on Divine grace in Christ. The scriptural idea of the Church is found in such passages as Romans xii. 5, ' We, being many, *are* (not, shall be, or, ought to be, but are) one body in Christ, and every one members one of another.' So also in Ephesians the same truth is stated as a fact, not as a hypothesis ; as a present reality, not as a prospective hope. The Church *is* the Body of Christ, and this is a fact that no differences or divisions can alter, or even affect. One community may excommunicate another, but if any person thus rejected is united by a living faith to Christ he is a member of Christ's Body, however much he may be cut off from visible fellowship. No part of the Church can exclude from the whole or from God. Men like Savonarola and Luther were excluded from a part, but not from the entire Church.

No idea has been more fruitful of error, or more serious in practical results than the identification of the Body of Christ with any visible institution or institutions. The words of Bishop Westcott are particularly valuable in this connection.

' It follows necessarily from what has been said that external, visible unity is not required for the essential visible unity of the Church. The promise of Christ does not reach to the unity of the outward fold at any time.' [1]

' The conception of unity based on historic and Divine succession in the religious centre of the world was proved to be no part of the true idea of the Church.' [2]

' No external organization can supersede the original relation in which the Society stands to its founder. The gift of the Holy Spirit was the outward sign of the elevation of humanity to glory at the right hand of God ; the sharing in that gift is the life of the Church ; the absolute oneness of the source from which the gift flows is the ground of essential unity in the congregations of which the Church is composed.' [3]

The one complete safeguard against all such errors connected with the unity of the Church is a fuller emphasis on the presence and work of the Holy Spirit of God. It is He Who unites us to Christ and to one another in Him, and in proportion as our life is truly Christian it will express itself in all those graces that find their source and spring in the Spirit of the living God.

Another ecclesiastical danger is that of rigidity in the forms of worship and organisation. This peril, as we have already seen, is the plain message of Montanism, Quakerism, and Brethrenism. In spite of all aberrations these movements represent legitimate assertions of the regenerated soul and the spiritual community. ' Where the Spirit of the Lord is, there is liberty ' (2 Cor. iii. 17).[4] And there is scarcely anything clearer in the New Testament than its emphasis on the liberty of the regenerated believer. Although liberty is far removed from licence, and although it may be difficult from time to time to express in proper terms the reality and limitations of liberty, the truth can never be disregarded with impunity by the Church. The soul that has learned the liberty wherewith Christ makes it free desires to stand fast thereby (Gal. v. 1), and is particularly sensitive

---

[1] Westcott, *The Gospel of the Resurrection*, p. 216.

[2] Westcott, *op. cit.* p. 217.   [3] Westcott, *op. cit.* p. 221.

[4] See note N, p. 281.

to anything that may check that freedom of approach to, and intercourse with God. There will always be difficulties in preserving the balance because the human mind is so apt to go to extremes, but in spite of the difficulty every effort must be made. The danger of the older, larger, and more thoroughly organised Churches is always in the direction of usurping the place of the Holy Spirit. But to guard against this will not mean undue individualism, because individualistic Christianity finds no warrant in the New Testament, and it may be said without any question or qualification that there is no future for Christianity apart from a unity of Christians. There have been, there still are, improper emphases on this truth, sometimes in Roman Catholicism, and sometimes from an entirely different standpoint in Ritschlianism, but the truth is undoubted that the Church is important and necessary for the individual, and that no man will ever be a 'saint' except in connection with the 'Communion of Saints.' Justification comes to a man solitarily and alone, but he is sanctified in relation to others. Christian character needs the Church for its development, and this is only possible in the Christian community. It is not without great significance that twice over in one short Epistle St. Paul associates himself with 'all saints' (Eph. iii. 18 ; vi. 18).

Nor will this insistence on Christian liberty lead to anything approaching what may be called ultra-spirituality, opposed to all organised Christianity. Here, again, we have to beware of falling into the fallacy that abuse takes away use. There are many indications to-day in support of Dr. Forsyth's pointed words that 'Free lances are futilities.' We must therefore beware of two extremes ; that of exaggerating the place and importance of the Church, and the opposite one of depreciating it. If we attempt to exaggerate the community we shall find that high views of the Church will often tend to low views of Christ, and will result in placing the Church between the soul and its Lord. On the other hand, we must foster Church fellowship, and emphasise to the full the value of the Christian community, and we shall do this in proportion as we allow the Holy Spirit His rightful place in the Church.

This will keep us from any exaggeration or depreciation, either of the individual or of the society. We shall rejoice to hear what the Spirit is saying to the Church, while we shall be equally thankful for what He is saying to the individual soul. We shall endeavour to glorify Christ as the Head of the Church, and at the same time rejoice in Him as the Lord of the individual. In our worship, our service, our fellowship, if we make room for the Holy Spirit and follow His leading step by step we shall find in that the safeguard against all extremes and the guarantee of a Christian life, love, and liberty that blesses men, builds up the Church, and glorifies God.

CHAPTER 32

CONCLUSION

As we recall the steps we have taken in the consideration of the Biblical teaching, the history of past days, the doctrinal formulation, and the application to modern needs, we cannot fail to see the imperative necessity of the Church and the individual emphasising the all-embracing importance of the Holy Spirit and His work. There are indications of this in the realm of religious thought, for it is being felt that the Holy Spirit has not received due notice and proper place in comparison with other aspects of Christian truth and life.

' The question is whether the full significance of our Lord's words concerning the Spirit has ever been adequately apprehended by His Church ; whether in this, as well as in other directions, there be not more light ready to break forth from God's Holy Word, when it is diligently and prayerfully pondered.' [1]

It has recently been said [2] that the doctrine of the Spirit is the hardest to reformulate to-day, that probably the time has not yet arrived for its full restatement ; and that Eucken and Bergson are preparing for it, by giving it a larger interpretation than the Church of Christ has yet generally conceived. There may be truth in this, because, as Dr. Swete has said :

' The same Holy Spirit Who taught the great writers of the ancient Church to conceive of Him in terms which served their

---

[1] Davison, ' The Person and Work of the Holy Spirit,' *London Quarterly Review*, p. 204 (April, 1905).

[2] Canon Masterman, Lectures at Liverpool on ' The Doctrine of the Holy Spirit,' 1912.

generation, may be leading us by other paths which He knows to be more suited to our feet.' [1]

But if it be true that in the New Testament ' the concep tion of the Spirit reaches its perfect end,' [2] it may be questioned whether we need wait for any further and fuller reformulation, or for any ' larger interpretation.' The writings of Eucken and Bergson are valuable as against the materialism of an earlier generation, but it remains to be seen, and, indeed, it may fairly be questioned, whether they have anything distinctive to teach us about a doctrine which is essentially one of the New Testament, and is only efficacious when kept in close relation to Jesus Christ. When Eucken rejects the idea of a Mediator, and insists upon our going direct to God, it would seem as though the criticism is correct that describes his Christianity as ' a Christianity without Christ,' especially as one of his admirers writes that he implies that Jesus was ' the unfortunate occasion and starting-point for a departure from pure monotheism and truly spiritual religion.' [3] If, therefore, it be accurate to describe Eucken's philosophy as simply a spiritual view of life without any relation to historic Christianity, it will not carry us very far, and we shall agree with Dr. Denney when he says that

' evidently Christianity will need the courage of its own experi-ences and conviction against Eucken, as against other philosophers who will not take Jesus at His own estimation.' [4]

The ' Spirit ' in the title of Eucken's book, *The Life of the Spirit*, is not to be confused with the ' Spirit ' of the New Testament ; it is concerned with *spirit*, not with *The* Spirit.

A little time ago Dr. Caldecott read a paper on ' The Religious Significance of Bergson's Philosophy,' [5] and after speaking in appreciative terms of Bergson's philosophy as a ' philosophy of spirit,' he admitted that we do not yet

---

[1] Swete, *The Holy Spirit in the Ancient Church*, p. 409.

[2] Wood, *The Spirit of God in Biblical Literature*, p. 269.

[3] Hermann, *Eucken and Bergson*.

[4] Denney, Review of Hermann's *Eucken and Bergson* in the *British Weekly*.

[5] *Record*, March 7, 1913.

know what his ethics will be beyond the fact that they will be 'ethics of freedom.' Further, that at present we cannot say that the idea of God is in sight, though Dr. Caldecott sees no peril ahead at this point. He holds that Christian believers are not warranted in asking whether Bergson's philosophy establishes revelation and redemption as we understand them, but 'whether it makes room for them.' Dr. Caldecott's conclusion is that whilst he may be over-estimating it, he finds very much even in its unfinished state which 'seems to him congenial with what Christian religion shows to us in its doctrine of the Holy Spirit and its doctrine of the spiritual life in man.' We are profoundly thankful for this assurance from so capable a thinker, but it may still be permitted to remind ourselves that, in Dr. Denney's words,

'The only Spirit which generates Christian experience is One which takes the things of Jesus and shows them to the soul. It is only by a ceaseless dialectical jugglery that we keep up the illusion that a historical religion can be independent of its origin and history.' [1]

The state of the Church to-day is another indication of the need of a re-emphasis on the doctrine of the Holy Spirit. There does not seem much doubt of the fact that the Church of God is not making proper progress. This is the conviction of thoughtful men in almost every part of the Christian world. The unconverted are not being won, the young people are not being kept, and even the children are not being gathered in. The Churches of all denominations are bewailing loss in the decrease of membership and the decline of conversions. Not long ago the Editor of the *Westminster Gazette* said : 'No one who attempts to look into the future can regard the present state of religion and religious bodies as either final or satisfactory. When we seek to discover the cause of this trouble, we cannot help feeling that beneath everything else the vital question concerns the spiritual life of those who 'profess and call themselves Christians.' Forsyth has rightly said that

'the arrest of the Church's extensive effect is due to the decay of its intensive faith, while a mere piety muffles the loss.' [2]

---

[1] Denney, *ut supra*.
[2] Forsyth, *The Principle of Authority*, p. 313.

It is widely believed that religion is losing its hold on numbers of people in various ranks of society where its power was formerly recognised. It is also urged that there is very little sense of sin because there is so little conception of God and eternal judgment. Is it not time, therefore, to face this problem, and endeavour to arrest the backward movement and turn it into a spiritual progress? It is unutterably sad to realise how little influence Churches have on the neighbourhoods in which they are situated, and to see the large numbers of people who never darken the doors of a place of worship, and are apparently, if not really, indifferent to the call and claim of Christ.

What, then, should be done? Every revival of spiritual religion has begun with a new conception of God, a recovery of the supernatural, a fuller revelation of the Person and Work of Christ and a deeper consciousness of the presence and power of the Holy Spirit. Unfortunately modern days are experiencing substitutes of various kinds for these eternal realities. Sometimes the priest is the substitute. In the Middle Ages when the consciousness of direct spiritual realities had become weakened the priest represented God, because God was only heard mediately by the individual soul. When the Reformation came, with its re-assertion of the introduction of the soul direct to God through faith, we know what a spiritual revival resulted, and whenever that consciousness of eternal realities has become lost, certain types of mind inevitably revert to the Church and the priesthood. But this is not the true solution of the problem; the Church and the priest are prominent when the consciousness of spiritual and eternal realities becomes weakened. The emphasis on the Holy Spirit and on His direct relationship to the soul in Christ is the supreme need rather than of any form of ecclesiastical mediation, which almost inevitably tends to set God aside.

Another substitute for spiritual realities is often found in the scholar, or philosopher, or critic, by those who are unable to accept the idea of the priestly function in the Church. A short time back a book was published, *The Greek Genius and Its Meaning to Us*, by an Oxford scholar, in which among other points attention is given to the contrast between the religion of the Greek and the religion of the Jew. The author points out that the Greek was enabled to exercise his religious and political liberty without being at all concerned with the idea of a Divine revelation.

' The Jew accepted the God that was revealed to Him, the Greek thought his gods out . . . , the Greek set himself to answer the question how, with no revelation from God to guide him, with no overbearing necessity to intimidate him, man should live.' [1]

An able writer, reviewing this book, remarked, ' That is the question we have to face now,' and recommended his readers to adopt this idea of life without any Divine revelation. This is typical of much to-day that is found in modern scholarship. Minds are either unable or unwilling to realise that the Gospel is a Divine revelation, a supernatural religion. They seem to think that everything in Christianity can be explained along the lines of history and evolution, and they are constantly trying to reduce the Gospel to such limits as necessarily exclude its supernatural element. Even Benjamin Kidd in his *Social Evolution*, while recognising the supernaturalness of Christianity, declared it to be irrational. But there are many things in life that cannot be solved by reason, or analysed by science, and the innermost secrets of this Divine supernatural Gospel are the redemptive work of Christ and the presence of the Holy Spirit. The deepest needs of humanity will never be solved by philosophy, scholarship, or criticism. Nothing but spiritual and moral sterility can be found in these directions.

Once again, to those who do not feel satisfied with the priest, or the scholar, the philanthropist is sometimes recommended. Great emphasis is placed upon social effort, and it is urged that Churches should be organised to improve social conditions, and to minister to social and economic needs. No doubt this is a timely and much-needed lesson, lest in our thought of bringing men to God, we fail to realise the need of social relationships and duties. But the deepest need of all is the conviction of sin, and no emphasis upon the social aspects of life will ever bring this about. Legislation will do much for human betterment, and it is the duty of the Church to emphasise the highest

[1] R. W. Livingstone, *The Greek Genius and Its Meaning to Us.*

social ideals and to help forward the best social improvement. But when all has been said, it is still true, as Forsyth remarks, that

'the prime object of the Church with its Gospel is neither to sweeten, spiritualise, nor rationalise civilization and religion ; but it is to conquer them.' [1]

Social reform can only come from spiritual reform, and the most clamant call to the Church is to proclaim the relationship and responsibility of man to God and the revelation of God to man. It is only in the presence and power of the Holy Spirit that sin will be realised and spiritual transformation effected. ' When He is come He will convince the world of sin . . . because they believe not on Me.'

Not, therefore, in the priest, or in the scholar, or in the philanthropist will the solution of the problem of arrested progress be found. The supreme need to-day is that of the evangelist and the prophet. If the evangelistic spirit were what it ought to be in our Churches a very great change would soon be effected. The supreme purpose of discipleship in the New Testament is that of personal service for Christ, the work of winning men to Him and to His Church, and this can only be done in the power of the Holy Spirit. As we contemplate the present condition of Christendom, we cannot help asking, ' Is the Spirit of the Lord straitened ? Are these His doings ? ' (Micah ii. 7). And the answer is a decided negative. It is the unfaithfulness of the Church to its supreme duty that is the cause of the present trouble. It is admitted by all that we are living in difficult and solemn days. The outlook depresses the earnest soul, for wherever he turns he is conscious of elements of evil and trouble, and of strange conditions in the Church and in the world. Callousness becomes more defined ; indifference more widespread ; the love of many waxes cold ; universal charity tends to tolerate many forms of false teaching, and as a result the clear witness of the Church to Christ is hindered. There is only one way of changing all this and of bringing back a life in harmony with New Testament principles ; it is by the declaration

[1] Forsyth, *op. cit.* p. 313.

of the ' Old, Old Story,' by hearts that know, and lives that value it. ' Not by might, nor by power, but by My Spirit, saith the Lord of Hosts ' (Zech. iv. 6).

Since, therefore, the explanation of all the foregoing in individual Christian lives has been given our duty is obvious. The supreme need is for clear thinking, definite teaching, holy living, faithful witness, earnest service, strenuous effort in the power of the Spirit of God. We must make the Holy Spirit dominant in our life.[1] Doctrine is power-less without experience. We must first receive the Spirit and then obey Him if we would understand fully and live adequately.[2]

The New Testament picture is that of a Spirit-filled Church, a community of Christians ' full ' of the Spirit of God, and herein consists the essential difference between life before and life after Pentecost.[3] Whatever had been the case previous to that time, it was nothing compared with the life of the Church then and afterwards. But the trouble is that so many Christians to-day possess an experience which is only on a level with the earlier dispensa-tions of the Old Testament and the Gospels. Although the dispensations of the Father and the Son are historically past, they are still experimentally present in many lives. It is not that, like the disciples of the Baptist, people have not heard whether the Holy Ghost has been given, but that they have never realised and entered fully into their inheritance. In the Old Testament dispensation from Abel to John the Baptist, there was of course a real life lived in the fear of God, with a genuine sense of sin, a strong belief in the coming Messiah, and a definite consciousness of immortality. Further, in the dispensation of the Son during our Lord's earthly ministry, there was a distinct advance on the previous period, for the disciples felt the power of the Divine Word in their Master's teaching, and enjoyed not a little fellowship with Him. But the dispensa-tion of the Holy Spirit ushered in at Pentecost was marked beyond all else in a threefold way. It was characterised

---

[1] Denio, *The Supreme Leader*, ch. xiii. p. 226.

[2] Humphries, *The Holy Spirit in Faith and Experience*, pp. 360-363.

[3] See note O, p. 281.

by (a) a rich personal experience : men were full of faith (Acts vi. 5) ; wisdom (Acts vi. 3) ; joy (Acts xiii. 52) ; and hope (Acts vii. 55). Then it was noteworthy for its (b) great personal courage, both of speech (Acts iv. 31), and of action (Acts xiii. 9). And as the outcome there was (c) splendid personal service in preaching (Acts ii. 4), and living (Acts ix. 31). There is scarcely anything more out-standing or more striking in the story of the primitive Church recorded in the Acts than the association of the Holy Spirit with every part of the life of the disciple and the community. Not only are men like Peter, Stephen, and Paul filled with the Holy Spirit (Acts iv. 8 ; vii. 55 ; ix. 17), but ordinary disciples have exactly the same experience (Acts iv. 31 ; xiii. 52), and almost every Christian grace is associated with the Holy Spirit, including wisdom (Acts vi. 5), comfort (Acts ix. 31), power (Acts x. 38), faith (Acts xi. 24), and joy (Acts xiii. 52).

This is God's purpose for all and at all times, and it is a disastrous error to regard it as a luxury for the few, or for spiritual occasions alone. When we read of Stephen being permanently full of the Holy Spirit ($\dot{\upsilon}\pi\dot{\alpha}\rho\chi\omega\nu$; Acts vii. 55), we may surely believe that such an experience is possible for all. Some time ago, the Bishop of Durham gave a simple yet striking testimony in regard to his own spiritual experience :

' Never shall I forget the gain to conscious faith and peace which came to my own soul not long after I had appropriated the crucified Lord as the sinner's Sacrifice from a more intelligent and conscious hold, from the living personality of that Holy Spirit through whose mercy I had obtained that blessed view. It was a new development of insight into the love of God, a new discovery into divine resources.'

This represents the essential truth of the Holy Spirit in relation to the Christian life. When we receive Him by faith, we make ' a new discovery in Divine resources,' and we find that our lives enter upon a higher plane of restful satisfaction, of calm confidence, of frictionless service, of deepening influence, and of ever-extending blessing. If only our faith will accept the Spirit we shall receive and experience His power. And then if only in faithfulness we obey the Spirit we shall maintain our position, and by never grieving (Eph. iv. 30), never resisting (Acts vii. 51), never quenching (1 Thess. v. 19), we shall repeat in all our experiences and emergencies the New Testament life of privilege, power, and blessing. We shall rejoice in God's rich provision of grace, fulfil His great purposes of grace, and glorify Him as the God of all grace in a life ' full of the Holy Ghost.'

NOTES

THE subject of the Holy Spirit includes a large number of subsidiary topics, and some of the most important of these call for special attention. The following notes are intended as suggestions for study, and references are given to books in which the questions are more fully considered.

NOTE A. THE DOCTRINE OF THE HOLY SPIRIT IN SEPARATE NEW TESTAMENT BOOKS

In order to obtain the fullest impression of the teaching of the New Testament on the Holy Spirit, it is essential to study the subject in each book by itself. The teaching of the Fourth Gospel has already been outlined, and also that of the Acts. It is of primary importance to give attention to the first eleven chapters of the Acts, where the presence and operation of the Spirit are so prominent. By way of further illustration, the following suggestions are given.

THE HOLY SPIRIT IN ROMANS

I. Salvation (ch. v. 5).
II. Sanctification (ch. viii.). Life (ver. 2); conduct (ver. 4); mind (vv. 5, 6); soul (ver. 9); body (vv. 11, 13); obedience (ver. 14); sonship (vv. 15, 16); pledge (ver. 23); power (ver. 26). See Elder Cumming, *After the Spirit*, ch. v.
III. Service (chs. ix., xiv., xv.). Sincerity (ch. ix. 1); love (ch. xiv. 17); hope (ch. xv. 13); consecration (ch. xv. 16); power (ch. xv. 19); prayer (ch. xv. 30).

THE HOLY SPIRIT IN GALATIANS

I. The Spirit Received (ch. iii.). For commencement (ver. 2); for continuance (ver. 5); for completion (ver. 14).

II. The Spirit Realised (chs. iv., v.). As to the past (ch. iv. 6, 29) ; as to the future (ch. v. 5) ; as to the present (ch. v. 16, 17, 18, 25).

III. The Spirit Reproduced (chs. v., vi.). Character (ch. v. 22) ; conduct (ch. v. 25) ; consecration (ch. vi. 8).

THE HOLY SPIRIT IN EPHESIANS

I. Facts. Sealing (ch. i. 13 ; iv. 30) ; introduction (ch. ii. 18) ; indwelling (ch. ii. 22) ; revelation (ch. iii. 5).

II. Consequences. Strength (ch. iii. 16) ; unity (ch. iv. 3) ; sensitiveness (ch. iv. 30) ; fulness (ch. v. 18).

III. Conditions. The Word (ch. vi. 17) ; prayer (ch. vi. 18).

See also Elder Cumming on 1 Cor. ii. (*After the Spirit*, ch. vi.).

NOTE B. THE GIFT OF TONGUES

This important subject can best be studied in the following works :

Scroggie, *The Baptism of the Spirit and the Gift of Tongues*.

Dawson Walker, *The Gift of Tongues*.

Swete, *The Holy Spirit in the New Testament*, pp. 73, 379.

Elder Cumming, *After the Spirit*, p. 10.

Denney, Article ' The Holy Spirit,' *Dictionary of Christ and the Gospels*, vol. i. p. 737.

Wood, *The Spirit of God in Biblical Literature*, p. 161.

Denio, *The Supreme Leader*, p. 33.

Humphries, *The Holy Spirit in Faith and Experience*, p. 205.

Davison, *The Indwelling Spirit*, pp. 81, 87.

Kuyper, *The Work of the Holy Spirit*, p. 133.

Swete, Article ' Holy Spirit,' Hastings' *Bible Dictionary*, vol. ii. p. 409.

Bartlet, *The Apostolic Age*, p. 13.

NOTE C. THE HOLY SPIRIT AND THE LAYING ON OF HANDS

The references to the laying on of hands in the Acts of the Apostles in connection with the gift of the Holy Spirit call for special attention. The first case is that of the Samaritans (ch. viii. 15), who did not receive the Holy Spirit independently of the Apostles at Jerusalem. Perhaps this was intended to prevent any rupture in the early Church, and any rivalry of

Samaria with Jerusalem. The second instance is that of Paul (ch. ix. 17), and the gift of the Spirit in this case was by the laying on of hands of one who was a layman, not an Apostle. The third is that of the disciples of the Baptist (ch. xix. 2-6), who did not know that the Holy Spirit had been given at Pentecost. The Apostle makes known to them the truth in Christ and also lays his hands upon them. It would seem from these that in each there was an intention to link the disciples with the existing Church in order that the truth of 1 Cor. xii. 13 might be seen : ' By one Spirit are we all baptized into one body, whether we be Jews or Gentiles.' The case of Cornelius and his company (Acts x. 44) shows that the Holy Spirit was given not by the laying on of hands, but while Peter was speaking. It is essential to study all the instances, and it will then be seen that the Holy Spirit was not restricted to the laying on of the hands of the Apostles, or to the laying on of hands at all. There was variety of method in this one definite gift. See Denney, Article ' The Holy Spirit,' *Dictionary of Christ and the Gospels*, vol. i. p. 737.

NOTE D. THE BAPTISM OF THE SPIRIT

The phrase, ' the Baptism of the Holy Ghost,' is so frequently used as to call for careful notice. As it stands, it is not found in Holy Scripture, though there are seven passages which speak of being baptised in (or with) the Holy Spirit. The first four of these are associated with the words of John the Baptist in stating the difference between his own baptism and that of the coming Messiah (Matt. iii. 11 ; Mark i. 8 ; Luke iii. 16 ; John i. 26, 33). Two others refer to the same distinction (Acts i. 5 ; xi. 16). The seventh is 1 Cor. xii. 13. In one passage (Mark i. 8) the preposition $\dot{\epsilon}\nu$ is omitted. But even the preposition may be fairly translated ' with ' according to a well known Hebraism, which makes $\dot{\epsilon}\nu$ stand for בְּ.

Then again, the reference to baptism in, or with, the Holy Spirit is plainly stated as the actual experience of every Christian without exception, and not at all as the special privilege of the certain number. This is absolutely clear in 1 Cor. xii. 13, and is implied in other passages. As the term ' baptism,' when applied to water, refers to an initial act which is never repeated, and is used of designation for, and introduction to a new sphere of relationship, it is perhaps best to interpret the phrase, ' baptised in (or with) the Holy

Ghost' as referring to the initial work of the Holy Spirit in uniting believers to Christ and to one another in Him (Acts ii. 33 ; Gal. iv. 6). If this is the true meaning, then the view that the baptism of the Holy Ghost is a second distinct work of grace after conversion is without any warrant in Holy Scripture, especially as the phrase, ' the baptism of the Holy Ghost,' is not found in the New Testament. But while believing that a Spirit-filled life is the privilege and duty of every believer, and that as a matter of personal experience it is often realised by means of a distinct crisis after conversion, yet much modern phraseology about ' the Baptism of the Spirit ' does not seem to be justified by the New Testament, which teaches that all who are born again have been baptized by the Spirit into the one body of Christ. Instead of seeking some exceptional and transcendental experience, it is rather the true duty of the believer to accept and yield quietly each day to the indwelling of the Holy Spirit for the purpose of Christian living.

See also Note E, ' The Fulness of the Spirit.'

Scroggie, *The Baptism of the Holy Spirit.*

McConkey, *The Three-fold Secret of the Holy Spirit.*

Biederwolf, *Study of the Holy Spirit*, ch. ix.

(Important for its statement of various views.)

Robson, *The Holy Ghost the Paraclete*, p. 149.

A. J. Gordon, *The Ministry of the Spirit*, p. 75.

Elder Cumming, *Through the Eternal Spirit*, p. 149.

Torrey, *The Baptism with the Holy Ghost.*

Moule, *Veni Creator*, p. 12.

Humphries, *The Holy Spirit in Faith and Experience*, p. 194.

Denney, Article ' Holy Spirit,' vol. i. *Dictionary of Christ and the Gospels.*

Wolston, *Another Comforter*, p. 221.

NOTE E. THE FULNESS OF THE SPIRIT

The word ' full ' and its cognates are frequently found in connection with the Holy Spirit, and a careful study of the usages on and after the Day of Pentecost is particularly important. Thus, the gift of the Spirit on the Day of Pentecost is described by the Aorist tense (Acts ii. 4). Then for the special work of testimony the Aorist is again used (Acts iv. 8). Similar usages are also found elsewhere (Acts iv. 31 ; ix. 17 ; xiii. 9). The Imperfect is also employed (Acts xiii. 52).

From these passages it is apparently taught that the filling of the Spirit refers to special enduements for special needs and emergencies. To put it in familiar words, ' One baptism, many fillings.'

The passage in Ephes. v. 18 calls for two remarks : (1) The use of the Dative and ἐν, not the Genitive, indicates that the Spirit is the Sphere in which, or the Agent by Whom, not the Person or Matter of Whom, we are filled. (See Bullinger, *The Giver and His Gifts*, p. 157.) (2) The context shows by the four following participles that verses 19-21 give the fourfold proof or result of the Spirit filling us : ' Be filled by the Spirit, by speaking . . . by singing . . . by giving thanks . . . by submitting.'

The supreme test and proof of the fulness of the Spirit is the Presence and Preciousness of Christ. The Spirit glorifies Christ, and the answer to the question, What is Christ to me now ?, is the infallible criterion of the fulness of the Holy Spirit.

Biederwolf, *Study of the Holy Spirit*, ch. x.

A. J. Gordon, *The Ministry of the Spirit*, p. 89.

Elder Cumming, *Through the Eternal Spirit*, p. 22 ; *After the Spirit*, p. 12.

NOTE F. RECEIVING THE SPIRIT

It is significant that the Holy Spirit in the New Testament is associated with the words ' giving ' on the part of God, and ' receiving ' on the part of men. But these are not the only expressions found. We read not only that God gives (Acts v. 32 ; xv. 8 ; 1 Thess. iv. 8 ; 2 Cor. i. 22) ; but of expressions such as ' came upon ' (Acts xix. 6), ' anointed with ' (Acts x. 38), ' poured out ' (Acts x. 45), ' fell on ' (Acts x. 44 ; xi. 15), ' baptized with ' (Acts xi. 16), ' received ' (Acts ii. 38 ; viii. 15, 17 ; x. 47 ; xix. 2). It would seem best to understand all these expressions as so many different ways of regarding the features of the same experience of the Spirit entering the believer.

Elder Cumming, *Through the Eternal Spirit*, p. 157.

NOTE G. SIN AND SINS AGAINST THE HOLY GHOST

A careful study of Matt. xii. 22-32 and Mark iii. 21-30 shows that our Lord was referring to a persistent and continuous attitude of deliberate and wilful sin against light, maintained in the face of all God's efforts to bring about a change. As the dispensation of the Spirit is the final and supreme provision of God for man, there remains nothing more to be done if anyone deliberately closes the eyes to the fullest provision made by God. ' The sin against the Holy Ghost is the full personal rejection of all the moral demand which the Holy Ghost makes through conscience. . . . It is the culmination of personal sin into a fixed attitude of wilful unrighteousness, and so it is the complete exhaustion of the pressure of the Holy Spirit.—And so it is unforgivable—it is everlasting moral ruin ' (Curtis, *The Christian Faith*, p. 343).

Biederwolf, *Study of the Holy Spirit*, ch. xii.

Smeaton, *The Doctrine of the Holy Spirit*, p. 183.

Elder Cumming, *Through the Eternal Spirit*, ch. xxv.

Robson, *The Holy Spirit the Paraclete*, p. 197.

Moule, *Veni Creator*, p. 19.

NOTE H. THE HOLY GHOST AND FIRE

Although the reference by the Baptist to the Messiah baptizing ' with the Holy Ghost, and fire ' (Matt. iii. 11) is often used to express the spiritual symbol of fire, as illustrated on the Day of Pentecost (Acts ii. 3), yet it is in every way better to regard the fire in this passage as expressive of future judgment, as indeed the context itself clearly suggests (Matt. iii. 10, 12). But see Elder Cumming, *Through the Eternal Spirit*, p. 162.

NOTE I. THE TWO PARACLETES

The use of the same word ' Paraclete ' to describe both the relation of our Lord and of the Holy Spirit to the believer (1 John ii. 2 ; John xiv. 6) is particularly significant. The best treatment of the various aspects of the truth will be found in Clemance, *The Scripture Doctrine of the Holy Spirit*, ch. ii. The subject is also discussed by Swete, *The Holy Spirit in the New Testament*, p. 372 ; R. C. Morgan, *The Outpoured Spirit and Pentecost* ; Robson, *The Holy Spirit the Paraclete*, ch. i.

NOTE J. THE FRUIT OF THE SPIRIT

It is noteworthy that the term is singular, not plural (Gal. v. 22, 23), indicating that each part mentioned is included in the generic term ' fruit,' like a cluster of separate grapes. All the aspects refer to character rather than to conduct; what we *are*, not what we *do*. The nine elements are divisible into three sections of three each. (1) In relation to God; ' love, joy, peace.' (2) In relation to our fellows; ' long-suffering, gentleness, goodness.' (3) In relation to ourselves; ' faithfulness (not faith), meekness, self-control.' The contrast between the ' works ' (plural) of the flesh is particularly significant.

Elder Cumming, *Through the Eternal Spirit*, ch. xv.

NOTE K. HOLINESS

As the title of the Spirit most frequently used in the New Testament is the Holy Spirit, it is natural that holiness should be considered in close and intimate connection with the Spirit of God. Among other works the following call for special notice :

Davison, *The Indwelling Spirit*, ch. viii.
Elder Cumming, *Through the Eternal Spirit*, ch. xiv.
Walter Marshall, *The Gospel Mystery of Sanctification*.
Beet, *Holiness : Symbolic and Real*.
Andrew Murray, *Holy in Christ* and *The Spirit of Christ*.

NOTE L. THE HOLY SPIRIT AND THE SACRAMENTS

In relation to Christian Baptism the book of Acts records three different aspects of teaching. (1) The Holy Spirit as coincident with baptism with water (ch. ii. 38 ; cf. ix. 17). (2) Baptism apparently without any gift of grace or the Spirit (ch. viii. 14-17). (3) The gift of the Holy Spirit before baptism with water (ch. x. 45-48). Any true view of the Holy Spirit in relation to the Sacrament of Baptism must include and explain all these three aspects. The other question in this connection is the meaning of ' water' in John iii. 5. (1) In any case it is surely not possible to interpret it of Christian Baptism, which was only instituted nearly three years afterwards. (2) The analogy of chs. iv. and vii. must be observed where water is used as a symbol of spiritual blessing, the latter connected with the Holy Spirit. (3) The repetition by our Lord of ' born of the Spirit ' twice, without mention of water, seems to suggest the predominance of the Holy Spirit in the passage. (4) The phrase in the original has one preposition, not two, indicating a complete idea, and not two separate thoughts or sources. (5) The analogy of Ezek. xxxvi. 25 and Psa. li. 7 may perhaps have been in our Lord's mind in recalling Nicodemus to his assumed knowledge of the Old Testament Scriptures, and if ' water ' meant baptism Nicodemus might well have been surprised. (6) If water means baptism, it can only refer to John's baptism with its outward expression of inward repentance towards God.

Denney, Article ' Holy Spirit,' *Dictionary of Christ and the Gospels*, vol. i. p. 737.

Swete, *The Holy Spirit in the New Testament*.

Elder Cumming, *After the Spirit*, p. 37.

It is impossible to avoid noticing that the Holy Spirit is never once found in the New Testament connected with the Holy Communion, and although in the early Liturgies an Epiclesis is found, there are clear indications that its primitive form was a prayer for the Holy Spirit to come upon the communicant rather than upon the elements.

Woolley, *Liturgy of the Primitive Church*, pp. 93-120.

Upton, *Outlines of Prayer Book History*, pp. 12-21.

NOTE M. TEMPLES OF THE HOLY GHOST

The relation of the Holy Spirit to Christians under the figure of the temple is found in 1 Cor. iii. 16, 17 ; vi. 19 ; and Eph. ii. 20-22. See also John ii. 21. The presence of the Holy Spirit in this sense seems to be at once individual and corporate.

Elder Cumming, *Through the Eternal Spirit*, ch. xxiii.

NOTE N. THE LIBERTY OF THE SPIRIT

This subject is one of great importance and great difficulty, and calls for careful, balanced teaching.

Davison, *The Indwelling Spirit*, ch. vi.

Hopkins, *The Law of Liberty in the Spiritual Life*.

NOTE O. THE DISPENSATIONS

It is important to study the revelation of God along the lines laid down by Holy Scripture, when it will be found that from the Creation to the Coming of Christ the Father is pre-eminently in view. From the Coming of Christ to the Day of Pentecost the Son comes into prominence. Then from

Pentecost onwards we have the dispensation of the Holy Spirit, with the individual and the Christian community under His guidance and control.

A. J. Gordon, *The Ministry of the Spirit*, ch. i.
Andrew Murray, *The Spirit of Christ*, p. 15.

NOTE P. THE GIFTS OF THE SPIRIT

The subject of spiritual gifts is fully discussed in 1 Cor. xii., on which leading Commentaries, like those of Ellicott, Edwards, Godet, Evans, and Robertson and Plummer should be consulted. Three things are to be distinguished. (1) The gifts which are to be regarded as special equipments for service. (2) Ministries which are to be regarded as opportunities for exercising gifts. (3) The operations which would seem to refer to the inner experiences of the Holy Spirit in the heart corresponding to the outward ministry and the Divine equipment (vv. 4-6). See also Wolston, *Another Comforter*, p. 251.

NOTE Q. SPIRIT AND THE SPIRIT

The question whether the presence or absence of the definite article in the Greek implies a distinction of meaning is variously interpreted. It is hardly possible to doubt that some difference is intended, though, as Dr. Swete says, the exact meaning must be gathered from the context. Perhaps the best, or at any rate the most general view, is to regard the presence of the article as referring to the Person, and the absence of the article to the specific gifts or operations of the Spirit. This appears to be the view favoured by Dr. Swete.

Swete, *The Holy Spirit in the New Testament*, p. 395.
Elder Cumming, *Through the Eternal Spirit*, p. 353.
Bullinger, *The Giver and His Gifts*.

NOTE R. PRAYER AND THE HOLY SPIRIT

Three different subjects need attention :

(1) Praying *to* the Holy Spirit. No instance of this can be found in the New Testament, and perhaps it is due to the fact that the Holy Spirit is regarded as having already been given to the believer as the indwelling presence of God, and that therefore prayer to One Who dwells within may not have been considered suitable. It is probably best to direct our prayers

to God without distinguishing particularly between the Persons of the Trinity.

(2) Praying *for* the Holy Spirit. It is certainly striking that after the Day of Pentecost no instance is found of prayer for the Holy Spirit. As Swete significantly says : ' The attitude of the primitive Church towards the Spirit was rather one of joyful welcome than of invocation ; the cry *Veni, Creator Spiritus* belongs to a later age, when the Spirit was sought and perhaps expected, but not regarded as a Guest Who had already come, and come to abide ' (*The Holy Spirit in the New Testament*, p. 96, note). It is in harmony with this idea that the New Testament teaches that the entire spiritual life of the believer is due to the Holy Spirit. The only passage that tends to warrant prayer for the Spirit is Luke xi. 13. But it may be questioned whether this text is properly interpreted of a time after the experience of the Holy Spirit on the Day of Pentecost.

(3) Praying *in* the Holy Ghost. The New Testament clearly teaches that the Holy Spirit is at once the sphere and the atmosphere of prayer (Eph. vi. 18 ; Jude 20). When the Spirit takes possession of the soul, He becomes essentially the Spirit of intercession, and the heart is drawn out in earnest prayer, the Spirit helping our many infirmities (Rom. viii. 26).

Davison, *The Indwelling Spirit*, ch. vii.

Biederwolf, *Study of the Holy Spirit*, ch. xi.

A. J. Gordon, *The Ministry of the Spirit*, p. 151.

Walker, *The Holy Spirit*, p. 196.

Andrew Murray, *The Spirit of Christ*, p. 195.

Mullins, ' The Holy Spirit in the Old Testament,' *Review and Expositor*, p. 252 (April, 1912).

NOTE S. EMBLEMS OF THE SPIRIT

Very much in the New Testament on the subject of the Holy Spirit is found in connection with metaphors and symbols of His presence and work. Among these are the Seal, the Oil, the Dove, the Wind, the Fire and the Water.

Biederwolf, *A Help to the Study of the Holy Spirit*, chs. v., vi., xi.

Elder Cumming, *Through the Eternal Spirit*, p. 241 ; ch. xx. *After the Spirit*, p. 4.

Swete, *The Holy Spirit in the New Testament*, p. 365.

F. E. Marsh, *Emblems of the Holy Ghost*.

A. J. Gordon, *The Ministry of the Spirit*, pp. 84, 94.

NOTE T. CONSCIENCE AND THE HOLY SPIRIT

The relation of Conscience to the Holy Spirit is at once important and difficult. St. Paul in Rom. ix. 1 implies that the conscience lives in the sphere of the Holy Spirit.

Elder Cumming, *After the Spirit*, ch. ix. ; p. 238.

Andrew Murray, *The Spirit of Christ*, p. 369.

NOTE U. PERSONAL GUIDANCE AND THE SPIRIT

Much important teaching is found in the New Testament in connection with the Holy Spirit as the Leader and Guide of the believer (Rom. viii. 14).

Elder Cumming, *Through the Eternal Spirit*, ch. xviii.

NOTE V. PROPHECY

As one of the Gifts of the Spirit, Prophecy is particularly important. See Denney, Article ' Holy Spirit,' *Dictionary of Christ and the Gospels*, vol. i. p. 737.

NOTE W. THE HOLY SPIRIT AND THE MYSTERIES

Recent scholarship has endeavoured to prove that Christianity is largely dependent on some ancient Mystery Religions for its ideas and practices. The subject has not yet been given much attention in English, but the following works will enable the student to study the subject on general lines for himself. A series of articles in the *Expositor*, ' St. Paul and the Mystery Religions,' by Professor H. A. A. Kennedy, April, May, July, September, October, November, December, 1912, and January and February, 1913 ; an article on ' St. Paul and the Mysteries,' by Sir William M. Ramsay, in the *Contemporary Review* for August, 1913. See also *Primitive Christianity and Its Known Jewish Sources*, by Clemen, Index, s.v. ' Spirit.' All the indications at present go to support the view maintained above that the New Testament doctrine of the Holy Spirit is unique as a Divine revelation, and cannot be attributed to any earthly and historical source.

NOTE X. THE HOLY SPIRIT AND EVIL SPIRITS

The fact that the same word ' spirit ' is used to describe the Holy Spirit of God and also unclean spirits of evil arrests attention. The subject though difficult and mysterious demands careful study. The present writer expresses the opinion after reading very much to the contrary that the *prima facie* view of the New Testament is that our Lord and His Apostles believed in the reality of demoniacal possession. It is also very difficult to doubt that various manifestations of evil during the ages of the Christian centuries imply and demand some force or forces beyond what is merely human. Spiritualism alone is a phenomenon that cannot be entirely explained by chicanery. The subject will naturally be studied first of all in connection with the New Testament passages dealing with demoniacal possession. Among the works on Spiritualism may be mentioned *The Dangers of Spiritualism*, by Raupert. Reference should also be made to *Demoniacal Possession*, by Nevius, and *War on the Saints*, by Mrs. Penn Lewis. In studying this most difficult problem attention will necessarily be directed first of all to the thorough exegesis of the New Testament, and then to the various phenomena of history, but it may not be altogether unnecessary to say that while giving the matter all possible care, the student should rigidly keep an independent mind in considering the various deductions and implications found in works on the subject.

NOTE Y. THE HOLY SPIRIT AND MISSIONS

Christian Missions should be studied first of all from the standpoint of Holy Scripture in order that the Divine purpose may be realised, and the subject viewed from the standpoint of the Divine perspective taught by the Holy Spirit in the Word. Then will come the consideration of the missionary work actually accomplished through the centuries. Among many other works the following may be commended for study :

A. J. Gordon, *The Holy Spirit in Missions*.

Tait, *Christ and the Nations*.

Pierson, *The Divine Enterprise of Missions ; The Acts of the Holy Spirit ; The New Acts of the Apostles ; The Modern Missionary Century*.

Davis, *Christ the Desire of Nations.*
Macdonald, *The Redeemer's Reign.*
Baron, *The Ancient Scriptures and the Modern Jew.*
Carus Wilson, *Redemptor Mundi ; St. Peter and St. John ; First Missionaries of the Gospel ; St. Paul ; Missionary to the Nations.*

For other topics connected with the Holy Spirit, reference may be made to the Notes in Andrew Murray's *Spirit of Christ,* and to additional chapters in the two works by Elder Cumming already mentioned.

BIBLIOGRAPHY

In addition to the authorities mentioned in each chapter the following may be consulted :

Bibliography and valuable Notes in Denio, *The Supreme Leader*, pp. 239-255.

Bibliography in Hastings' *Bible Dictionary*, vol. ii., Article ' Holy Spirit.'

Bibliography in *Dictionary of Christian Biography*, vol. ii., Article ' Holy Ghost.'

Bibliography in Elder Cumming, *After the Spirit*, p. 243.

Bibliography in Biederwolf, *Study of the Holy Spirit*. Grand Rapids: Kregel Publications, 1985. (Former title: *A Help to the Study of the Holy Spirit*.)

St. Basil, *On the Holy Spirit* (English translation with important notes by the Rev. George Lewis).

Tasker, *Spiritual Religion*. (A fresh and suggestive presentation.)

Kuyper, *The Work of the Holy Spirit*. (Very full and elaborate ; important introduction by Professor Warfield.)

Buchanan, *The Office and Work of the Holy Spirit*. (Notable for illustrative cases.)

J. S. Candlish, *The Work of the Holy Spirit* (A valuable handbook.)

Clemance, *The Scripture Doctrine of the Holy Spirit*. (A brief but suggestive treatment.)

Cardinal Manning, *The Temporal Mission of the Holy Ghost ; The Internal Mission of the Holy Ghost*. (Apart from Roman Catholic views, these contain some useful contributions.)

Selby, *The Holy Spirit and Christian Privilege.* (Fourteen suggestive, scholarly, and spiritual sermons.)

Morgan, *The Ministry of the Holy Ghost.* (Spiritual expositions.)

McConkey, *The Three-fold Secret of the Holy Spirit.* (One of the best spiritual expositions.)

Bishop Webb, *The Presence and Office of the Holy Spirit.* (Devout spiritual addresses from the standpoint of extreme Anglicanism.)

Kelly, *Lectures on the New Testament Doctrine of the Holy Spirit.* (Spiritual expositions from a well-known scholar among the Brethren.)

Arthur, *The Tongue of Fire.* (An able and forceful Methodist presentation.)

A. B. Simpson, *The Holy Spirit.* Two Volumes. (Devotional expositions, unfolding the doctrine in the Old and New Testaments.)

Ridout, *The Person and Work of the Holy Spirit.* Seven Lectures. (Expository and spiritual, from the standpoint of the Brethren.)

G. Campbell Morgan, *The Spirit of God.* (An outline of Biblical study.)

J. B. Walker, *The Philosophy of the Divine Operation in the Redemption of Man.* (An able discussion of the doctrine of the Holy Spirit.)

Daunt, *The Presence and Offices of the Holy Spirit.* (Donnellan Lectures in Trinity College, Dublin.)

Edited by A. C. Dixon, *The Person and Ministry of the Holy Spirit.* (A series of expository papers on various aspects.)

Andrew Murray, *The Spirit of Christ.* (Exegetical and devotional.)

W. J. Erdman, *The Holy Spirit and Christian Experience.* (Papers on the Gift of the Spirit in relation to the sonship of believers.)

G. Soltau, *The Person and Mission of the Holy Spirit.* (Expository and practical papers.)

Hare, *The Mission of the Comforter.* (Including valuable notes.)

John Owen, *The Holy Spirit: His Gifts and Power*. Grand Rapids: Kregel Publications, 1977. (The great Puritan work.)

John Goodwin, *Pleroma to Pneumatikon, or A Being filled with the Spirit*. (Another Puritan work.)

J. M. Campbell, *After Pentecost, What ?* (A discussion of the doctrine of the Holy Spirit in relation to modern Christological thought.)

Marshall, *The Gospel Mystery of Sanctification*. (An old and very valuable treatise.)

Beet, *Holiness : Symbolic and Real*. (A useful handbook.)

Hopkins, *The Law of Liberty in the Spiritual Life*. (A clear and cogent presentation.)

Wolston, *Another Comforter*. (Spiritual expositions by a leader of the Brethren.)

A. J. Gordon, *The Holy Spirit in Missions*. (A suggestive missionary study.)

Pierson, *The Acts of the Holy Spirit*. (Meditations on the Acts.)

Bruce, *St. Paul's Conception of Christianity*, chs. xiii.-xv.

H. W. Robinson, *The Christian Doctrine of Man*, Index, s.v. ' Spirit.'

G. B. Stevens, *The Theology of the New Testament*, Index, s.v. ' Spirit ' ; and pp. 213, 338, 431.

J. M. Campbell, *Paul the Mystic*.

Lowrie, *The Doctrinal System of St. John*.

Somerville, *St. Paul's Conception of Christ*.

Wilder, *Studies on the Holy Spirit*.

RECENT FRENCH AND GERMAN WORKS

Arnol, *La Notion de l'Esprit*. (1st Volume, la doctrine Paulinienne.)

Lombard, *De la Glossolalie chez les premiers chretiens*.

Tixeront, *Histoire des dogmes*.

Bovon, *Dogmatique*.

Goguel, *La notion johannique de l'Esprit*.

Lietgert, *Gottes Sohn und Gottes Geist*.

Titius, *Lehre der Seligkeit*.

Franck, *Das Wesen des Christenthums.*

Wernle, *Die Anfänge,* etc.

A. Ritschl, *Altkatolische Kirche.*

J. Weiss, *Schriften des N.T.*

Lietzmann, *Handbuch zum N.T.*

Feine, *N.T. Theologie.*

Weinel, *N.T. Theologie.*

Mosiman, *Das Zungenreden.*

Gunkel, *Die Wirkungen des Geistes,* etc.

Weinel, *Die Wirkungen des Geistes,* etc.

Kölling, *Pneumatologie.*

Nösgen, *Das Wesen und Wirken des Heiligen Geistes.* 2 Vols.

Glöel, *Der Heilige Geist in der Heilsverkundigung d. Paulus.*

Sokolowski, *Die Begriffe Geist und Leben bei Paulus.*

ADDITIONAL WORKS IN ENGLISH,
published by Kregel Publications

Baxter, Ronald E., *Gifts of the Spirit,* 1983

——————————, *The Charismatic Gift of Tongues,* 1982.

Bickersteth, E. H., *The Holy Spirit,* 1976.

Bullinger, E. W., *Word Studies on the Holy Spirit,* 1985. (Former title: *The Giver and His Gifts.*)

Gardiner, George E., *The Corinthian Catastrophe,* 1975.

Marsh, F. E., *Emblems of the Spirit,* 1974.

Unger, Merrill, F., *New Testament Teaching on Tongues,* 1974.

INDEX OF SUBJECTS

The numbers refer to pages

INDEX OF AUTHORS

The numbers refer to pages

INDEX OF TEXTS

The numbers refer to pages

Other books by W. H. Griffith Thomas

THROUGH THE PENTATEUCH
Chapter by Chapter

These valuable notes from the pen of a well-known Bible expositor take the form of a connected commentary on the Pentateuch. A helpful introduction to each book plus the excellent homiletical material will give the reader rich devotional and inspirational insight and knowledge into the Pentateuchal writings. A special section on how to approach the study of the Bible will be an additional source of blessing.

OUTLINE STUDIES IN MATTHEW

This book takes the form of sixty studies touching all twenty-eight chapters of Matthew and is presented in expanded outline form. The studies include, in each case, introductory remarks and concluding applications. The reader will thus find in this volume a connected, devotional exposition of the biblical text.

OUTLINE STUDIES IN LUKE

"The author's clear, crisp straightforward style joined as it was with wisdom, both theological and devotional, gave his expository works classic status. Bible students seeking refreshment and teachers seeking resources will both be delighted with this work."   —J. I. Packer

THE APOSTLE JOHN: His Life and Writings

"Some books are dipped into or skimmed through; some are read thoroughly, but only once; W. H. Griffith Thomas' books are purchased, kept and re-read.

"In *The Apostle John,* clarity is not Thomas' only virtue, but it is certainly one of his strongest. A clear analysis of chapters, with memorable outlines makes the flow of thought easy to follow. His English style is outstanding, and the apt (but not excessive) use of 'alliteration's artful aid' makes this an excellent outline study, not only of the Apostle John's life, but of his Gospel, his Epistles and the Book of Revelation."   —Arthur L. Farstad

STUDIES IN COLOSSIANS AND PHILEMON

Warren W. Wiersbe, in the Foreword to this book, says that this is "one of the best expositions available, not only for the advanced student but also for the average reader who wants to gain a working knowledge of this important Epistle."

The excellent homiletical material, together with informative outlines, give the reader rich devotional insight and practical knowledge in the study of Colossians and Philemon. Two appendices on the life and work of Paul and a general survey of Paul's Epistles enhance the value of this work.

THE APOSTLE PETER: His Life and Writings

"*The Apostle Peter* has two major parts: the first deals with the life and character of Peter and the second with the truth revealed in his Epistles. Accordingly, the reader will find a comprehensive spiritual evaluation of the Apostle Peter, including a discussion of many aspects of his life and witness, and a fine devotional exposition of 1 and 2 Peter." —John F. Walvoord